Praise for *North of Ithaka*

"Imagine being able to reclaim your ancestral home two generations after it was lost. That's exactly what Eleni N. Gage did."
—*USA Today Weekend*

"Through this moving family memoir, Gage allows us to be present at her rite of passage across that 'psychic barrier' from American to Greek, at the exorcism of a tragic past and at the blessing of her reborn family house."
—*The Sunday Times* (UK)

"A monument to family history and an enthralling year spent in Lia."
—*The Daily Telegraph* (UK)

"Told with an expert's attention to detail and all the wit and bewilderment of a young urbanite dropped into a strange, old world setting, *North of Ithaka* is part travel memoir, part family saga, and part story of self-discovery. . . . One of those few books that only comes along every couple of years that qualifies as a 'must-read' for all Greek Americans."
—*Greek America Magazine*

"Eleni brings to life a part of Greece that . . . is worth a trip; if not an actual trip, a literary one."
—Rita Wilson, actress and producer
of *My Big Fat Greek Wedding*

"An inspiring coda to [her family's] tragedy."
—*Odyssey* magazine

"Part personal memoir, do-it-yourself-manual, historical novel, family saga, and tourist guide, *North of Ithaka* tells of Gage's attempt to put her cultural confusion to rest by exchanging the skyscrapers of New York for the mountaintops of her ancestral village."

—*The List* (Scotland)

"*North of Ithaka* is a sort of cross between *Captain Corelli's Mandolin* and *Driving Over Lemons* . . . a monument to family history and an enthralling year spent in Lia."

—*The Daily Telegraph* (UK)

"A fascinating portrait of a part of Greece seldom seen by tourists."

—*Dorset Echo*

"[*North of Ithaka* is] a tale far removed from those popular villa-restoration comedies and abounds with setbacks, superstitions, love, and the often suffocating bonds of heritage."

—*The Australian News*

NORTH

OF

ITHAKA

A Granddaughter Returns to
Greece and Discovers Her Roots

ELENI N. GAGE

ST. MARTIN'S GRIFFIN

NEW YORK

Map by David Cain

www.stmartins.com

Library of Congress Cataloging-in-Publication Data

Gage, Eleni N.
    North of Ithaka : a granddaughter returns to Greece and discovers her roots / by Eleni N. Gage.
        p. cm.
    ISBN 0-312-34028-1 (hc)
    ISBN 0-312-34029-X (pbk)
    EAN 978-0-312-34029-2
    1. Gage, Eleni N. 2. Gage, Eleni N.—Family. 3. Greek American women—Biography. 4. Greek Americans—Biography 5. Lia (Greece)—Biography. 6. Lia (Greece)—Description and travel. 7. Greece—Description and travel. 8. Gatzoyiannis, Eleni. 9. Greece—History—Civil War, 1944–1949—Biography. I. Title.

E184.G7G34 2005
949.5'3—dc22
[B]

                                                    2004062864

First St. Martin's Griffin Edition: May 2006

10 9 8 7 6 5 4 3 2 1

To the villagers of Lia, past, present, and future

CONTENTS

ACKNOWLEDGMENTS

Thank you to everyone who made my life in Greece full of adventure, full of knowledge, especially my friends and family in Lia, Ioannina, Corfu, Athens, and all over Epiros. And to everyone in the United States who shared in my experience, whether they visited, listened to my stories, read my e-mails, or offered their unsolicited opinions on my stay: my incredibly involved parents, NickGage and Joanie, my fearless sister Marina, the tantalizing trio of Katherine, Kay, and Arlene, the peripatetic duo of Elsa and Anna, the larger-than-life-sized Thitsas and their husbands, and the unfailingly supportive Eleni, Efrosini, and Themis Nikolaides.

Many thanks to the people who wanted to hear the story of my idyll in Epiros in the first place: Andy McNicol and Joni Evans. To Katherine Fausset, Nathan Lump, Natasha Wimmer, and my parents for reading early drafts and making invaluable suggestions with as much diligence as if it had been their jobs to do so. And to Nichole Argyres for editing the book with as much care and affection as if it had been a friendly favor and not another day at work.

To everyone who offered their support with such generosity, I wish I could give you all a place as exciting and welcoming as Lia to call home.

Other countries may offer you discoveries
in manners or lore or landscape.
Greece offers you something harder—
the discovery of yourself.

LAWRENCE DURRELL,
Prospero's Cell

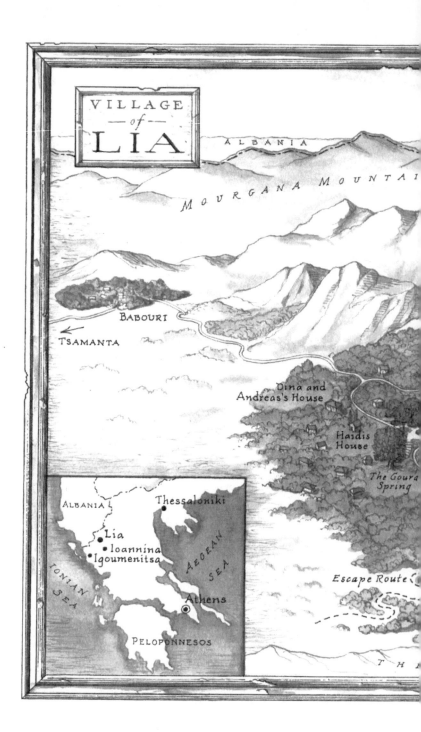

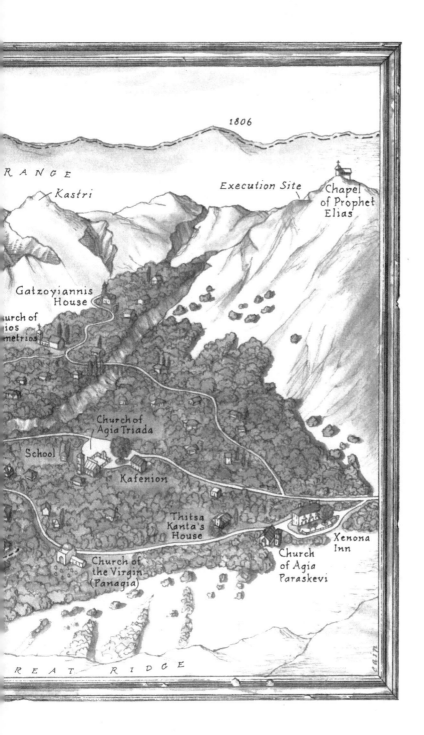

1806

RANGE

Kastri

Execution Site

Chapel
of Prophet
Elias

Gatzoyiannis
House

urch of
ios
metrios

Church of
Agia Triada

School

Kafenion

Thitsa
Kanta's
House

Church of
the Virgin
(Panagia)

Church
of Agia
Paraskevi

Xenona
Inn

REAT   RIDGE

December 6

I'm trying to crucify three oranges. Unfortunately, this talent isn't part of my skill set. I can't work out how to attach the slippery, swollen fruit to the wooden cross without impaling them, which would make juice and pulp spurt everywhere, all over my carefully chosen skirt and onto the stone courtyard, where it would lie in sticky trails and be tracked into the house by my guests.

The thing is, I've never decorated a rooftop cross before. It wouldn't have occurred to me to do so now if Foti hadn't told me, just a few days ago, that in Greece, once the roof of a new house is complete, the chimneys built and the shutters and other finishing touches in place, the owner of the house adorns a wooden cross with oranges and money-filled handkerchiefs, then plants it like a flag on top of her new roof. The workers then scramble onto the roof to retrieve their booty, completing a ritual that signifies that the house is finished and ready to receive its happy inhabitants.

I had thought a simple housewarming party would do the trick. (That's how I inaugurated my New York apartment after all, to celebrate my new status as the proud owner of a thirty-year mortgage and a home slightly larger than a restaurant's walk-in-freezer.) So I asked Father Prokopi to make an announcement in church last Sunday inviting everyone in the village to the Gatzoyiannis house for the blessing of the home. Then I heard about this cross. And in the year I've lived on this mountaintop, I've learned that if a ritual exists, it's wise to observe it—otherwise, you risk provoking the wrath of fate, the saints, or, worst of all, your fellow villagers.

So yesterday I drove down the mountain to the nearest city in search of handkerchiefs, filled them with twenty euros each, and knotted them onto the cross, which is now leaning against the stone pillar that holds up the veranda's slate roof. Crisp white linen with subtle blue borders, the money-filled handkerchiefs are now waving in the breeze like sails. That was the easy part.

Wire! There's a tangle of wire under the mulberry tree, where the builders must have tossed it. It's going to have to do. I grab the wire and twist it around the cross's arms, then around and around the oranges themselves. No muss, no pulp. Perfect.

Of course, I'm probably doing it all wrong. For all I know, the rusty wire counteracts the good luck of the ritual for reasons too ancient for me to guess. It's not just a simple question of a perfectly decorated cross, I think, as I sit on the stone steps to the front door, staring down at the mountain peaks rising like waves in the distance. Maybe renovating this house was wrong in the first place. And the party—a potential disaster! I've been running around to find just the right foil-wrapped sweets for the event, and I never stopped to wonder if the villagers even want to see the finished house, to come to a place where their friends and relatives were imprisoned, tortured, and killed—thirty-seven of them buried right here in the front yard. In my eagerness to return the villagers' hospitality, I had ignored the fact that most of them had avoided visiting the house so far.

Legally, I had every right to rebuild this home, which now looks cozy and benign, like the stone cottage of a noble woodcutter in a fairy tale. Before the Greek civil war in the late 1940s, my family's house stood on this land, so it's mine to do with what I will. But during the conflict, the Communist guerillas occupied the village and took over the house as their headquarters. The basement stable, where my family kept sheep and goats, became a jail where the soldiers herded prisoners. Our garden was turned into a makeshift burial ground. The thirty-seven bodies were removed from their shallow graves after the war; neighbors who knew the victims still remember the stench that filled the air.

My grandmother was among the last prisoners kept in the basement; by the time of her execution the yard was too full of corpses, so the condemned were marched to a ravine on the next mountaintop to be shot. After the war, her house was abandoned; its roof rotted and the house collapsed onto itself, as if to bury the memories of all it had witnessed. *The ruins scared me when I visited the village as a child and haunted my dreams once I left—crumbling piles of rocks whose decaying, misshapen forms seemed to represent my family's tragedy. None of my relatives wanted to see the house stand again. My aunts begged me not to move there to reconstruct it, then warned I'd be threatened by wild animals, homicidal intruders, and dark curses if I defied them. Because of their fear of the house, and the traumatic memories it held, they had ignored the building for half a century, letting it shrink into ruin. So my aunts were shocked that, as a member of the next generation to live away from this seemingly cursed home, I was determined to rebuild the house, both as a monument to my grandmother and, for myself, as a tangible link to my family's past and our village. I wanted to transform my relationship with our shadowy, sorrowful history from ignorance and fear to something I could understand, or even control. I was decades away from being born when my grandmother's death took place. But by rebuilding her ruined home, perhaps I could restore a fragment of the devastation her murder had caused.*

Still, in all my planning, I had never envisioned the day when I'd welcome to the house dozens of people who have a much longer history with it than I do—and perhaps an even deeper emotional tie. My guests were children during the war. How will they feel when they see the house that they remember as a prison resurrected as a home? Will they burst into tears, as my aunt did upon seeing it? Or will the sight of the house inflame old hatreds, jealousies, and political schism, the tiny pricks of envy, gossip, and suspicion that itch under the skin of any villager, and that over fifty years ago grew into betrayal as villagers jealous of my grandmother's relative wealth and husband in America denounced her at her trial, ensuring her execution? My housewarming party could easily turn into a screaming fight like the shouting matches I've witnessed over Greek coffee in the kafenion.

I'm probably a fool to be hosting this gathering. I wanted to thank the villagers, who have tolerated and fed me all year and taught me their skills, from rolling out phyllo dough to picking oregano, from reading the future in coffee grounds to placating angry sheepdogs. But although they welcomed me as an outsider, perhaps they'll resent the way I—a hopelessly citified, twenty-seven-year-old New York journalist—built a home here, reviving a past that belongs more to them than to me, and re-creating a place that symbolizes the village's tragic history. The land may belong to my family, but perhaps this ruin wasn't mine to rebuild. After all this time, I don't want the villagers to stop thinking of me as their neighbor and suddenly see me as an audacious American trying to slap a happy ending onto a Greek tragedy.

The cross is ready now. But am I? An old woman hobbles through the gate toward me, up the stone path leading to the house. She is one of the wizened, fragile widows who live at the other end of the village and leave their homes only for church services and feast days. With her almost translucent skin and halo of white hair, she looks like a cotton puff stuffed into a black dress and kerchief.

"Oh, my child," she sighs, a tear trickling out of one of her turquoise eyes. "I have memories here, and not just a few."

NORTH

OF

ITHAKA

ONE

RESTORATION

<<Κάθε αρχή και δύσκολη.>>
"EVERY BEGINNING IS DIFFICULT."

My aunts said I'd be killed by Albanians and eaten by wolves. Of course, that only made me more determined to go. Determined, but a little wary. Maybe more than a little. It all started the weekend after Thanksgiving 2001.

"Lenitsa, you put on weight?" Thitsa Lilia asked as she cut into another sticky piece of pecan pie, untroubled by the fact that she currently weighed at least twice what I did. She was perfectly at ease with her appearance, if not mine, as she sat gossiping with her sisters. Three of my four aunts were clustered around the kitchen table of my parents' house in Worcester, Massachusetts, scrutinizing me as they ate the leftovers of Thanksgiving's desserts.

"I don't think so." I shrug. "It might be the sweater."

"Of course it's the sweater. You got a beautiful figure, just like your aunt," said Thitsa Kanta, referring to herself. She was the slimmest of the sisters, partly thanks to a lifetime of stomach trouble and partly because she worked to maintain her image of herself as the polyester-clad femme fatale who returned to Greece to visit after the war looking "like a movie star," she said, with short, permed hair instead of long braids. Today all the *thitsas* had carefully maintained bouffants that were almost as high as their self-esteem. But right now anxiety cast a cloud over Thitsa Kanta's perfect world. She sighed. "I don't know why you not married yet, twenty-seven years old and single."

"Maybe you join the church group when you go back to New

York," Thitsa Olga suggested. The eldest and shortest, she had a medium-size build and a chestnut-colored bouffant, as opposed to her sisters' blond. "They got lots of Greek boys there."

"Maybe," I answered. There was no point in telling my *thitsas* I hadn't asked for their dating advice. Most people use the term *Greek chorus* figuratively. Well, I have the real thing, live and in person, a supporting cast made up of my four aunts: Thitsa Olga, Thitsa Kanta, Thitsa Lilia, and Thitsa Tina. I never used the proper Greek word for aunt, *thia*, in talking to them; it just seemed too grand. Our relationship was a mini-society that called for the use of the diminutive ending "itsa," a habit which made sense physically as well as psychologically. None of them is over five feet tall—in fact, they resemble Flora, Fauna, and Merriweather, the fairy godmothers in *Sleeping Beauty*, more than any chorus in a Greek tragedy. But they fulfill the same function: commenting on any action taking place in my life, interpreting oracles, explaining the past, and making predictions for the future.

As I started boiling my Greek coffee in a copper *briki*, my father burst through the kitchen door. "Look at this," he bragged, brandishing a black-and-white photo. In it, my father is thirty-eight years younger and twenty pounds slimmer, standing in front of his parents' house, which has not yet fallen into ruin.

Every year on my summer trip to Greece, I made a pilgrimage to Lia, faithfully visiting the shell of this house, which I thought of as the Gatzoyiannis house, after our original last name. I loved seeing the people in our village, who showered me with hugs, kisses, and stuffed squash blossoms. But my family never stayed more than a day or two, and I was always a little glad when we left Lia to head to an island where the vacation could really get started. Our visits to the lost home made me anxious, because when the wind blew over the toppled stones, rustling the branches of my grandmother's prized mulberry tree, I wasn't sure if the house wanted me there. I knew that people had been tortured and killed in the house and buried in the yard. But it wasn't just the knowledge of this fact that made the grounds seem ominous. It was the appearance of the fallen house itself. The ruins were forbidding, especially when seen through the arched frame of the *exoporta*, the outer door to the courtyard in front of the house. The wood of the door had rotted away, so I could step through the stone frame and onto a path to nothing, where the house once stood. All that remained was a collection of grim piles of gray stones swallowed by moss, and a rusted metal window frame smothered in swells of ivy. But in my father's old photo, the house still looked like a home. Rain had already damaged the roof in some places, but the outer door was still sturdy, and he leaned against it, smiling, wearing an open-collared shirt and excessive sideburns.

"Wow," I said, looking up from that tanned young man to my father's face, now covered in a bushy gray beard. "You look girly. You're so skinny! And that shirt!"

"Not *girly*," he insisted. "Byronic—that's the word you're looking for."

"Lenitsa, bring that here so your old *thitsa* can see," Thitsa Olga demanded.

Staring at the photo, I felt as if a spotlight had been directed onto a dark corner of my mind, revealing the outline of an idea that had been hovering there, indistinctly, for years. Maybe it was time to extend those stopovers in Lia long enough for me to develop a new relationship with the village, one that was as rooted in the present as in the past.

Whenever I toyed with the idea of staying long enough in Lia to resolve my conflicted feelings about the place, I fell back on the same excuse not to go—what would I do there? The image of the home in the photo was the answer to my question; I could move to Greece and rebuild the crumbled house, transforming the ruins into a home again so that if my grandparents' ghosts ever wandered back, they would recognize it as their own. It would be a constructive use of time, with a tangible result. And along the way, perhaps living in the village where my grandmother had spent her whole life would help me feel as if I knew this woman I had never met. I carried her name, but I'd never known her. Living among my grandmother's neighbors might help me understand my namesake, my father, my aunts, and even the Greek side of myself better.

After all, there was nothing to keep me here. As my aunts pointed out, I wasn't married. And I was growing increasingly bored with my little job, my even tinier apartment, and the slow parade of would-be soul mates who marched proudly into my view to the fanfare of trumpets but turned out to be sweaty and silly when I saw them up close. Lost in my thoughts, I made my way to the table slowly—too slowly for Thitsa Kanta, who grabbed the photo by one of its serrated edges before I sat down.

"Look at NickGage's hair!" crowed Thitsa Kanta, differentiating her brother from her other significant Nick, her son, NickStratis. "He looks like a drug dealer. But so handsome!" She sighed. "Lenitsa, we all old now. Your father, your *thitsas*."

"You can see part of the house behind him," I said, pointing to a small room sticking out to the right of the front door, a little L-shaped addition to the square frame of the gray stone house. "What's that?"

"That was the *plistario*," Thitsa Olga said. "Where we wash ourselves. We fill a water barrel and it had a pipe and a thing at the end where water comes out."

"A spigot?"

"Yeah, that," she continued. "And there was a *fourno* where we cook, roast lamb at Easter. One side of that room was open, with a tin wall for the rain." I tried to imagine a teenage Thitsa Olga loading a pan into the beehive oven, her long braids swinging.

"And next to that room?"

"That was the *mageirio*, where we cook in winter," Thitsa Lilia answered. "It had a fireplace, where our mother make the corn bread in the *gastra*, that covered tin pot you put coals on top. We had pallets next to the fireplace, to sleep on in spring and fall. We sleep outside in summer, in the Good Room in winter."

I knew the house had only four rooms, not counting the basement where the goats and sheep were kept, but my aunts had managed to turn it into a whole country that they journeyed around seasonally, just like their flocks that had spent summers up on the mountainside and winters down in the valleys. The *thitsas* had never told me about this pseudo-nomadic aspect of their childhood. And I had never asked, because their youth held so much sorrow that it seemed to lurk under the surface of even the most pleasant memory, making the past volatile, shaky ground on which to wander. Even the happiest occasions weren't safe. When a friend of mine got engaged, I urged the *thitsas* to sing the traditional wedding songs of our village, which they did, smiling as their shrill voices rose in unexpected harmony. Then I felt horrified and guilty when Thitsa Olga burst into tears, sobbing that her own mother hadn't been there to sing at her wedding. But that Thanksgiving weekend I felt brave enough to venture forth. "And next to the *mageirio?*" I prodded.

"Oh that was the *palia kamera*, the Old Room," Thitsa Kanta explained. "That was the first room, built when my grandparents get married long time ago—a hundred and fifty years. It was small, just a cabinet and a door to the hallway."

"So the hallway ran all the way from the front door to the back door?" I asked.

"Oh, yes," Thitsa Lilia replied. "Outside the back door was a tree that made so many apricots. Farther on we had the chicken coop, past that the outhouse. On one trip from America, Patera brought a toilet seat up the mountain."

"But we wouldn't sit on it!" Thitsa Kanta giggled. "We weren't used to it, so we just stand on the seat."

"When visitors come, we drink coffee in the Good Room," Thitsa Lilia said. "It was on the other side of the hallway, opposite the *palia kamera*. On one wall was the fireplace and on the other wall Mana had the iron bed Patera brought set next to the window. You can jump from the bed out the window onto the veranda."

"Beyond that was the courtyard?" I asked.

"Oh, yeah, it was nice and flat, Patera had it covered in concrete," Thitsa Olga recalled. "In summer we bring our pallets and sleep outside, and we hear the shepherds playing their pipes. It was so beautiful! When I think of those times, I cry."

All three *thitsas* were misty-eyed, recalling the fragrant apricot tree, the haunting music of summer nights. This was the moment to spring an early Christmas present on them, to turn my hazy idea into an actual plan, to say it out loud so that I would be forced to follow through in order to save face.

"Guess what! I'm going to quit my job, move to Lia, and rebuild the house," I announced.

"What? You crazy?" three voices shrieked in unison.

"You gonna get killed by Albanians and eaten by wolves!" Thitsa Lilia wailed.

"Scorpions, they gonna hide on your pillow to bite you!" Thitsa Olga keened.

Thitsa Kanta rose from the table. "I'm going home now," she announced. "I can't listen to this, or I get sick—you know I have the acid reflux."

Thitsa Kanta always got physically sick in times of stress. When she was conscripted into the Communist army at sixteen, she couldn't keep any food in her weak stomach and fainted so often during target practice that they eventually sent her home. It may have been then that she realized a shaky stomach can get you out of many sticky situations, but I never imagined that the mere mention of my moving to Lia would be enough to make her ill. Now she was rising up to her full five feet, quivering with rage or nausea. "You go back to New York, back to your good job, and when you come home for Christmas, you tell us you changed your mind and you gonna stay right here and find a nice husband." She strode out the door, with Thitsa Lilia and Thitsa Olga marching behind her.

I was shocked. The *thitsas* are always urging me to do Greek things—date Greek boys, go to the Greek church, then sit around our kitchen table with them, drinking Greek coffee and eating Greek sweets (but not so many that I get fat and repel the aforementioned Greek boys). So when I told them I was leaving my job and apartment in New York and moving to Greece to live in the village where they grew up, I thought they would be delighted. Now, watching their reactions—which were extremely loud, even for the *thitsas*—I realized I had been as blind as Oedipus by refusing to see their fear of Lia and all the violence that they had witnessed in the placid-looking village.

Over the next month they continued to raise objections in the shrill, piercing voices they had cultivated shouting to one another across mountaintops back in Greece. Thitsa Olga called me to wail, "Aren't you scared of ghosts? How can you go to that house?" Each time Thitsa Lilia came to my parents' house to watch the Greek TV channels they got via satellite, she casually mentioned the mountain wolves or the desperate Albanian refugees walking across the border and into the village, no doubt in search of Greek American girls to kidnap for ransom or shoot out of bloodlust. My father was more supportive—he offered to buy me a gun to combat said wolves and Albanians. My mother, who isn't Greek but is easily terrified, worried that as I lay in bed I'd be smothered by falling ceiling plaster caused by goats jumping off the mountainside onto the street-level roof of my great-grandparents' house, where I planned to live while the Gatzoyiannis' house was being rebuilt. Thitsa Tina didn't say anything—as usual, she wasn't speaking to the others because of some sisterly squabble—but hers was a *disapproving* silence. As for Thitsa Kanta, she simply appealed to a higher power: "I'm praying to God that you'll meet a Greek boy, get engaged, and stay here."

I shouldn't have been surprised by their reaction. The house I wanted to rebuild had been the scene of musical summer nights, but it was also the site of the violence that shattered their family forever. My aunts remembered suffering in Lia during the German and Italian invasions of World War II, the years of starvation and conflict culminating in the arrival of Greek Communist guerillas who occupied the village during the civil war immediately following WWII. The soldiers sent local women on grueling work details, trained the girls for combat, and ultimately began to take all the children from their parents to deport them behind the Iron Curtain. The guerillas were losing the war, but they hoped if they resettled and indoctrinated the children and trained them to be soldiers, they might win a larger victory.

After hearing about the deportation plan, my grandmother and namesake, Eleni, plotted her family's escape to America, to join her husband, who had gone to work there before the start of WWII. But she was forced to stay behind for a work detail on the June night in 1948 when three of my teenaged aunts and my father, who was then nine years old, fled Lia. They walked down their mountain and across the mine-filled no-man's-land until they reached the nationalist soldiers' camp up on the next ridge. From there, the children were sent to live in a refugee camp and subsequently sailed to join their father. My grandmother, alone back in Lia, was arrested, imprisoned, tortured, and executed for planning her children's escape. Along with thirteen others, she was shot by a firing squad in the mountains high above her house, and their bodies were thrown into a ravine.

With four of her children in a refugee camp, and one, fifteen-year-old Thitsa Lilia, threshing wheat for the guerillas in a distant village, my grandmother spent her final weeks without her family but in her home. The Communist guerillas had taken over my grandparents' house to use as their headquarters shortly after they arrived, an occupation motivated by both practical and political reasons. With its four rooms, the house was the largest in the village. But the guerillas also wanted to punish my grandmother for having a husband who worked in America, so they evicted her and her family. The Good Room became the guerillas' office, and the basement a makeshift jail where the soldiers corralled prisoners accused of disloyalty or spying for the nationalist troops. As many as thirty-one at once were crammed in so tightly that they were forced to sleep sitting up, their hands bound in front of them.

It was in the basement of her own home that my grandmother spent her last days, wondering if she would be the next to be called up into the *palia kamera*, the Old Room built for her in-laws' wedding, to be tortured or taken into the yard to be shot and buried, like dozens of others, under her apricot tree. The entire building bore witness to the inmates' suffering. A teenage girl escaped out of the *palia kamera* by knocking the rusted metal bars out of its old window. The soldiers watched the captives in the basement by looking through a trapdoor in the floor of the Good Room. But it was the basement where the prisoners lived in terror and pain, and the basement ruins that frightened me most, even though I swore to my aunts that I wasn't scared. Each time I visited the ruins, I would approach the gaping hole of the foundation, choked with vines, nettles, and scrub pine, and stare through the hollow window casements into the twelve-by-fifteen-foot space. I never climbed down into the basement area—it was too overgrown. But when the wind blew down the mountain through the cypress trees around the church of Saint Demetrios, the moaning sound made me think of the prisoners' cries. I wasn't frightened of wolves or Albanians, but Thitsa Olga was right: I was scared of ghosts. This was why I needed to go: to reclaim the house from its ruins and myself from my fears, and the much sharper fears, sorrow, and memories of my aunts and father.

By now, the house had been empty for fifty years. After the guerillas retreated behind the Iron Curtain, taking all the surviving villagers with them, the Gatzoyiannis house stood deserted. For a few years after the war it was used by Greek nationalist soldiers assigned to patrol the Albanian border at the top of the mountain, in case the guerillas who had kidnapped Lia's children or had been deported behind the Iron Curtain after the war mobilized forces and returned. But by 1953 the fear of invasion had diminished, and the nationalist soldiers, too, abandoned the house. When my father first returned to visit in 1963, the roof had sprouted leaks. Rain dripped between the slate roof tiles, rotting the wood below so that the roof caved in and the house crumpled. By the time I saw it as a child, the house had tumbled down.

My aunts and father didn't destroy the house themselves. But their neglect of it encouraged its decline. I knew that my aunts resented their home for turning on them. Their happy memories there were so eclipsed by the tragedy that followed that each insisted, "I never want to see that house again." Although the ruins scared me, too, I felt it wasn't the house's fault. Each time I stood at its shell, surrounded by piles of stones, I sensed that the house had been as much a prisoner as the people crammed inside. It compounded my family's tragedy that the home my grandparents had loved was now nothing more than the ruins of a prison.

My aunts' feelings weren't a factor when I made my impulsive decision; it hadn't occurred to me that they would get so upset. But now, seeing their reaction, I was still determined to go. My father had restored his grandparents' home—the Haidis house— and organized the building of a village inn. But although he had an architect draw up plans to rebuild the Gatzoyiannis house of his childhood, he could never bring himself to start construction. I understood my aunts' violent opposition and my father's reluctance— they remembered the site as their mother's prison. But I was convinced that the house needed to be restored to a home. My aunts and father could not be turned back into the children who jumped on beds and fell asleep to shepherds' lullabies, but the house could be rebuilt as it was before the war.

The *thitsas* resented their old home, but their feelings about the village weren't so cut-and-dried. They spent most Sunday afternoons listening to radio broadcasts of music from the region and calling old friends and relatives to wish them happy nameday and hear the latest gossip from the village: who was making moonshine, how the restoration of a church was going, whose child was getting divorced (a horrible thing, but it happens to so many families these days), or having a baby boy, may he live for them.

Sorrow about what had happened in the village pushed my aunts away from Lia, but love for the villagers and their homeland wouldn't let them go completely. As for me, I couldn't explain exactly what it was that drew to me to Lia, why I needed to explore my ancestral land. I knew it was my fear of sadness and guilt that my own life had been relatively sorrow-free that made me feel relieved each time I left Lia, but I couldn't say why I yearned to return and live there. I knew only that this place was integral to the emotional history my family shared. It was a place where my aunts, father, grandparents, and all who had come before them belonged, and I wanted to make space for myself there, too. When I waxed philosophical, I reasoned that this was the essential dilemma of immigrants and their children, who shuttle back and forth between two homes, feeling disloyal about belonging to one more than the other. My need to go to Lia seemed unnatural to my aunts. The generation that leaves a country always wants to assimilate and move forward, while those of us in the new homeland can't resist looking back, like Orpheus, to see from where we came.

For my aunts, however, nothing was philosophical; they were taking my defection personally. When it became clear that they couldn't stop me, the *thitsas* became resigned to my leaving. They didn't like it. But since I am as intractable as anyone else from Epiros, our native province, there was nothing they could do. (In Greek, when you want to say someone is stubborn, you call him or her an Epirote-head.) So my worried friends and family members started offering advice. My roommate in New York suggested that I fill a tin can with coins and shake it at any attacking goats, to scare them away. My mother gave me a key chain that also functioned as a rape whistle and high-powered flashlight. Thitsa Kanta, as concerned with my standing in the villagers' eyes as with my physical safety, said, "Just dress nicely, and close your windows when you change clothes."

I nodded at everyone with a smile that meant "I'm too nice a person to tell you that you're being ridiculous." I was sure I'd be safe living in the renovated pink stone house that had belonged to my great-grandfather Kicho Haidis. Lia is home to only 140 families, and although there really are both wolves and Albanian refugees, the crime rate is basically zero. This compares quite favorably with Manhattan, even post-Giuliani. At first glance, Lia looks like not only a safe village but also an enchanted one, with a natural beauty so lush and overripe that it's almost embarrassing. Year round the steep mountainsides explode with green overgrowth and riots of wildflowers, and in spring enthusiastic mountain streams gush right over the road. It's enough to make you want to tell Mother Nature to rein it in a little; she doesn't need to try quite so hard.

Lia's dramatic beauty masks a history of turmoil. The village has always been a scene of oppositions. Even geographically, it narrowly missed being split in two. When the borders of Albania were ratified in 1913, the province of Epiros was cut in half. Today one half is in Greece and the other section, Northern Epiros, is Albanian. Lia is on the Greek side, but just barely, and when communism first fell in Albania in 1991, illegal immigrants started escaping over the mountaintop border into Lia, only a kilometer below it, in a constant stream.

My aunts don't care much about borders, treaties, or politics. They remember Lia as a place of violent hostility between villagers during the civil war of 1946–49. The locals were sharply divided in their political loyalties, and at my grandmother's trial some of the villagers testified against her. After growing up and becoming a journalist, my father wrote a book about those years. Like me, the book is named after his mother, Eleni. Before moving to Lia I had never read it or seen the film based on the book. When my friends found out, they were always incredulous. "You're kidding," they would say. I always answered, "It just hits too close to home."

Since the age of six I knew I wasn't willing to read the story of my grandmother's life and death. My family lived in Athens when I was three to seven years old as my father investigated the events. I still remember the time a middle-aged man from Babouri, the village next to Lia, stopped by the house we were living in, gave me a bar of Ion chocolate, then went into the living room and told my father how he watched his own parents be tied to a tree and shot during the civil war. I sat on the stairs, eating the silky chocolate in its red, white, and pink wrapper and listening, unnoticed but terrified. It was then that I decided to avoid sad-looking old Greeks and their traumatic memories as much as I possibly could.

After four years in Athens, we moved to Worcester, Massachusetts, where my father and his sisters had come to join their father, and where they all still lived. By the age of thirteen, I had noticed that other kids didn't agree to have dinner with their parents' friends "but only if no one mentions Albanian internment camps." Our house in Worcester was a favorite stopping point for Greeks looking to rescue relatives stuck behind the Iron Curtain or to unburden traumatic memories of war-torn childhoods along with others who could understand their pain. I felt sorry for these wounded people, but, I have to admit, a tiny bit annoyed that they were disturbing my viewing of a *Three's Company* rerun. So I decided that my parents weren't doing a very good job of sheltering me from life's harsher side. It was up to me to shield myself from unpleasant realities. I became obsessed with Technicolor movie musicals. (And I was shocked—shocked!—when they didn't have a happy ending. Why did no one warn me that the king dies at the end of *The King and I?*) I read all the *Anne of Green Gables* books. And when I imagined myself grown-up, I looked just like Marcia on *The Brady Bunch.* None of my friends had murdered grandparents or nightmares about rotting piles of stone surrounding gaping holes that had swallowed up their family's home. Why did I? Our family history was easy enough to ignore if I made a conscious effort to do so, leaving the room when my aunts started reminiscing about growing up, or spending the local premiere of the movie *Eleni* in the cinema lobby so that I wouldn't have to watch the torture scenes. I quickly learned that a little proactive vigilance could stop a lot of nightmares from forming.

At the same time, I knew that tragic memories weren't the only inheritance of Greece my aunts passed on to me. I was fascinated by the transplanted Greek village culture that surrounded me in Worcester. Since my mother isn't Greek (she's from Minnesota), she pointed out that my aunts' quirky habits and superstitions were actually folklore that had been passed on through generations and had survived the long boat ride across the ocean. This was my inheritance. I shouldn't hand my aunts soap, scissors, or a knife, because that would cause an argument. Occasionally I'd find a putrid garlic clove tucked into the pocket of my good coat, where Thitsa Olga slipped it during church, to protect me from the evil eye. And when Thitsa Lilia opened my bedroom door to wave incense around as I studied for January exams, I knew she wasn't doing it for ambience but to exorcise evil spirits on Saint Basil's Day.

Perhaps because of the dark shadows lurking in my family's past, I was always eager to have luck on my side and evil spirits out of my bedroom. I became more intrigued by Greek folklore as I grew older, and often felt torn between two equally compelling realms. I loved the sitcom-safe American pop culture and yearned to be like the blond, well-adjusted icons I admired. But part of me was irresistibly drawn to the darker mysticism of my aunts' beliefs and customs. Although I never understood the motives behind my aunts' machinations, I was intrigued by the rituals themselves, by how relieved and reassured my aunts seemed when they wafted incense throughout the house or repeated an incantation guaranteed to remove the evil eye. So when I got to college, I put my cultural confusion toward class credits, studying folklore and mythology, with an emphasis on modern Greece. Once I graduated, I moved to New York and started a career that combined my interest in rituals with my relentlessly optimistic desire to focus on the lighter side of life, writing about celebrities, weddings, and beauty products for women's magazines.

After five years in New York, I had an apartment, a career, and all the free makeup a girl could ever want. But I still felt as if something was missing from my life. I knew that as much as I was steeped in my family's hybrid culture, I was neglecting a part of our past, a history I had spent years trying to ignore. I felt as if there was a part of myself I had yet to meet, the part that somehow belonged in Lia while the rest of me felt relieved each time I drove out of the village toward the ferry boats that would whisk me away from the mountaintop I couldn't help but fear. As I approached an age when I could no longer consider myself "growing up" but rather "grown-up," I felt compelled to confront the complete history of my family, to examine the sorrow that existed back in Greece, and the joy as well. Maybe facing my past would somehow jump-start my grown-up future and provide the piece that seemed to be missing from my present existence.

So as 2001 ended, I began preparing for my move to Lia. My friends didn't really understand why I was so willing to trade *Sex and the City* for introspection in Epiros. My career was finally at a point where I had an assistant instead of being one, they pointed out, and now I was going to run off, in my miniskirt and mules, to a village where a woman wearing pants was unheard-of just a generation ago? I explained that I was doing it for my family, to transform the ruins of past generations into a home for future ones. But the real reason was even more personal. Having spent my girlhood living among my family's ghosts, and my adulthood trying to avoid them, I felt driven to return to the site of my ancestors' home to seek out the shadows of my past and turn them into protective spirits for my future. I wanted control over a past I couldn't change. And I hoped to integrate the American and the Greek sides of my self into one well-adjusted whole.

Of course, I didn't tell anyone that—it all seemed too pathetically earnest, too 1970s divorcée: "Yeah, it's real important that I go live on a mountain and *find* myself." So I wrapped my earnestness in irony, referring to my plans as "my little odyssey." Just as Ithaka provided a psychological home for Odysseus even though he spent most of his adulthood away from it, so Lia loomed in my mind: as a home from long ago that would require much effort to be reached. Odysseus had spent ten years after the Trojan War trying to get home to Ithaka, a small island southwest of Epiros; I could take ten months to journey through my family's home. My catchphrase worked; most of my friends just assumed I was getting back to my more scholarly roots, reviving my interest in folklore. And I half believed it, too.

Still, it was obvious that I had a split personality—at least to anyone who looked at my official documents. My American self, Eleni N. Gage, had a blue U.S. passport that would permit me to live in Greece for only three months without registering as a foreign alien at a police station every so often. But because my father was born in Greece, I was entitled to a maroon and gold passport as Eleni Gatzoyiannis, which would permit me to stay indefinitely. So throughout January, February, and March of 2002, I spent at least one morning a week at the Greek consulate in New York, sighing dramatically as the passport officer informed me of new documents that Mr. Natsis, the all-powerful official in charge back in Ioannina, required. I had hoped to reconcile both sides of my personality into a well-integrated whole, but I couldn't even get them official identification. "I'll take my papers and deal with this when I get there," I snapped at the clerk. Clearly, if Eleni Gatzoyiannis was going to be found, it wasn't going to be at the consulate in New York.

I wasn't surprised by this setback; Greek bureaucracy is notoriously, well, byzantine. But it forced me to acknowledge that my odyssey might not be smooth sailing. Walking away from the consulate, I remembered something from one of my Greek literature classes. In Homer's *Odyssey*, Odysseus gets to Ithaka and is delighted to have reached home. But in Nikos Kazantzakis's retelling, Odysseus finds Ithaka disappointing and feels trapped, wishing he were still at sea. As the weeks sped on, I began to worry that my odyssey would end up a letdown. What if I went to reclaim my Greek past and, after a year of loneliness, didn't like what I found? But it was too late for second thoughts; I had already rented out my bedroom in my apartment and quit my job, stubbornly eradicating my life in New York.

Then, in the round of medical checkups I conscientiously scheduled before setting off for the remote mountain village, my doctor found a tennis-ball-size cyst on my right ovary. This was nothing to worry about, she assured me. Women get cysts all the time. But after my laparoscopic surgery and the tumor's biopsy, it turned out that my cyst wasn't a friendly garden-variety growth. It was a low-malignant potential cyst, a rather rare type of tumor that isn't cancerous but isn't completely benign, either. A follow-up CT scan showed that I had two small cysts remaining on my ovary. These might just be normal cysts that would clear up on their own, the doctor explained. But if blood tests indicated elevated levels of cancer hormones, they could be low-malignant potential tumors as well and would have to be removed, delaying my trip even longer.

Normally, this medical misadventure would have terrified me. But right now I was a woman obsessed. I was so wrapped up in planning my departure that my medical troubles just seemed like a hassle, an unfair delay. My initial departure date had been March 21, the fifty-second anniversary of the day my father and aunts had arrived in America. It had all seemed so perfect, so circular, and now this had put my odyssey on hold. I was frustrated, raring to go. But as I waited for the results of my blood tests, part of me started whispering in my ear, in Greek, "Can't you recognize an omen even when it kicks you in the gut?" I had assured my aunts that my surgery was routine and successful so that they wouldn't worry. They didn't know about the complicated results of my biopsy, but maybe it was a sign that they were right about the misguided foolishness of embarking on my trip. They had taught me to look for omens in the first place, to see ladybugs, spilled water, even broken dishes as good luck, and Tuesdays, scissors left open, and a heap of black residue left at the bottom of a coffee cup as unlucky. Maybe this tumor was a warning that Lia was somehow inherently evil, a place that brought misfortune to all who lived there—or even contemplated living there.

The Eleni N. Gage who smiled in my blue American passport knew it was a coincidence that this health problem was revealed just as I was due to leave for my trip—and a lucky one, too, since I had taken care of it before setting off. If I hadn't caught it, the doctor said, my ovary might have twisted around it and exploded when I was on a mountaintop miles from medical care. But the Greek side of me insisted that there are no coincidences. This was the hand of fate trying to keep me away from Lia, from reclaiming my past. It might even be divine intervention; the obstacle God sent in response to Thitsa Kanta's prayers for a man—or some other unexpected turn of events that would make me stay.

I needed reassurance from people who didn't live their lives trapped in the thrall of omens but also wouldn't think I was ridiculous to consider them. So I called my parents to float my theory that if one prays for a suitor to keep one's niece from going to Greece, God thinks it's hubris and sends a tumor instead. They found that unlikely. My father explained that the thitsas didn't really want to sabotage my trip, they were just worried about me because of the horrible experiences they associated with Lia. "We all go to the village in our nightmares," he said. I knew that. Even I sometimes visited the village in a recurring nightmare in which I followed a neon blue dragonfly up a hill to find myself at the windswept piles of rocks that were the ruins of my grandparents' house, about to fall into the gaping crater that was once the basement. That's when I'd wake up. This dream was part of the reason I was so determined to see Lia in the stark light of day, to incorporate it into my everyday life instead of relegating it to vivid memories, hazy dreams, or stopovers between island-hopping, short visits that were protected by the unreal enthusiasm of vacations.

The next morning my doctor called. The tests were good. I was free to go to Greece—as long as I had ultrasounds every few months to make sure that the remaining cysts weren't growing; if they disappeared or stayed small, they were most likely normal growths. I boarded a flight that afternoon. The people around me on the plane shifted their legs over their under-the-seat bags and complained to the surly stewardess about the lack of blankets. I just sat there, grinning. Just when I had finally become ready to face my fears, it seemed as if fate wouldn't let me do so. But there I was in midair. Not my oncologist, not the Greek consulate, not even the all-powerful alliance of my aunts could keep me from moving to Lia. I was about to embark on my odyssey, to become a native in the village of my family's past, and perhaps even change my future.

TWO

FORWARD BACK

<<Πρέπει να βρέξεις κ ώλο για να φας ψάρι.>>

"YOU HAVE TO GET YOUR ASS WET TO EAT FISH."

April 1

I've finally made it to Greece, but what with acquiring a rental car, a Greek cell phone, and a few signed documents from the U.S. consulate here in Athens, it will be at least a week before I get to Lia and see the ruins that will, I hope, become a house. So I'm forced to settle for the next-best thing: a meeting with the man with the plan, the architect, George Zervas.

He had a set of drawings waiting for me at the hotel when I arrived, with a note saying that after all this time, he is excited to begin the house's renovation. Actually, it didn't say exactly that. In Greek, there is one word for renovation, and another, αναπαλαίοση, for re-old-ation, making something old again. I suppose that's what we're doing—since I can't go back in time, we're bringing the past into the future by restoring the ruined Gatzoyiannis house to its original, intact state.

Of course, I've never seen the house standing, so to me, it's all new. And Zervas has it all there in the drawing: windows framed by wooden shutters stare out from the second floor, under a sloping slate roof. The old gray stones that once formed the original house are stacked on top of one another, a free-form puzzle of random shapes. It looks as cozy as a gingerbread house, as strong as the Great Wall. And, this being April 1, about as likely to be real as any other April Fool's Day joke. Maybe if I could get in touch with Zervas, I'd actually believe that re-old-ation is possible.

———

"It's so beautiful!" I exclaimed as George Zervas unrolled his plans across the lacquered coffee table in the lobby of the Athens Plaza hotel and made a sweeping gesture with his small, elegant hand. "I can't wait until it's finished. How long do you think it will take?"

Zervas shrugged, his gray mustache twitching. "The sooner we get started, the sooner it will be finished," he replied. "Beyond that, I couldn't say. Time is just a construct." He leaned back, the better to expound on his philosophy. "I've been able to break the boundary of time, like scientists are always trying to do. It's easy—just don't wear a watch!" He added that he also didn't believe in cell phones, computers, or answering machines—anything that allowed the outside world to intrude on his thoughts.

I smiled weakly. If you're about to start a re-old-ation project, I suppose you want an architect who doesn't believe in linear time. But I'd budgeted only ten months to oversee the rebuilding of my grandparents' home. A birth takes only nine months—why should a rebirth take much longer? Now that I knew my ethereal architect had broken the boundary of time, I was starting to get nervous.

"The design is so rustic, just like the original house," I said. "It can't take that long to stack the stones that way, can it?"

"When you're my age, you realize *long* is a relative term," the seventy-something Zervas responded in his elegant, reedy voice. "Not everything is as simple as it seems. Did you know there's not one straight line on the Acropolis? It's all ellipses, parabolas. There were four or five great architects when Pericles commissioned the Parthenon. He chose the design most based on mathematics."

I'd been to the Parthenon many, many times and had never noticed any parabolas. But I was already finding the rebuilding of our own house to be less than straightforward. In theory, we shouldn't be planning to rebuild the house at all—like my citizenship, the project was not yet officially recognized by the Greek bureaucracy. First, the plot of land on which the ruins stood had to be legally confirmed as being neither forestland nor an archaeological site. That shouldn't seem difficult to resolve; there were houses above, next to, and below the land, and a house had stood on the spot from at least 1870 to 1953. But both the Greek forestry and Archaeological Services make their own rules. Getting the okay to build a house is like getting into the college of your choice: you need a great application. An engineer has to arrange the required papers into a packet, sign off on it, then pass it on to the forestry and Archaeological Services. These august bodies can then take months, or even years, to approve the plans. Or not. I could only cross my fingers that it would all work out in the hands of an engineer Zervas had recommended.

Zervas, an elfin man whose eyes darted around the room looking for a wider audience, could not be bothered to discuss the approval process. He was busy uniting entire planes of thought.

"Architecture is the practical and the spiritual coming together," he opined, inspired at the thought of the Parthenon. "It *is* poetry."

Knowing more about folklore than about architecture, I tried to steer the conversation toward more familiar terrain. "Do you think we'll find the lost treasure of Ali Pasha when we dig up the ruins of the house?" I teased. Ali Pasha was the Albanian vizier who ruled Epiros for the Turks from 1778 to 1822 and is said to have buried his ill-gotten gains somewhere in the area he governed—why not my basement?

"Oh, I know where his treasure is already," Zervas replied, sipping his coffee. "It's in Ioannina, in the old city, but not at his palace. I used a divining rod to detect it."

I was only slightly surprised that Zervas, who lived in his own surreal world, had treasure-dowsing powers that matched his skill at outwitting time. "Then what?" I asked. "Did you dig it up?"

"Oh, no. If I had wanted to dig it up, I never would have found it," he explained patiently. "So many others have tried to find it, to profit from it, and failed."

This logic sounded as circular as the walls of the Parthenon. "Don't you want to be sure you're right?" I asked.

Zervas shrugged. "Ali Pasha cursed the treasure so it moves when you try to unearth it," he explained. "That's the legend, anyway. Some men dreamed that they had found the treasure, so they went to the place they saw in their dreams and dug until they came upon a large chest. They slid ropes under the trunk, then climbed out of the pit to pull it up. But as they tugged, the rope snapped. 'No matter,' said one man, 'We'll come back tomorrow night.' But when they did, there was no trunk, no pit, no ropes. It was all gone." Zervas hugged me good-bye and started strolling toward the thick glass of the lobby door, about to pull his own disappearing act.

"Wait," I called after him. "When are you coming to Lia?"

He pivoted. "You find the workers, sign a contract for the house, then I'll come. Just call when you need me. Who knows what buried treasure we'll find?"

His smile was so encouraging, it wasn't until he was gone that I realized I couldn't call him once I assembled a team; he never answers his phone. I was eager to start and my architect was as elusive as Ali Pasha's legendary treasure. But at least he was excited about the rebuilding, which was more than I could say for the seventy-something crowd in America. In fact, all over Athens, I was getting kudos from strangers who were as astonished as my *thitsas* at my plans, but much more encouraging. "Bravo! An Athenian girl would never go live for a year in a village," a taxi driver commended me when I told him my plans. "I wish I could return to my village on Zakynthos, but I made a mistake I'll pay for the rest of my life. I married the wrong woman and moved to Athens. Now we're divorced; I can no longer fish with my father. I drive this stupid cab to pay her alimony."

During the rest of the ride, the cabbie proved to be as chatty as he was bitter. He was typical of his countrymen in his longing for his lost home. The concept of a natal village occupies a major place in the Greek psyche. It is the alpha and the omega, the beginning and the end, both in theory and in practice, because the village is where many Greeks were born before they moved to a big city and also the place they hope to retire to, to eventually die and be buried there. This is a Greek's cherished goal, to lead a life that ends up where it began—not a straight line, but more of an ellipse.

Since wars and industrialization drove Greeks into cities in the middle of the last century, fewer and fewer people have been born in a village. But even those who have been born in a city return to their family's village for holidays, which accounts for the huge traffic jams at Easter, when everyone streams out of Athens. Of the almost 11 million people living in Greece, 4.5 million live in Athens. But everyone wants a place to consider home, somewhere that represents a romanticized past. According to a Greek song about *xeniteia*—life in a foreign place—"the bread of exile is bitter." But today most Greeks live in a kind of exile from their village. Although they may really prefer the comforts of their city apartment, they pay homage to their village as having the purest air, the cleanest water, even a key to their own personality. This is why urban Greeks return to their village in summer, or leave their children there with grandparents on vacations. And it is why I was moving to Lia.

By the time the cabbie dropped me off at the car rental office, it wasn't my village I was concerned about but rather the car that would take me home. There she was, a silver Hyundai Accent, the only automatic the company had. (I can't drive a stick shift, a major handicap in Greece.) I named her Asymina—Silver One—because of her coloring. I should have named her Asyminoula because she was compact and adorable and I knew the intense Greek passion for cuteness. Everybody and everything that is good in the world gets a nickname formed by adding a diminutive ending to the existing word. At a gas station, the attendant confided that he had trouble with the 'roulas. "The what?" I asked, thinking perhaps he was dating twins, say, Stavroula and Dimitroula. "You know, the euroulas? The new currency?" Of course! The petite and personable euro!

I drove Asymina past the urban sprawl of Athens to Rion, where I backed Asymina onto the ferry across to Antirion as twenty Greek men shouted advice. It was too early in the year for tourists, so sailing with me were a rowdy soccer team, a Gypsy playing a guitar, and an old woman sitting under a poster showing the euro denominations and the slogan "The Euro: Currency of a United Europe—Get to Know It!"

Back on dry land, I drove through mountains and fields, past fish farms and *tavernas* covered in wisteria. As the seven-hour trip stretched on, I began to have some doubts about my mission. What if Zervas never showed up in Lia? What if the car broke down and I had no idea what to do with it? And where was I supposed to find workers for the house?

I desperately started looking for omens, but all I saw were dramatic road signs, which had no words, just pictographs that could be understood by any citizen of a united Europe. They were yellow triangles bordered in red, with a black image in the middle showing, say, a sheep, a curve, a skidding car, a cow, or the silhouette of a man walking across the highway with his arms akimbo, signifying, perhaps, "disoriented old people cross at random here." In extreme circumstances the highway patrol lined up several signs in a row, with one exclamation point at the beginning and another at the end, as if to say, "Careful! You might skid around this curve and send a sheep flying into a disoriented old person crossing the highway at random. So watch it!"

As the shadows lengthened across the road, I realized it was too late to worry about my future. I was already there, at the bridge over the Kalamas River, the turning off point for Lia. I was entering deepest Epiros. After the Iron Curtain closed, its proximity to Albania made Greek Epiros a political hotspot. When my mother first visited Lia in the sixties, it was in an area known as the Forbidden Zone, and as a non-Greek, she had to get special permission to cross the Kalamas after passing through a military checkpoint. I was born in 1974, the year they dissolved the Forbidden Zone, so to me it all sounds very sexy, like the lambada, the Forbidden Dance. And the area still has a bit of an off-limits, Forbidden Zone feel. Border guards sometimes wait at the foot of the bridge, scouting for cars ferrying illegal immigrants from Albania, and camouflaged sentry posts flank the river. When I turn onto the road that winds up the mountains to Lia, I have the sense I'm going where not many people have gone before, to search out new worlds.

Lia sits on an isolated mountain in Epiros, the most remote province of Greece. The name comes from the word *apeiron* (infinity), which may be a reference to the seemingly endless rows of mountains reaching to the sky. Epiros is the least urbanized, least touristed region of Greece and was the last province to win independence from the Ottoman Empire—in 1913, after 460 years of Turkish domination. When my grandfather set sail for America in 1910, he threw his hated Turkish fez into the ocean. A man with strong feelings about fashion, he was inspired to emigrate as a teenager after meeting an Epirote in a three-piece suit that the well-dressed man said he bought in a place called Ameriki. My grandfather had left Lia itself in 1902, at the age of nine, to work as a traveling tinker's apprentice.

Now, a hundred years later, I was staring at a sign that read LIA, 24 KM, feeling that I was almost home. Most foreigners imagine Greece as a scattered chain of islands, with whitewashed houses rising like opals from volcanic cliffsides. But for me, Greece would forever be this tiny village of waterfalls gushing over mountain paths, and gray stone houses balanced on sloping hillsides against a background of shifting shades of green.

I had always been awed by the village. When I was very young, before most of the houses in Lia modernized, even using the outhouse felt like an adventure. But I was always glad to get back to flush toilets and the less tangible luxury of peace of mind. Although the village had changed over the years, my feelings toward it were the same. I loved the beauty of Lia—the cool mountain air and riot of wildflowers. But I still thought of the village with the same mixture of wonder and trepidation I felt as a seven-year-old when my mother took us on nature walks to distract us while my great-aunt killed the Easter lamb and hung it from a tree to drain its blood. Since then, I sensed there were grotesque surprises suspended all over Lia, as if it were a haunted village in a Grimm's fairy tale. On the somber stopovers in the village that punctuated our pleasant trips to Greece, I felt as if we were visiting a memory, not a place. Now I wanted to experience life in Lia long enough to cure my mysticism and ambivalence about the village.

I drove up the winding road, flanked by waves of hunter-green mountains occasionally interrupted by clusters of houses, bright lavender Judas trees, and herds of rowdy sheep so woolly that they looked as though they might bounce down the mountain if you hit them. When I drove through a village, the sound of my car lured curious children out of doorways, and old men in coffee shops turned to look up from their backgammon. I noticed the crushed carcass of a truck that had rolled off the road, sticking out of the mountainside like the gnarled trunk of an olive tree, and I zoomed past a shepherd woman chatting away on a cell phone.

Finally, after endless hairpin turns, I spotted the sign that read, ENTERING LIA. WELCOME TO OUR HOSPITABLE VILLAGE. I drove through the village as the sun began to set, softening the sharp contrast between the blue of the sky, the dark green of the mountains, and the early, lime green leaves of the trees. As I passed the playground and the Xenona Inn, which had not yet opened for the season, I rolled down the window to smell the village air, a scent I associated with woodsmoke, fragrant dirt, and herbs we didn't have back in the United States. I continued on to the town square, bordered by the *kafenion*, the church of the Agia Triada (Holy Trinity), and the stone building where my father went to school, which now held offices for the village and the border police. My aunts had told me that during the civil war, a man had been tortured to death in that building; I remembered and sped on, through the heavy mist, turning past the Goura, a spring covered by a plane tree so old that it has been declared a national monument. Then I arrived on the road that ran along the hillside just above my great-grandfather Kicho Haidis's home, where I would live while rebuilding the Gatzoyiannis house. I parked under a walnut tree, behind an old white van used by the neighbors, Dina and Andreas, who were traveling fabric salesmen. Είδη προικός, it said in block letters on the back door. "Dowry supplies": everything a woman needs to get set up in her new life. A good omen, I told myself, trying to forget about the haunted schoolhouse and the fact that I'd be living in the house below all alone.

The van was parked on the main road. You could drive this road for miles without seeing another car, but in Lia it was the equivalent of a major highway and was the first horizontal road in town. When my father left in 1949, he had never seen a wheeled vehicle; people didn't use them, because everyone climbed up footpaths dug into the mountainside like scars. A vertical village, Lia grew from the top down. Sitting in the center of the Mourgana range, it wraps itself around the necks of two gray and green mountains. From the abandoned border guard station above town, you can scale footpaths up to either peak. At the top of the shorter path is the church of the Prophet Elias, the patron saint of the village. Near the peak of the other is Kastri, where the walls of a *kastro*, a castle dating from the third century B.C., rise in massive blocks of crumbled majesty.

I unloaded my oversize wheeled suitcases from Asymina and dragged them down the main road, which bisected our neighborhood into two sections I called uptown and downtown. The entire neighborhood was known as Motsala, after the spring that gurgles out of the mountain just past the outer door to the Haidis house. My grandmother, then Eleni Haidis, grew up in this house. At nineteen, she was working in the garden by the spring when a thirty-two-year-old visitor strolled up the path and noticed her. A Liotan who was now a fruit seller living in Worcester, Massachusetts, he was wearing a really great-looking suit. He would soon become her husband, continuing to work in the United States and visiting every few years. Absent husbands were the norm in Lia as men left the rocky village to work as traveling tinkers or found jobs abroad, returning once a year or a decade to father children. Their wives and families awaited them, sometimes too trustingly; one woman waited for her husband for seventy years, until her death. In the meantime, he had started another family in America.

The Haidis home was where I'd live while rebuilding the uptown Gatzoyiannis home. A two-story building with a courtyard made of pink stone, the Haidis house still had its original gray keystone over the door. It read <<Κόπιασε, φίλε>> ("Rest, friend"), and it must have had magical powers of attraction, because by the time I lugged my bags down the steep path, I already had my first guest. Dusk was falling and the house was rapidly veering from cozy to gloomy, so I was delighted to see Foti Tsandinis at the door. He once owned a pizza place outside Worcester, and I recognized his shiny pate and tiny blue eyes. When Foti's wife was diagnosed with cancer, she quit chemotherapy and went to Lia with her husband to live out her remaining two years. Now a widower, Foti was president of the group of Liotes who ran the Xenona Inn. As if to advertise that he had lived in America, Foti was wearing an all-denim ensemble—jeans, denim shirt stretched over his ample paunch, and denim jacket, accessorized by a leather cap, as it was still chilly.

"I thought I'd see how you're doing," he said, kissing me hello. "I promised your aunt I'd keep an eye on you." That explained how he found me like a heat-seeking missile the minute I arrived. This was the work of Thitsa Kanta. Her husband, Thio Angelo, was the brother of Foti's deceased wife, so they were related by marriage. Furthermore, she had told me that when these senior citizens were children and Thitsa Kanta and Thitsa Lilia were too tired to herd their sheep up the mountain, Foti, a shepherd boy who was even poorer than they were, would do so in exchange for bread. Now, seventy years after watching over Thitsa Kanta's sheep, Foti felt responsible for herding her misguided niece.

"Great!" I exclaimed, although I was taken aback—not so much that Thitsa Kanta was checking up on me but that I was so pathetically glad to have the company, even though I had no idea what to talk about with my unexpected guest. So, like a good Greek hostess, I quickly offered to make him some coffee.

Unfortunately, the stove had other ideas. Although the stove lights went on, the burners did not heat up. Glad to see that his presence really was needed, Foti looked at the fuse box and flipped a switch. Suddenly, we were enveloped by the same darkness that shrouded the two empty houses in the neighborhood.

I realized that although the house had a large decorative candle, I had no matches. Then I heard footsteps on the road above. My uphill neighbor, the church cantor Spiro Karapanos, was enjoying his evening stroll. I called to him and he threw down a lighter. With his white hair, round glasses, and sport coat, Spiro looked like a professor, but he was actually a retired railroad worker and knew a thing or two about fuses. He ambled down, handed me a bouquet of purple wildflowers, flipped the fuse box back on, then moved on to the stove. Spiro seemed on the verge of identifying the problem when Foti invited me into the courtyard to admire the stars. Obediently, I followed but maneuvered us back inside just as Spiro was wrapping up the stove's shredded electrical cord, chewed through by a greedy mouse. Apparently, Foti had been trying to distract me from seeing a roasted mouse carcass. Although my aunts were oceans away, it seemed I now had some overprotective new uncles. I tried to let that thought comfort me as Spiro and Foti sauntered off into the darkness and I plugged in my electric radiator. But I was still a little lonely, so I decided to call Thitsa Kanta to let her know the bodyguard she had appointed for me was already hard at work.

"Foti invited me to stay in his spare room, but I'm not scared in this house," I lied.

"*Ah pa pa!*" she huffed. "You can't stay alone in a man's house, not even if the man is Foti. What everyone else gonna say?"

"Well, nothing," I ventured. "It seems like everyone else is asleep. It's really quiet here. But I'm not scared."

"Scared of that house—you should be scared of the whole village," Thitsa Kanta said. "You think they asleep, but they sneaky. They would watch you got to Foti's house, and then they lie about you. The villagers' lies killed my mother, you know."

I knew; during my grandmother's trial a few villagers testified that she had hidden treasure from the Communists, a charge that helped condemn her to death. But I also knew that those who had testified hadn't returned to the village.

"None of those people are here anymore, Thitsa Kanta," I protested, suddenly getting tired. "If they're even alive."

"Sure, they not there, but plenty of people who hate us are still there," she insisted. "Hate you, too, even though you a nice girl, because you American and my niece."

"Like who?"

"Like Kokkinos. When he own the *kafenion*, people come looking for my mother's house, he tell them your father's book all a lie."

I burst out laughing at the memory of the grimacing old man who used to run a shop my siblings and I called "the Communist Kafenion," a place we would run past frantically in hopes of avoiding his grim stare. I hadn't realized until now that the man who ran it had a last name that literally translated to "red."

"Hah, you laugh now, you think it's funny. We'll see if you still laughing after staying there a few months." Thitsa Kanta huffed.

"I don't think it's funny, I'm just laughing because I'm so tired," I said.

"I know, honey." Thitsa Kanta brightened up. "You go to sleep now. But first tell me who else you see besides Foti. Anyone ask about me? You tell them hi for me, but only if they ask about me first." I assured her I would and then settled down to bed.

That's when it started—a scrabbling noise like hundreds of dice rolling. It must be the goats on the roof that my mother had warned me about. Why hadn't I taken Foti up on his invitation? I rose from the bed, my flashlight/rape whistle in hand, and opened the door. There was no one in my courtyard, no goat on the roof, and the street above the house was still and dark. I felt as if I were the only person in the world, which would explain why the blinding moon was so intent on shining down on me. Then I heard it again, a cavalcade of scraping and thumping. The noise was coming from inside the ceiling. Anything that fit in there was too small to hurt me, I reasoned. And maybe the noise would keep away ghosts.

The next morning the sky was the clear, bright blue of the ceilings of some Greek churches, and as the clouds rolled off the road in smoky wisps and settled into the valley below, I felt full of energy, relieved to be alive. So I drove up to the neighborhood of Perivoli, where my grandparents, aunts, and father had once lived. The term *high-rise* took on an entirely new meaning in Lia. The area of Perivoli, "the Orchard," embodies the literal sense of the phrase, set in the halfway point in between the neighborhood of Mesochori (Middle Village), which is a measly 675 meters above sea level, and the *kastro* at the top of the mountain. Perivoli's landmark is Agios Demetrios, a gray stone church ringed by towering cypress trees, where, my aunts told me, my grandmother lit a candle every day. I stopped to light one myself. The church door was locked, a situation I'm sure my grandmother never encountered back when Lia was full of people appealing to Agios Demetrios and the church was in constant use. So I lit one of the candles lying in the sand-filled stand in front of the locked door. It was the best I could do.

A few meters up from Agios Demetrios were the remains of what was once my family's home. Although it was eerie and abandoned, the ruined building had an overgrown cragginess that was impressive. But now as I stared at the gorgeous decrepitude, my early-morning confidence crumbled like the house itself and I wondered if I should let sleeping shells of houses lie. The home had sat in ruined piles for years, left to rot by those who had actually lived there. Now here I was, a person who had never even seen the house intact, about to disturb the sorrowful quiet of the ruins, to tear up this earth all over again. Suddenly the idea of digging up this bloodstained soil and disturbing the resting ruin seemed like a colossal act of hubris. Maybe it was naive to reconstruct a house where so many had suffered and died, to try to wrap our family history up into a Technicolor happy ending. Thitsa Kanta's words from the night before ran on constant playback in my head. "There is hate in that village," she had warned me before hanging up. I wondered if the sweet-faced old villagers I had seen as I drove into town had testified against my grandmother and helped destroy this house that I planned, perhaps foolishly, to rebuild. In the clear light of morning in Lia, my plan to reclaim my Greek past seemed so presumptuous. So American.

I was still questioning the wisdom of my odyssey when I arrived back at the Haidis house and found that my neighbors, Dina and Andreas, had returned from a trip selling dowry supplies and visiting with their grandkids. It was the second marriage for both of them; each had two children from a first marriage. Several years ago Dina's son had died in a car crash, and the previous summer, in a coincidence that shows fate's cruel lack of imagination, Andreas's son was also killed in an auto accident. The couple were still wearing black mourning clothes. Dina, a handsome, middle-aged woman with chestnut hair pulled tautly into a ponytail, brought some *pita* (savory stuffed pie) over for me. She told me that Marianthe, a friendly old lady who lived near the Xenona, had recently lost her son to a heart attack and her husband died of cancer and grief fifteen days later. Dina's grandson had played with Marianthe's granddaughter the summer before. When Dina told the eleven-year-old that his friend lost her dad, too, he replied, "She has the same black fate I do."

When I was eleven, none of my fellow sixth-graders worried about fate. But the belief in fate is so prevalent in Greece that it has even shaped the language, as τύχη, which means "luck" or "fortune," is the root of many words, including *success* (επιτυχία), *failure* (αποτυχία), *happiness* (ευτυχία), and *misery* (δυστυχία). The word τύχη itself comes from the goddess Tyche, who had the power to determine men's fortunes. According to Robert Graves's *The Greek Myths*, "Tyche is altogether irresponsible in her awards, and runs about juggling with a ball to exemplify the uncertainty of chance: sometimes up, sometimes down."

Dina's examples of unfair, tragic fates in the village filled me with apprehension. I could have been drinking with my friends at the wine bar near my apartment in New York instead of listening to a catalog of recently deceased Liotes. Was it possible that the villagers shared an unlucky fate, and if they did, was I making myself part of that dark future? As for my present, it was looking increasingly bleak. I had no working stove and was about to go to bed hungry.

But Dina invited me to dinner that night; I soon learned that if the people of Lia were overly cursed with tragedy, they were blessed with an acute ability to enjoy life's small pleasures, everyday blessings such as tasty food, strong wine, and the company of friends. Dina and Andreas lived across the path from me in a whitewashed house that Andreas had expanded from a one-room shack into a village compound. It had a complex irrigation system to water the garden and feed two pools: one for a fish hatchery and the other for their grandchildren's visits. It also had a greenhouse, a grape arbor, a man-made waterfall, a tin roof because Andreas liked the sound it made when the rain hit it, and, that night, a fire in the fireplace. Crowded around the table with us were Dina and Andreas's yapping Pekinese, Ruda, and two strangers with faces that were almost as round and well scrubbed as our dinner plates. Dina introduced us. Also new immigrants to Lia, the men were Albanians, a father-and-son team who lived in Dina and Andreas's freestanding extra room next door. They were working around Lia in hopes of earning enough money to bring over the rest of their family: the mother, Xalime, and single youngest daughter, Dorina. Vladimiros, the father, was in his forties, with elegant mannerisms and a good command of Greek, although he tended to mix up genders, much to everyone's amusement. Netvil, the son, was fifteen, and went by "Net."

"I'm going to baptize Net this summer," Dina announced as the boy blushed. He and Vladimir were Muslim Albanians, unlike the ethnic Greeks living in Albania, who are called Northern Epirotes and are Orthodox Christians. "He insisted only I could do it," she confided. This was a great honor, as being a godparent had social, not just religious, significance. By baptizing Net, Dina would become his second mother, responsible for his welfare in the eyes of the church and the village. The only problem, Dina said as she pivoted between the stove and the table on which our plates were set, was that Net didn't want to change his name, but you need the name of a saint to be baptized in the Orthodox Church.

"What about Nectarios?" I asked, digging the obscure saint's name from deep in my memory bank. "He could use Net as a nickname."

"Great!" said Andreas, who, despite a certain lack of teeth, retained the wiry, tobacco-riddled good looks of a retired Marlboro Man. "Net, ladies love that name."

Net seemed pleased with his new Christian name and I was feeling optimistic, too. Maybe fate sent these men my way on purpose.

Zervas had told me to find workers for the house, and Vlad and Net needed jobs—I could hire them, at least to dismantle the ruins so we could recycle the stones.

As we drank vast quantities of wine and *tsipouro* (the homemade moonshine favored by Vlad and Andreas) and ate roast chicken, I asked Dina how she had met Andreas.

"At thirteen I married a man my parents chose, then had two kids, and got divorced," Dina began, tossing her ponytail. "By seventeen, I was single and living with my parents and children in Lamia. Andreas sold fabric and he kept coming around to the spring where we women would wash our clothes."

"I gave her some materials for a dress, you know, to make an impression," Andreas interjected.

"I bought that material!" Dina insisted. "But he kept hanging around me, and I got embarrassed, worried about what people might think." She shrugged. "So I married him."

Thirty-three years later, the match seemed to be working out. Dina and Andreas formed the social hub of the neighborhood, being among the youngest of the few families who lived in Lia year-round. Over dinner, we made plans for the spring and summer: trips to take, festivals to attend, meals to cook, schemes that got more outlandish as the moonshine diminished. Then I walked back across the way, only to realize that whatever lived in my ceiling was having a dinner party just as raucous as the one I'd left. The next day Net crawled into the attic to evict my uninvited guests. He pulled himself through the trapdoor in time to see several squirrels scurry out, just as an electrician from Ioannina arrived to fix the stove.

Those first few weeks, when I wasn't fighting vermin or unpacking, I hung out at the *kafenion*, the unofficial headquarters of any Greek village. A *kafenion* always contains a TV tuned to the news, sports, or a beauty pageant; a freezer full of ice cream; and lots of old men playing cards and debating loudly. Ours also had some groceries for sale, a potbellied stove in the middle of the room, a potbellied owner married to a petite Northern Epirote sylph named Stella, and their dervish of an eight-year-old son, Costa. It was frequented by a gang of regulars, including a friendly, kerchiefed, toothless lady who had given birth to a daughter thirty-odd years ago but never had a husband. Self-propagating, like Zeus from whose head Athena sprang, she had crossed the gender divide and spent her days sitting in the *kafenion* with the men while the rest of the women worked.

The *kafenion* was Lia's business and commercial center. On Mondays, Wednesdays, and Fridays, at about ten A.M., the postman came to have a coffee and pass out the mail. Although the population of Lia swelled to about three hundred in summer, in winter there were only some fifty full-time residents, and Liotes who were in the *kafenion* collected mail for their missing neighbors. In any case, the village was too small to have street names, so home delivery was not an option.

The postman was in his late thirties, dark-haired, handsome, and well liked but overshadowed by the blond lady doctor who came on Tuesdays and Fridays. Greek medical residents are required to spend a year doing an agricultural rotation, and this was hers. She filled prescriptions, listened to complaints, and looked sexy in her tight jeans all at the same time, and was therefore justly revered. I liked to imagine she and the mailman, who overlapped on Fridays, were involved in a passionate affair, because he always smiled shyly as he handed her rolled-up copies of *Agricultural Doctor* magazine as if they were long-stemmed roses.

On Sundays there was church, of course, but since the village had four churches and just one priest, who was also responsible for two other towns in the tri-village area, we waited to hear the church bells ring to learn where the service would be held. On Thursdays and Saturdays there were no scheduled activities, but Lia had plenty of unplanned visitors, such as the Gypsies who drove through town in their trucks, hawking everything from live chickens to plastic tables, blasting Greek tunes over loudspeakers.

Slowly I adjusted to the daily rhythm of Lia. I had been worried that village life might bore me after New York, but Lia was such a small village that just by virtue of being there you were instantly wrapped up in any excitement that happened. In New York I felt that there was always something fascinating going on, and I had to go out and find it; in Lia I began to feel that there was always something exciting going on and, like the Gypsy peddlers, it would come find me.

There was so much to do just getting settled. During the day, I tried to wrest control of the house from squirrels and ants or worked in the garden I was planting, with Dina's help, on the four small terraces that climbed up the courtyard wall. A hopeless city girl, I asked questions like "So, tomatoes grow aboveground, not underground?" But Dina didn't laugh; she just showed me how to place seeds deep into holes in the dirt, then surround them with *kopria*, goat dung she bought from a shepherdess named Iphigenia. She was so confident that the garden would be a success that she suggested we plant a clove of garlic, just in case, to ward off the evil eye attracted by the admiration and jealousy of passersby on the road above.

I also spent time entertaining unexpected visitors who arrived in a steady stream, bearing gifts of homemade *pita* or bread. I don't know if they assumed that as an American, I was inherently unable to cook, were glad to see a young person in the village, or were just curious about the newcomer. But my aunts had taught me my duty as a hostess, so I kept a doily-covered tray at the ready, and on it I would serve coffee, water, or juice and spoon sweets that a kind neighbor had given me. Spoon sweets are candied fruits or fruit rinds preserved in their own gelatinous juices. They must be difficult to make, because homemade ones are always served with great pride, so although I find them cloying, I always force myself to eat a few bites.

Once the kind, gossipy, bread-bearing ladies went home to cook dinner, I would sit on the veranda, watching the sunset. As dusk fell I would stare at the horizon, missing my aunts and even the grandmother I had never known, wishing they were there to enjoy the beauty of this place. With mountains all around, the sunset wasn't a ball of fire flaming out on the horizon, just long, slow, quiet shifts of light and expanses of pink in the distance. In New York, surrounded by high-rises, I never saw the sunset, which was my favorite time of day. I had lived in New York for almost six years and was just starting to get settled here in Lia. But sitting on my veranda, with a view that stretched for miles in all directions, I could almost convince myself I belonged in the village.

After dark I would go out in search of dinner, usually to Dina and Andreas's, where every meal was a masterpiece. A few times a week I would join Foti and a gang of garrulous local men to drive the hazardous mountain roads to *tavernas* in neighboring villages. My favorite nightspot was Louie's Grill in the diplomatically named village of Agoi Pantoi (All Saints). Another reverse immigrant, Louie had spent eleven years in Australia, then returned to open a *taverna*, where he served his own wine, squirted into carafes from a Poland Spring water dispenser. His *taverna* was decorated with wall plaques, each bearing the face of a philosopher and a limerick about the great thinker's relationship to wine, such as "They all had lots of ladyfriends / ten or twenty-five / But Plato who didn't drink at all / He had only . . . five."

On these nights of booze and lamb chops I realized that in the winter and early spring, the village is a cross between a frat house and a retirement home. Every night men between fifty and, well, I don't know, but my great-uncle lived to be 107, pile into cars and go to a *taverna*, where they eat fried cheese, drink moonshine, and insult one another happily. Their wives are dead, in Athens babysitting the grandkids until school lets out, divorced (in one rare case), or home doing something useful. It was an exact reversal of Lia's prewar situation, when the village was filled with women raising children, and the men were all off working in Athens or America.

I was surprised at how much I enjoyed both my daytime, female endeavors and my nighttime, male adventures. But my favorite part of the day was just after sunset, when I would walk alone from the Haidis house at one end of the village to the playground at the other end, twenty minutes away. The Xenona was still closed, but the stroll took me through my new neighborhood. One day as I walked back home, mulling over what I should plant in my garden next, I almost bumped into a white-haired old man with a cane, shuffling along. I jumped back, excusing myself, then stared at his white mustache and narrow eyes, trying to figure out where I had met him before. He pivoted left as quickly as he could and started hobbling toward his house, a yellow-painted old building that still had the word *kafenion* painted above the door. It was Kokkinos! And when he appeared in front of me as just another frail old man I forgot to be scared of him. "Good night," I called out.

He turned to stare at me, then nodded quickly before shuffling inside, as his petite, kerchiefed wife waved at me from inside the dark room. I walked on quickly, flushed with my victory. I had flashed him the eager smile I gave to all Liotes I met on my evening walks, those I recognized as well as those I didn't. People in Lia were proud of their ability to hold grudges for generations, not speaking to those who had done them wrong, a talent at which Thitsa Kanta excelled. But I knew exactly who that man was when I smiled at him, the Communist Kafenion owner, a looming villain from my childhood, although in my memories he was much taller and the mustache was more of a handlebar. Reality had cut him down from a hulking figure to a stooped old man, but when I recognized him, I smiled to show I belonged there as much as he did with his grimly set forehead. Whatever our history, we were neighbors now. I reached the playground just as it got dark, then turned home, walking briskly, but not hurrying.

Two weeks after I arrived, Foti called me with a late-breaking bulletin: the Xenona was open. I wandered over and introduced myself to Nikki and Fanis, the new innkeepers. Nikki told me that she had been born in Lia but left as a teenager, moving to Germany to live with her sister. In Germany she met and married Fanis, another Greek immigrant, a truck driver turned businessman, and together they had lived all over Africa before moving to Athens when their children were ready for high school. Now those children were married, and Nikki and Fanis had come back to Lia to rent the inn. With their smattering of German and English, they were determined to turn a profit by increasing visitors to Lia, which normally attracts outsiders only on holidays and in hunting season.

"Africa—how exciting!" I exclaimed.

"It was," answered Fanis, who was tall and debonair, with impeccable posture. "I'll tell you a secret if you promise not to tell anyone else—they'll never believe me." I nodded and he leaned forward. "Once, in South Africa, I danced with Elizabeth Taylor. It was a fancy dinner party and she grabbed my hand and pulled me to the dance floor, saying, 'Come here, Zorba.'" He sat back and smiled.

"Is that why you came back?" I asked Nikki, a no-nonsense woman with short reddish hair and toffee-colored eyes. "So Fanis wouldn't run off with Elizabeth Taylor?"

"No." Nikki laughed, looking up from the sink. "We moved to Athens so our children could grow up in Greece. And we came here because, well, this is home. My brother had lived in South Africa, too, but when he was dying of cancer, he asked to be brought back to Lia. As soon as the ambulance crossed the border from the next village, he died." She nodded, proud of her brother's stubbornness and excellent timing. "There's a shrine erected to him right on that spot."

I suddenly understood why no one there seemed surprised that I, too, had made my way back to Lia. My friends thought I was quixotic, adventurous to move to this tiny village; my family thought I was crazy. But not one villager asked what I was doing there, and I loved no longer having to explain myself. The Liotes simply took it for granted that I would want to be there, where my family began.

After a few weeks I had to trek to Ioannina, the nearest city and the capital of the province. Built on a lake at the foot of several mountains, Ioannina was an hour from Lia and was home to our family friends George and Kaity. My father is their son's godfather, so we are related in the eyes of the church. They were ecclesiastically bound to help me with the annoying tasks of relocating.

Shortly after I arrived, George took me to see Mr. Natsis, the passport official/puppetmaster who had made me run all over Manhattan to gratify his bureaucratic whims. Natsis had recently decided that I had to sign, in front of him, a statement expressing my desire to become a Greek citizen—those documents that had been faxed from the consulate in New York were irrelevant. So George and I typed one up and arrived to find Natsis stooped over coffee in a tiny room littered with folders. It was like seeing the Wizard of Oz behind the curtain. This little bald man had made me, and all five marble floors of the Greek consulate in New York, tremble?

Natsis glanced up from his folder. He looked like a typical Greek civil servant—miserable. In a country where the average worker is lively to ebullient, I couldn't help but notice that every government clerk is ashen-faced and unsmiling. In Greece, the waiters are amused, the soldiers are raucous, the priests, jubilant. But the civil servants are grim, harried, worn out by the pressures of shuffling papers until two P.M. five days a week (except for strikes and holidays). They're exhausted by the endless toil of creating hoops for the fearful public to jump through in order to achieve their unrealistic goals of building a house, obtaining a visa, or mailing a package. George put my paper in front of Natsis. I signed it with a flourish.

"You should have had this from the start, from the *proxeneio* in New York," Natsis spat, stamping the document.

"I did! They faxed it to you!" I insisted, wanting credit for my wasted mornings. But George hustled me out of there before Natsis could take an even stronger dislike to me. Led by George, who seemed to be on a first-name basis with everyone in the city, I moved on to a computer store to make history. I was ordering a computer we all believed would be the first in the entire Mourgana range. It would connect me on my mountaintop with the outside world. For such a trailblazing machine, the salesman explained, it made sense to get the most expensive model, with a low-radiation flat screen.

"I'll get the Internet, way up in my village?" I asked. But the salesman assured me it would work and he'd deliver it once the components arrived from Athens. No, he didn't take credit cards or checks. Cash only. I could pay the 1,600 euros upon delivery. The main task I wanted to accomplish in Ioannina would be far less expensive but much more difficult. Although he couldn't bring himself to start the project, my father longed to see his childhood home rise again, so he offered to fund the reconstruction. But the rebuilding was up to me, and I felt that before I could start, I needed to read the book *Eleni*. I knew I wouldn't be able to do it in Lia, alone in the house where my grandmother had been born, a house that might be full of ghosts (if a few noisy squirrels didn't scare them away each night). And I didn't want to read it in the home of one of my neighbors, however kindly they seemed. Thitsa Kanta had warned me that no one in the village was above suspicion, anyone could turn against you as quickly as some villagers had betrayed her mother. And I'd been in the village only a few weeks. I didn't know my new friends well enough to know how friendly we really were. I had conquered Kokkinos, forcing him to acknowledge my greeting. But by the time I had returned to my house and the village was completely dark and silent, it no longer seemed like a victory, just a near collision with an addled old man who probably wasn't sure if I was his granddaughter, a visiting social worker, or an enemy.

So I told George and Kaity I planned to visit with them for a few days. I wanted company, but really, I needed the distractions of a city to put some distance between myself and the story I could no longer avoid. I needed to walk outside and be a stranger, not a neighbor, and I couldn't do that in Lia.

I grew up hearing my family's story from my aunts' tearful reminiscences or overheard laments. But I consciously tried to spare myself from too many painful details. Now that I was about to reconstruct my grandmother's home, it was time to learn about the life she spent there. I felt I couldn't start rebuilding the house until I had a sense of its past. So I began to read *Eleni*. The first section was fun, and had me laughing to myself as I read about my aunts as children; their strong personalities were formed even then. But as the story intensified, I could read for only an hour at a time, with the promise of one of Ioannina's many distractions at the end of each chapter. I read up to the part where Eleni says good-bye to her children, knowing they will escape while she has to remain behind. Then I went to Diethnes, a sweetshop my grandfather frequented, and treated myself to *kaimaki* ice cream, vanilla with rosewater sauce. I returned to Kaity's and went to bed to read some more. The escape chapters were easy, because of the suspense, but I trembled as I turned the pages. I stopped before the section called "Retribution," because I knew I couldn't handle it in the dark. If I continued reading, I would spend the rest of the night awake, staring at the ceiling, waiting for daylight to trickle in from under the curtain. Instead, I flipped through a Greek *Vogue* I had bought at the local bookstore.

The next morning I finished reading *Eleni* as Kaity bustled around, preparing breakfast, making reassuring kitchen noises by rinsing plates, squeezing orange juice, and lifting hardboiled eggs out of a pot with a clinking spoon. It was horrifying to read about my grandmother's capture, imprisonment, trial, torture, and execution by firing squad. My stomach felt hollow, my throat dry, and my brain fevered as every noise, smell, and sight that confronted me when I looked up from the page seemed a thousand times more acute than normal. It was as if any present distractions clashed irrationally and inappropriately with the terrifying world of the past that I was immersed in while reading. But once I had finished absorbing the book, knowing exactly what took place helped me separate the story from myself. The shadowy, incomplete childhood vision I had of my family's history had been replaced by a reality— a horrific reality, but something concrete and contained.

Once, on a family visit to Lia, my father had gotten out of the rental car to greet an old friend and left the unfamiliar stick shift in neutral. The car rolled backward, its wheels inching out over the edge of the mountain road before one of us slammed the shift into park. It was August, and my mother, with her usual glass-half-empty charm, later said to me, "I was thinking how weird it would be, given your name, if you died in the same village as your grandmother on exactly the same day." She had articulated my unspoken, unrealistic, but seemingly possible fear that Lia's tragic past could somehow erupt and overtake our safe present.

Reading the book reassured me that the situations it described were historic events that happened once, not a cycle that would keep happening, even if you put people with the same names in the same place. Now I was glad to be reclaiming the home, transforming it from the ruins of a prison to a house where people could be happy again. I knew I couldn't change my family's past, but at least I could reshape my relationship to the village where it took place.

A week later, after my visit to Ioannina, I was back in Lia when the computer guy arrived as promised. "Wow, you live really high up," he observed.

"Yup." I didn't want to chitchat—I wanted to check my e-mail.

"Well, I bet it's nice and quiet here," he said, starting to put the machine together.

"Yeah, that's why I really need the Internet for work."

I was not at my friendliest. My brave face began to crumble as he kept trying, and failing, to make an Internet connection. After getting to know—and like—my kindly neighbors, I believed that Thitsa Kanta was wrong in her sinister view of Lia and that my time there would be pleasant as well as productive. I might even enjoy my time in Lia instead of wishing that the rebuilding would proceed faster. But I still wanted an escape valve, a link to my old life in New York, to my friends, and their now-exotic-seeming lives full of office intrigue and tortured romances. While he typed futilely, I panicked quietly, pacing around the living room and swearing softly in English. I could tell he wondered if it was the altitude or the isolation that had gotten to the crazy American woman.

When he gave up, shrugged, and asked to be paid for his time, I explained that I didn't want a doorstop, or even a typewriter, that cost 1,600 euros. If he couldn't hook it up to the Internet, he had to take it back. He looked confused—return policies are as popular as credit cards in Ioannina. And he was just an attractive nineteen-year-old who didn't want to deal with a hysterical American on a remote mountaintop when he could be back in Ioannina, drinking a café frappé on the harbor and calling his friends masturbators, that most cherished of Greek insults.

After consulting his boss via cell phone, we decided I would keep both the cash and computer, and he'd come back next week to try again. He took off, leaving me quivering with frustration.

I had no ties to the outside world, but I told myself I couldn't panic about that until the computer boy returned and the Great Internet Experiment finally, officially failed completely. Luckily, my neighbors were starting to seem less like a Greek spin-off of *The Golden Girls* and more like potential friends, fascinating companions with decades' worth of stories to tell. One night Dina invited me for dinner, tempting me with the promise of *lachanopita*, a vegetable pie containing ten different kinds of greens, including nettles. I arrived to find Andreas and an elderly raconteur named Vangelis Panagiotou drinking wine mixed with Coca-Cola, the libation of choice for male Liotes. A dashing widower with an impossibly high forehead I came to recognize as Epirote pattern baldness, Vangelis made up in stage presence what he lacked in teeth.

The conversation at Dina and Andreas's was always as exciting as the mixed drinks; a few nights before, they had been polling guests for names of women who might be interested in marrying the son of some clients of theirs in Arta, who was rich and handsome but had been a little, well, nervous, ever since a cabinet fell on his head during an earthquake more than twenty years ago. But that night, the main topic was the house I was about to start building—the men remembered it when it had belonged to my grandmother. Vangelis called her Kichina Gadzoyanova, a village nickname created by feminizing my grandfather's nickname, Kicho, and their last name.

"Kichina had a great house," Vangelis said, dipping a kiwi slice into his wine and Coke. "Kicho sent money from America to make a cement courtyard, so it was straight and flat, like no other yard in Lia." He even remembered attending my father's lavish baptism as a six-year-old boy. "It was the first time I saw cement and the first time I ate white bread. Everyone ate *bobota*"—corn bread—"but Kichina paid for white bread to keep us kids satisfied while the grown-ups ate inside."

I smiled. This was only the second time I'd met Vangelis, but I felt that he'd known me since before I was born, that we shared in the same communal history of this small village. Vangelis also recalled the Haidis house I now lived in as it was originally, before it was burned during the Second World War by the Germans, who tossed an old woman, a distant relative of mine, into the flames because she refused to leave her goats. Later, when George told me they unearthed her skeleton while renovating the place, it became harder to convince myself that the sounds I still heard in the night were squirrels.

"Where have the years gone?" wondered Vangelis, shaking his head at me. "I remember your grandmother, Kichina Gadzoyanova, standing in her yard as clear as day. She looked just like you, blond, blue-eyed."

Andreas choked up recalling how he saw the guerillas lead her, battered, unable to walk, and tied onto a donkey, to the yard of the Haidis house to point out where she had buried some "treasure," a few by-then rotted blankets she had saved for Thitsa Olga's dowry. "Those were ugly times," he said. "Toward the end of the civil war, we kids joined my father in Ioannina, but my mother stayed behind to take care of the house. When the retreat orders came, the Communists took everyone to Hungary, and it was six years before my mother could return. We all met her boat in Igoumenitsa."

"But she was always afraid, my mother-in-law," Dina added. "She lived in fear until the end of her days."

To a small degree, I knew how Andreas's mother felt. I was happy to be talking to people who remembered my grandmother. This was why I had come to Lia, to live with people who knew my family and to make a place for myself in our village. But although

I had now read about the details of my grandmother's life, I still got nervous when villagers talked about the war, as if the past could creep into the present and envelop us, and our convivial dinner party could degenerate into the tense world of neighbor against neighbor, which seemed so vivid when my new friends discussed their wrenching pasts. So I was glad when Andreas brightened as he reminisced about my great-grandfather Kicho Haidis, who, also being named Christos, had the same local nickname as his son-in-law. "He was sneaky," Andreas said, laughing. "When they dismantled the Motsala spring to rebuild it, they found a hose he had trained to go to his fields. 'It just drew a little water,' he said when they caught him."

"All the old-timers were sneaky," added Vangelis. "They had to be cunning to survive under the Turks."

Years ago, they told me, sneakiness was the mother of invention in Lia, where most men were itinerant tinkers, traveling around, mending pots. They developed a dialect called *alafiatika*, to talk to one another without customers understanding. The *kalantzides*—tinkers—had names for all the important things in life: *tsakta* is "bread"; *shoro*, "wine"; *tchukali*, "meat." *I'm cracking the code!* I thought triumphantly. My neighbors trusted me enough to teach me their secret dialect, and if we spoke the same language now, I'd have to trust them, too.

As glad as I was to be learning Lia's secret language, I still longed to be able to communicate with the world at large. But it had been hubris, I reasoned, to think that I could be a one-woman technology center there in the Mourgana mountain range. So when the computer boy returned, I greeted him sullenly and read, with my back toward him, as he worked. I couldn't watch. He interrupted me. "Could you come here a minute?" I got up, slowly. "I want to show you how to connect to the Internet."

"It works?" I gasped. He wagged his finger at me. "You should have more faith." He took off, still chuckling at the foreigner living so high up that new modems couldn't recognize her slow Internet connection and he'd had to come back a second time with an out-dated model.

I'd never been so happy to see a handsome man leave. He was right; I needed a more positive attitude. I could live in Lia while working with editors and cyberchatting with friends in New York; my plans were slowly being realized. Now that my computer worked, I was ready to take care of more important business. I called Thomas—the only local contractor and the man I planned to hire to build the Gatzoyiannis house—and told him I was ready to negotiate prices. As he strutted up to the house, I was glad to see that Thomas was only about fifty—young for Lia—and muscular. If anyone in Lia was up to the task of rebuilding my grandparents' home, it was this guy. Short and sturdy with black curly hair and ice blue eyes, one of which wandered a bit, Thomas looked as if he would have wrestled in high school, if he hadn't quit school as a teenager to work in construction.

Our summit meeting took place on the porch of the Haidis house. Thomas said the house could cost as much as 30 million drachmas, but he would do it for 25 million. (It was clear that he hadn't gotten to know the euro.) I insisted that was several million more than the prices I had been quoted in Athens. (Of course, Thomas, as the only contractor for miles around, had a certain home-field advantage over an Athenian import.) Our referee, Foti, who was Thomas's godfather but my Thitsa Kanta–appointed protector, kicked at the stairs of the porch and removed his leather cap.

"Those guys in Athens would hire Albanians under the table, then do it for less because they don't pay taxes or health insurance, and all the profit goes—*tsak!*—right in their pocket," Thomas objected. "I live here, so I need to run an honest site—I can't have investigators coming up to check on me all the time."

"I want it to be a good deal for us both," I insisted. "But I don't want you to take advantage of me because I'm an American—or a woman. This is a small house you're building, not a villa!"

"Can I make a suggestion?" Foti interrupted, putting his cap back on. "Why don't you both draw up some budgets, think about it for a few days, and decide after Easter—building won't start until after that anyway." He had a point. It was mid-April, Easter was just a few weeks away, and we would all be busy with church services until then. I was new in town, I needed to make friends, not enemies. We agreed and shook hands.

Having triumphed over technology and avoided an ugly confrontation, I was proud of conquering the Mourgana range. This lasted until, after an orgy of e-mail checking, I went downstairs and stepped, ankle-deep, into the water that had flooded my basement kitchen. Squirrels and kitchen floods weren't major obstacles in rediscovering my homeland—after all, Odysseus battled angry Cyclopses and duplicitous nymphs during his odyssey. But the vermin and the stagnant water still posted a problem for me—especially since I didn't have a superintendent to call for help. Odysseus had his crew to aid him. By now I had mine. I rounded up the usual experts to battle the lake in the kitchen. Foti thought it had flooded because of the rain. Spiro said there was a leak. Finally, Fanis arrived from the Xenona and, proving to be as nimble a plumber as he had been a dancer squiring Elizabeth Taylor around South African society, replaced the rubber joints that hold the pipes together; they had frozen over the winter, then burst when I ran the water, causing leaks.

After my advisers left, I pulled back my comforter to put new pillowcases on the bed. There it was: a large black scorpion, curled up on my pillow like a mint at a fancy hotel. On closer inspection I realized it was dead and threw it in the trash. Now that I was alone, even a dead scorpion seemed like a bad omen. If Thitsa Olga was right about scorpions, were my other aunts right about Albanians, wolves, and ghosts? I took my blanket and slept on the banquette in the living room, leaving the light on.

I was still lying there the next day when Vladimiros knocked on the door. I had told him I wanted to see anything he found while tearing down the old walls, no matter how useless it seemed. Even a shard of pottery would be valuable because it had belonged to my family. And I was still hoping, just a bit, that he might find the treasure of Ali Pasha. But what he had in his hand was far more exciting. When he'd lifted up the rock above the house's original cornerstone, he had uncovered a Turkish coin. I turned it over in my hand—it was bronze and concave, with Arabic-looking writing and a curlicue design that resembled a flower. I had learned that back when the house was built, masons would place a coin on the cornerstones of a house to make it *siderenio*, strong as metal. I knew the Gatzoyiannis' house had existed when my grandfather's elder brother was born in it in 1870, during the Turkish occupation. If I could decipher the coin's date, which was not written in modern Arabic numerals, I would have a better idea of the date of construction. The coin was a clue that would lead back in time and also a sign that I was finally moving forward toward uncovering my family past, starting to round the bend that would close my ellipse.

THREE
DIVINE INTERVENTION

<<Αφού μπήκες στο χορό, θα χορέψεις.>>

"SINCE YOU'RE STANDING ON THE DANCE FLOOR,

YOU'RE GOING TO HAVE TO DANCE."

April 23

I'm sitting on a boulder, watching Net stack the stones that cover the courtyard of the Gatzoyiannis house in neat piles, ready for reuse. Heaving a pick and a spade, Vlad and Thomas are digging trenches about three feet deep. They're really just deepening the original foundation of the house so that we can pour concrete. I'd join in, but when it comes to lifting boulders, I'd be more comic relief than any real help. So I'm writing in my journal, taking pictures, and patting the stray dog that followed me up here. All of which I can do while eavesdropping.

"Net, you should be in school, jackass!" Thomas yells to the boy. "You don't want to be my age and working with your hands, ruining your back."

"School expensive," Net says, shrugging. "I like work, to make money."

"All money gone in the pyramids," Vlad explains to Thomas. He's told me this before—like so many Albanians, he lost all his savings by investing in crooked pyramid schemes whose collapse led to rioting in Albania in the late 1990s.

"School's free—the government pays," answers Thomas, who has no children but many devoted godchildren in villages throughout the Mourgana. "They'll even pay for a cab to take Net back and forth to school in Filiates." He turns to the boy. "You're shy, because you make mistakes in Greek. But by September you'll have muscles and money from working all summer, and speak Greek better than I do. Eleni, what do you think?"

Finally, a situation where I can help. I put down my pen and look up. "I think he'd be the most popular boy on campus."

Greece is not for spectators. It's as if the entire nation has been raised to believe that in the University of Life, participation counts for 90 percent of your grade. I learned this the first time I tried to parallel park in Ioannina. It soon turned into a group effort, with coaching from local shopkeepers who shouted directions and pantomimed jerking the steering wheel in the hope that I wouldn't crash into their window displays. I welcomed the help—I'm a team player. It was the critical commentary that stung. First, a jowly truck driver rolled down his window to say, "You don't know how to drive, my girl." Then several girls in halter tops honked at me, sure I was giving lady drivers a bad name. Finally, a man in a BMW spat, not at *me* but at the wheel of my car as I blocked the one-way street.

But even when I wasn't starring in the slapstick comedy that is driving in Ioannina, I was often sucked in for audience participation. Once, as I circled the block looking for a spot, I witnessed an argument in front of the ATM machine. It started out between two guys but soon involved a screaming woman, a priest, and the police. As I backed into a makeshift parking spot wedged between a Mercedes, a Fiat, and a large blue fruit truck stopped in the middle of the street, a matron in a passing car rolled down her window and asked, "What's going on?" I thought she was commenting on my driving until she added, "Over at the bank—what's happening?"

All I could say was "I don't know." In New York I had carefully honed my avoidance reflex, learning to turn away from any unpleasantness in the street, no matter how loud or foul. Collision between two taxis? Not my problem. Hirsute college student selling pot? At least he's showing some initiative. Homeless man defecating in the middle of Saint Mark's Place? I can't see you; I am suddenly engrossed in the body-piercing options on display at the end of the street.

Once I arrived in Greece, I quickly realized there were no sidelines for me to stand on anymore. There was always some kind of festival, political scandal, or local gossip everyone talked about so much that I got sucked into caring about it to. And so each time I heard church bells in the morning, I'd bound out of bed, determined to find whatever service I might be missing. (Church in Lia is never boring—children spend the liturgy chasing one another around the nave, the occasional snake slithers in to be stomped on by a vigilant church council member, and parishioners interrupt services with theological debates; once, a visiting Liote got into a screaming fight with Sofia the lady cantor, sixty inches of religious fervor with curly gray hair and a Minnie Mouse voice, debating when it is appropriate to take Communion.) I even feigned interest in soccer and studied national politics in case I needed to take part in a heated debate. With so much of my time devoted to excavating my family's difficult past, I sought out any distraction that didn't have to do with my history.

The spectacle that demanded the most audience participation of all was Easter. I arrived in Greece shortly after Lent started. My family observes Lent in America by following Greek Orthodox customs: not eating meat, dairy products, or anything higher on the food chain than shellfish. To be honest, we usually shorten our fasting period from the full forty days to Holy Week itself, and then outdo ourselves trying to find delicious combinations that are kosher, so to speak, such as shrimp in lobster sauce. Now that's exactly what all theologians say you shouldn't do, turn Lent into a forty-day shellfish banquet. But I felt okay about bending the rules. After all, the main point of fasting is not to approximate Jesus' suffering, which would be impossible, a Sunday school teacher once taught me, but to de-emphasize the physical and nurture the spiritual side of life, to act as a constant reminder that this is a special, somber time of year. This is also why weddings, baptisms, and other celebrations aren't held during Lent.

Apparently, my family isn't alone in trying to turn Lent into a culinary adventure. En route from Athens to Lia, I stopped at a roadside McDonald's to use the bathroom and spotted two huge posters advertising the specials that were available to help us celebrate ΜcΣαρακοστή (McLent), a happy marriage of the commercial and the spiritual. On a bright green background were printed the words EVERYBODY READY? and then in different colors and fonts, fAstIng. "Fasting is an old tradition and an opportunity to try something new," explained a paragraph under this eye-catching headline. "Now old and young alike can avidly follow the custom and enjoy the renowned McLent!" At the bottom of the paragraph was the slogan "Surrender to McDonald's!"

I hadn't spent Lent in Greece since I was seven years old, so to me, McLent was a new and exciting endeavor. I soon realized that even more Greeks were following the buildup to Easter than the windup to the World Cup that obsesses the nation every fourth summer. Approximately 95 percent of Greece's population is Greek Orthodox, and since the religion is so common, it has become commonplace, something that fits easily into everyday life, without too much soul-searching required. For me, in America, Greek Orthodox Easter meant a weekend of celebration, capped off by a huge feast at my parents' house, to which I invited interested non-Greek friends who had nothing else to do that weekend. But in Greece, from the first day of Lent, Easter fever was everywhere, including on TV, which was clogged with ads for various types of *lambades*, the decorated Easter candles that godparents buy for their godchildren to take to church on Sunday. I hadn't known *lambades* were such a big deal, but I was glad to learn, because it provided me with a conversation starter for chatting up kids: "What does your *lambada* look like?" The smallest children, whose parents still had control over them, were carrying traditional versions, decorated with ribbons, flowers, or wooden boats. The ones with purchasing power, four-year-olds and up, lobbied for *lambades* decorated with the colors of a favorite soccer team for boys, and for girls, the internationally adored Barbie.

By the middle of Lent, I had acquired my fair share of Easter decor, including red candles in the shape of eggs (red to symbolize the blood of Christ) and a table runner embroidered with red eggs and yellow chicks. But I still needed some more prosaic household items, such as a garden hose and small dessert plates on which to serve spoon sweets. So I headed to Filiatés, an old Turkish city that had aged, quietly, into a provincial Greek town. At forty-five minutes away, it was the nearest commercial center to Lia. I parked in front of a fountain on the main square and went straight to the aptly named παντοπωλείο, the "everything store." The garrulous old man behind the counter said he had anything I could ever want—but since it was all massed in dusty piles, I had to tell him what that was and then he would search for it. The man's body was as frail as his personality was robust. Thin, tall, and stooped, he was as speedy as one would expect a seventy-four-year-old man with an intravenous port in his arm to be. As he shuffled around, lifting up toasters and place mats in search of my dessert plates, he told me about himself and his recent illness. But he also wanted to learn about me. Was I married?

I wasn't. In New York, this response often invited a crinkly-eyed smile of reassurance: "A good man is hard to find in this city!" But the wise Everything Man saw the decision to marry as a unilateral one on my part. "Find someone to share your bread with," he advised. At that moment my cell phone rang; Kaity's number lit up.

"Hello, girlfriend," I trilled. (Kaity and I called each other girlfriend despite our twenty-five-year age difference; I did the same with my frequent playmate in Lia, a six-year-old named Popi.)

"Where are you?" Kaity asked from her third-floor apartment in bustling Ioannina.

"In Filiates, at the everything store."

"Find a church and go to it," she said, issuing an emergency bulletin. "It's the holiday of the Hairetismous, the Greetings to the Virgin Mary."

"Oh." I paused, racking my brain. "Is this a major holiday?"

"Not really," Kaity said. "But I'm not calling because of the service. See, if you take a flower off the garland that surrounds the icon of the Virgin Mary and sleep with it under your pillow, you'll dream of the name of the man you're going to marry."

I knew this kind of practice is not sanctioned, or even condoned, by the church. But with a belief in fate and a belief in God both being so fundamental in Greece, it was only natural that the two would intertwine like the vines that were beginning to grow on the grape arbor in my yard. I told myself I was interested in this ritual only as a folklorist. But the truth was, sleeping on the banquettes of the Haidis living room had me wishing there was someone to share my bread with in the kitchen. In New York, with so many distractions, I liked being single and I had little patience for men who, once I started dating them, quickly became more annoying than appealing. I'd broken up with my last boyfriend after he proudly announced that he refused to tell people his age. (It was twenty-eight, I learned, thanks to www.anybirthday.com—too old to be so affected and too young to have something to hide.) My aunts said I was too picky, but I preferred to call myself "independent," and on good days in New York I thought of myself as a shorter, blonder version of Mary Tyler Moore tossing her ill-advised beret into the air. But in Lia, I wished, just a little, that I was rebuilding the house with a partner. So I packed up my purchases, paid the everything man, and asked directions to the nearest house of worship in order to find out if the Virgin Mary planned on sending Mr. Right my way.

I found the large, newish church just past the main square. In front of the altar the priest was intoning behind the flower-framed icon of the Panagia, the All-Holy One. All of Filiates was there— harried mothers and dutiful fathers with toddlers in tow, toothless crones, and clusters of tough-looking teenage girls wearing denim. I stepped in line with a row of older women heading toward the altar. Each kissed the icon, although none took a flower. But why would they? These women were grandmothers; they knew who they ended up sharing their bread with and were probably already sick of him by now.

It was finally my turn. I kissed the icon, grasped a white carnation, and was about to escape. Then I felt the eyes of the faithful boring into my back. Here I was, a stranger in a pleather raincoat— I couldn't be seen stealing flowers from the Virgin Mary! I dropped my carnation back onto the icon, trying to make it seem as if I had picked it up accidentally, on account of a strange tic of the hand.

Then I crept back to the entryway of the church and hid behind a carved wooden iconostasis, glumly watching a gang of teenage boys in track pants come and kiss another, silver-covered icon of the Mother and Child. Following one buzz-cut head as it dipped down, I noticed that two flowers had been placed behind the icon— a white carnation and a deep pink, almost red, rose. A second chance! As I stood there, debating whether the Virgin Mary wanted me to take the rose, a young mother lifted her chubby four-year-old up toward the icon.

"Aren't you going to kiss it?" she asked. He reached up enthusiastically, took the icon in both of his meaty little hands, tipped it toward himself, and gave it a big, loud smack—knocking the rose onto the table right in front of me. It was divine intervention. I snatched up the rose, my heart pounding so loudly that I could hear it through my sweater, through the pleather, and over the priest's chanting. Then I sauntered out, holding the flower, expecting to be stopped by the men who were standing behind the candle booth. But no one made a move. My rose and I were home free.

It wasn't until I was safely on my way to Lia that I noticed how intensely fragrant the rose was, an almost miraculous combination of incense and rose essence. I did put it under my pillow that night but didn't hear any names in my sleep, at least not any that I remembered. I was disappointed but not disheartened. Receiving messages from saints was new to me. If I paid attention, I was sure I'd eventually learn to listen properly.

The tomato plants in my garden were now so tall that Dina had to show me how to stake them. But my popularity with some of the nonvegetable inhabitants of Lia wasn't growing quite so rapidly. Dina had started the staking project while I was in Filiates, and she told me that Net had strolled by on the road above and laughed at her for struggling with the long sticks. "Eleni doesn't have real stakes," she explained.

"If she doesn't know how to tend her own tomatoes, maybe you should let them rot," he replied.

"I told him, 'That's a fine thing to say about someone who is employing your whole family!'" Dina scowled. "And he said, 'I was just kidding.'"

Net was always nice to me but so awkward that I felt uncomfortable myself. Maybe he was joking in some culturally relative brand of humor you had to be Albanian to really understand. Or did the boy really want to curse my tomatoes and, by association, me? Like me, he was a newcomer there. But his comment made me wonder about the native Liotes. How did they feel about my bumbling presence, an ignorant New Yorker always in need of advice and agricultural instruction?

With Easter coming, I was too busy preparing for the holiday to stew about Net's remark. On Palm Sunday I woke up to the kind of cataclysmic storm that explains why the ancient Greeks called the Mourgana range and its surroundings the *Keraunon Oroi* (Thunder Mountains). That Sunday's storm was way scarier than the Disney World roller coaster of the same name. But Palm Sunday is the kickoff for Holy Week, and as a newly minted Liote, I was not going to let mine get rained out. Religion was a major component of everyone's daily life there, not just a convenient end to a Sunday drive. And I wanted to be a part of the action. The villagers were teaching me to plant vegetables and navigate Lia's social scene—I wanted to show them I was an eager pupil. So I was determined to start Holy Week off right, by going to church and receiving palm fronds in memory of those that were showered on Jesus on his entrance to Jerusalem. Most people place the palms behind the icons on their mantel, where they are said to bring good luck the entire year. I was not about to let a little rain—or even the gushing torrents that were pelting Lia—jeopardize a year's worth of luck. Since moving to the village, I had somehow become superstitious. In New York I didn't bend down to pick up lucky pennies on the sidewalk. But in Lia, alone in the Haidis house, I felt I needed any divine help I could get.

I ran up the slick path and squished, sopping wet, into my car to drive through the thick, wet fog toward Agia Paraskevi, the church at the end of the village, next to the Xenona. I had barely set out when I saw the village president, Nikolas Skevis, hobbling toward me with his cane, water coursing off his raincoat. I pulled over to offer him a ride. That's when he broke the news. "There's no church," he said, shaking his head as drops of water hit me through the open window. "Father Prokopi is sick. He went to the hospital yesterday."

I was stunned. The storm was bad enough, but a sick priest during Holy Week is like the Grinch stealing Christmas. "What about Easter?" I asked.

"We'll see how he feels," Nikolas replied, puttering onward.

As the dice-size drops turned to hail and started bouncing off the windshield, I assessed the situation. If Father Prokopi stayed sick, we would never get a substitute priest during this, the church's busiest time of year. There are forty-two villages in Epiros that have no priest at all, Father Prokopi told me once when he was bemoaning that young men don't want to become priests. ("It's their girlfriends," he confided. Orthodox priests can marry, and most, like him, do. "Girls today don't want the pressure of being a priest's wife.") I was going to have to take Easter week into my own hands. My only option was to continue on to the village of Lista, six kilometers away, and get palms there.

I inched on through opaque fog, and by the time I got to Lista, church was over. Father Vangelis, a petite priest with a white beard and bright blue eyes, was enjoying coffee with his flock in the *kafenion* across the street. I walked in and every head turned to assess the sodden newcomer.

"Are there any palms left?" I asked, breaking the silence.

"There are always palms on Palm Sunday," Father Vangelis replied, rising from his chair with ecclesiastical elegance. "Let's get some." I followed him up a slippery ramp to the Church of the Dormition, which he unlocked. As I stared at the sky-blue ceiling, Father Vangelis seized a huge bunch of palms that had been adorning an icon. "Bring these back to everyone in Lia," he said beatifically.

Back in Lista's *kafenion*, the proprietress served coffee and tried to stir up discontent. *"Pappoulis,"* she asked Father Vangelis, "is a priest even *allowed* to be sick during Holy Week?" It was clear that news of Father Prokopi's illness had raged through the tri-village area. Clutching my coffee cup for warmth, I leaned in to hear Father Vangelis's reply. He raised his hands as if in benediction. "Father Prokopi has an intestinal problem; that's what the hospital told him," he reported. "Now, you can perform a service with a 104-degree fever, but if you've got an intestinal problem and you have to keep running back and forth to the bathroom, it can't be done."

Toula, a well-coiffed, middle-aged blonde who was the president of the Civic Society of the nearby village of Glousta, sprang out of her chair and stalked over to our table. Glousta was the third village in Father Prokopi's roster. He didn't have a car, so he had to walk from church to church or depend on the kindness of his parishioners to give him a ride. But since Glousta was located significantly down the mountain off the main paved road from Lia, and even farther from Father Prokopi's home in the village of Babouri, it was his least convenient location. A former teacher, Toula was used to being in charge—and she was not about to let Easter bypass her village. She sat next to Father Vangelis, pulled out a pen and notepad, and started pressuring him to perform Glousta's Holy Week services.

"Father Prokopi will be fine by then," he assured her.

But Toula would not be moved. "Even so," she argued, "if he's not feeling well, it's too far for him to come."

Father Vangelis knew there was no escape. He began to barter. "Well, you people from Glousta will have to drive the *gerontakia*"—little old people—"from here in Lista over to Glousta for the Resurrection—I'm not doing another one here," he commanded.

That was fine by Toula, as long as the service was in her hometown.

"And the congregation can't leave right after the Resurrection on Saturday night," Father Vangelis continued, sensing he had the upper hand. "Everyone has to stay to the end of the liturgy." This was a major demand, as all over the world, Greeks rush home immediately after the Resurrection at midnight in their desperation to end the seven-week Lenten fast, thus leaving a lonely priest chanting to an empty church.

Toula agreed to his terms—what else could she do? A deal was struck. It meant that Father Vangelis would be driving all over the mountain range, but the people of Glousta would have Easter after all. As I left, I wondered how old he was and how he could move so quickly in his long gown. But mostly I wondered about our own Holy Week. In some towns there were two services a day during Holy Week. But with a priest shortage and the intestinal flu that smote Father Prokopi, we Liotes were in serious trouble.

On Holy Monday I drove to Filiates, which was teeming with women carrying huge trays of *koulouria* (braided Easter cookies), to be cooked in the massive ovens at the bakeries. I was on a mission of a less-culinary sort, heading to the municipal registry, where I picked up the ID number required for my Greek passport. After five months, I now had all the materials necessary to become a Greek citizen. It was a minor Holy Week miracle. I took my hard-won ID number and drove over treacherous mountain passes to the town of Metsovo. There I could find both a fax machine to send my ID number to the consulate in New York, which would issue my passport and mail it to me, and Holy Week services that I'd be unable to attend in spiritually underprivileged Lia.

Metsovo is to Lia as Elizabeth Taylor was to Joan Collins circa 1960: a larger, more glamorous role model. A mountain village full of gray stone mansions, it has always been central for travelers, lying on the most logical route from Epiros to Thessaly and Macedonia. Most Metsovites speak Vlachiko, an unwritten language of Latinate origin, as well as Greek. Some historians theorize that the Vlachs are descendants of Roman soldiers who were stationed in Metsovo, and others think Vlachiko was developed to trade with the Romans who traveled the route. Today Metsovo is a thriving tourist town with a ski lift, cheese factory, and vineyard. But I was there to visit some old family friends who had a fax in their home and promised they could find a liturgy or two for me to hit. I slid along Metsovo's cobbled streets to the church for the Holy Tuesday service, which was attended by dozens of older women in traditional Metsovite costume, a heavy black skirt, breast-hugging black vest with bell sleeves embroidered in scroll-like designs, embroidered apron nestled just under the bust, and a headscarf. The outfit is adorable but tends to make the wearer look squat and pyramid-shaped; I was glad wearing it wasn't required for entry into church.

The next morning I took advantage of my proximity to healthy priests yet again, attending church to have holy oil dabbed on my forehead. This time, the churchgoing ladies were walking around clutching bouquets of leafy green branches. Elena, my hostess, explained that the plant is called *mai* and you pick it on May first to "catch the May" and gain control over the month. May is thought to have dangerous magical properties, perhaps because the word for "May" resembles the word for "magic," *maghia*.

"They say you shouldn't get married in May," Elena continued.

"Because it's bad luck?" I asked.

"No, because you might be driven mad by lust and make a hasty decision."

Surrounded by nothing but toothless old men in Lia, I didn't want to be driven mad by lust in a Maenad-like frenzy. And I wanted to celebrate Easter like the Epirotes around me, to really be a part of the event. So I asked around and determined that the source of the *mai* was just outside of Metsovo on a hill that slopes up from a crossroads. Approaching the hillside, I noticed a shepherd lying on the grass, and figured I'd ask him to point out the magic plant. But when I got closer, I realized he was fast asleep. I was on my own. I picked the green stuff that looked the most like the branches the crones were carrying. When I arrived in Lia triumphant, my arms full of *mai* to craft into a May wreath for our door, Vladimiros came up to greet me.

"Your tooth hurt?" he asked.

"No," I said. "Why?"

"Oh, because in Albania that plant is very strong for cure

toothaches. But it also makes rash," he said, rubbing his forearms as if they itched.

He had brought his wife, Xalime, to meet me, having just gotten the cash and papers together to bring her over the border from Albania. She didn't speak a word of Greek and had been very carsick on the mountainous roads. But at the sight of my wreath, hung proudly on the veranda, a huge smile spread over Xalime's face and she pointed at it, rattling away to Vlad. I couldn't tell if she was admiring the wreath or mocking it. I had tried to fit in with my fellow worshippers, but it seemed that I had failed. At least, I hoped, I might get points for effort. I left my imperfect wreath on the veranda, where, in true Easter spirit, my kindly neighbors admired it politely.

The next day I awoke to another minor miracle: church bells. Father Prokopi's health had improved enough for him to perform the morning service for Holy Thursday, when the souls of the dead are said to rise and walk among us for the next fifty days. I followed the sound of the bells to Agia Triada, where he read the names of Lia's departed—who, at that point, seriously outnumbered the living Liotes—and gave Communion to those who were present in the flesh as well as in spirit.

As I left church I noticed that, apart from any dead villagers who might have been walking among us, Lia was suddenly full of Liotes who had moved away and were back to celebrate Easter. The empty houses in uptown Motsala were now full, and outside one of them stood a four-year-old boy. <<Να σου πω>>, he would call out to passersby. "Let me tell you." It's a useful phrase for starting a conversation, as it builds suspense. I took the bait. "What?"

"There was a scorpion in the house!" he exclaimed.

"No!" I gasped. Sensing a responsive audience, he continued to wax poetic. "Yes! And Daddy killed it. He stomped on it like this. *Paf! Paf! Paf!*" The *paf*s were accompanied by frenzied hopping. "And then I stomped on it. *Paf! Paf!* ..."

I could have watched the scorpion slaughter reenacted all morning, but the boy got called inside by a harried-sounding mother. All mothers were harried, as the entire village was busy with Easter preparations. Some people had gone to clean relatives' gravestones. Others were baking more Easter cookies or, like me, dyeing eggs in traditional Liotan style: arranging leaves, wildflowers, and stalks of grass artistically on white eggs; wrapping the eggs in a square of cut-up panty hose; tying the fabric with dental floss; and dropping the shrouded egg into a pot of red dye. Once the eggs have been boiled and the panty hose removed, they are entirely red except for a white pattern where the leaf used to be, and a star where the fabric was tied up. (Panty hose and floss are recent innovations; cheesecloth and string were the norm in pre-Hanes Lia.) I finished polishing my eggs with olive oil just in time for more church.

Holy Thursday's evening service features the reading of the twelve Gospels, twelve sections of the Bible that recount Christ's passion. In Father Prokopi's case, it was the twenty-four Gospels, because he performed the same service in Babouri first, before being driven over to Lia to read the twelve Gospels to us. It would have been a grueling task even when he was a recently ordained, strapping young priest in the best of health.

Now just a few years away from retiring, Father Prokopi read the Gospels seated in front of the altar. A slim man with a white beard, white hair, and the sorrowful blue eyes of a saint about to be martyred, Father Prokopi looked even more holy than usual as he sat upright in his wooden chair. He had dark circles under his eyes and a raspy voice due to his illness, but he fulfilled his duty—and Lia's spiritual longing—beautifully, never once sneaking in a condensed version of a scripture.

The service's high point is the description of Jesus' crucifixion, when a wooden figure of Christ on a cross bearing three candles is carried around the church three times and hammered into a stand on the middle aisle. We all held our breath as Antonis, the church council president, disentangled the candles from the chandelier. Then a huge taper fell onto the stone floor. It lay there, sputtering, until several old ladies pointed it out and Antonis retrieved it. Unfortunately, this climax takes place in the middle of the service; after it, you've still got six Gospels to go. I have to admit that most of us left ailing Father Prokopi alone to finish reading the Gospels to a few faithful old ladies, including one who was kneeling on the stone floor, knitting away.

I thought the knitting lady should have been paying a little more attention to the service, but I was in no position to judge, as I went across the street to the Xenona for some après-church booze (another Lenten no-no). There I found two scholars from Archaeological Services who were doing research on the area and had just climbed down from Lia's *kastro*. It would take lots of work to uncover, they said, but there was definitely something important there. An ancient coin from the far-off island kingdom of Thassos had been found near the *kastro* a few years ago, indicating that ancient Lia was once a prominent trading community.

Finally, I had official confirmation of what the locals had been telling me—that Lia had a long, illustrious history. I hoped the archaeologists would find more artifacts of historical importance, but not in the yard of the Gatzoyiannis house, because then we would be forced to stop building and turn the property over to Archaeological Services. A few years ago a man in Glousta stumbled upon a royal tomb from the Hellenistic era while trying to build a garage. Now the golden crown and earrings that were unearthed are on display in the Archaeological Museum on Corfu, and the poor man still doesn't have anywhere to park.

All the archaeology talk was starting to make me nervous when Father Prokopi strolled in, exhausted. He had finally finished the twelve Gospels times two, and I told him he deserved some refreshment. He pulled up a chair and ordered some tea. It being Holy Thursday, Father Prokopi was thinking of his beloved deceased parishioners, who are much more easily satisfied than the living Liotes.

"Human beings, we need meat, milk," he said, gesturing to the table in front of us. (It contained neither, it being Holy Week and all, but he was speaking figuratively.) "The dead, may their memory be eternal, all they ask for is a *Trisagion* service in their memory and that we light a candle to them once in a while."

Dead saints, apparently, can be somewhat more demanding. Father Prokopi told me that Agios Athanassios had once visited him in a dream, moaning, "They've abandoned me. Help." So now Father Prokopi was busy renovating the monastery of Agios Athanassios, on a hilltop below Babouri and Lia, in order to prepare it for a monk from the Peloponnese to take up residence. The monastery had been abandoned since its last inhabitant, a toothless, hundred-year-old nun, died twenty years before.

"She was a simple old nun," Father Prokopi told me. "One day her herd of cows was missing. So she prayed to Agios Athanassios, '*Effendi*, either you bring me my cows, or I burn you to the ground.' In a half hour the cows were back. It was a miracle."

This story fascinated me. First, because the nun called her patron saint *effendi*, which means "master" in Turkish and is the way village women addressed their husbands during the Turkish occupation. Second, it didn't seem super-holy to threaten to burn a monastery. Perhaps our friend the nun was a pyromaniac?

"I guess even saints feel fear," I said.

"No, the saint was rewarding the nun," Father Prokopi explained patiently. "The story shows how much faith she had in him."

This wasn't Agios Athanassios's only miracle. "When my father was sick and couldn't walk, I let him spend the night in Agios Athanassios," Father Prokopi continued. "The next day he walked all the way back to Babouri himself."

I could write off the cows as bovine practical jokers, or a coincidence. But Father Prokopi wouldn't lie, so his father's recovery represented a bona fide miracle to me, a testament to the power of faith. Having spent the past month worshipping with the Liotes, I was starting to believe anything was possible, and was beginning to feel like a Liota myself. I headed home, happy to be living in a village where miracles still took place.

In larger villages the women and girls spend all Holy Thursday night decorating the epitaphion, singing the Virgin's Lament as they tie flowers to a carved wooden bier that represents Christ's coffin. But in Lia there weren't many ladies young and strong enough to stay up all night, singing and arranging flowers. So Good Friday morning found me and a few other women in the clifftop church of Agia Paraskevi, preparing blooms to decorate the epitaphion as Father Prokopi read from the Bible and an energetic twelve-year-old boy tugged on the rope in the tall stone bell tower, sending chimes ringing out over the sloping fields below. His sister begged the bell ringer to stop the cacophony, but Antonis, as church president, said the boy didn't have to stop until he got tired, which seemed unlikely to happen that Easter.

We women were under the supervision of Spiridoula, Lia's honorary soccer mom. The wife of the contractor Thomas, and the village's youngest full-time female resident, Spiridoula was a born leader, with a sturdy figure, sensibly short blond haircut, and the ready smile of a woman who always knows what she wants to happen and is confident that it will. She merrily shouldered many major civic responsibilities, including overseeing the epitaphion decor. Several men were in attendance, too, listening to the service, and when the priest got to an important part, Spiridoula would signal to us to put down our knives and carnations and listen for a few minutes.

At the end of the service, as Father Prokopi read about Jesus' descent from the cross, Antonis removed the statue of Jesus from the cross in the middle of the church. Then Father Prokopi stepped out of the altar with his shoulders wrapped in the pall (a gold-embroidered purple cloth that represents Jesus' body), which he placed on the epitaphion, where Spiridoula strewed flower petals on top of it.

"Make a beautiful epitaphion, ladies," he said. "I'll see you tonight."

Before leaving, Father Prokopi surprised me by dropping to his elderly knees and scooting back and forth under the epitaphion three times. A few men followed suit, then Spiridoula shooed them out of the church so that the older, skirt-wearing ladies could crawl laboriously under it as well without inviting voyeurism, and then kiss the pall, now covered in rose petals. The book *Greek Calendar*

Customs explains that people crawl under the epitaphion "in order that its Grace may touch them," but the ladies told me that it brought good luck in the coming year.

With the men gone, our concentration on decorating intensified. Spiridoula had even brought a lantern to put inside the crown on top of the epitaphion so light would shine through during the evening procession. She had bought pink, white, and red carnations; other people donated voluptuous roses from their gardens, and the red and pink flowers along with the orange centers of the daisy chains made the epitaphion look vaguely Indian, like an adorned litter from a maharajah's palace. But we weren't done yet. Some men shyly offered white wildflowers as filler, which met with the Spiridoula seal of approval, and I had brought blue irises from Dina, who wasn't participating in Easter festivities because she was still in mourning for Andreas's son. "They always use my irises on the epitaphion," she said. "Since I can't bring them this year, you will."

Visitors kept dropping by, following the custom of seeing as many epitaphoi as possible; the more you visit, the better your luck for the coming year. I crawled under the epitaphion, too, and Spiridoula tipped me off that people take flowers from the epitaphion home with them after the evening service to save as *filakta*—protective amulets. "In five minutes it will be naked again," she said, smiling. She didn't care that all her hard work was ephemeral; after the procession, the epitaphion has fulfilled its mission, bringing beauty and luck to all of us.

Having outdone even her triumphs of previous years, Spiridoula left. I stayed alone in Agia Paraskevi for a few minutes to admire our handiwork. Two old women, both less than five feet tall, came in, dropped on all fours, and crawled under it deliberately, like inchworms. "The epitaphion looks beautiful," one said, latching onto the bishop's throne to hike herself up to a standing position. "But you forgot the daphne."

"Is daphne supposed to be good for the epitaphion?" I asked tentatively.

"Daphne has been considered 'good' for over three thousand

years," she replied, and hobbled out, shaking her kerchiefed head as if thinking, *What a rookie!*

I knew daphne—or laurel, in English—was an important plant. I just didn't know what it looked like. A wood nymph named Daphne, who was being pursued by Apollo, successfully prayed to be turned into a laurel tree in order to protect her virtue. The Olympic victors were crowned with daphne, and the Pythia at the oracle of Delphi inhaled the smoke of burning daphne to induce visions. But I hadn't realized Jesus wanted daphne, too. I was not about to make an executive decision, run out and collect what I thought was daphne, then add it to the epitaphion without Spiridoula's approval. After my mishap with the *mai*, I suspected I was just as likely to pick poison ivy, so I decided not to mention our oversight to Spiridoula.

That evening we all assembled in the *plateia* in front of Agia Paraskevi for the funeral procession of Christ. But although the church bells had rung, indicating a service was starting, Father Prokopi was nowhere to be seen. We stood around, holding our Good Friday *lambades*. Finally, a car stopped and a figure in a long black robe and stovepipe hat started running toward us, with a crowd of churchgoers cheering him on like he was a marathoner rounding the halfway mark.

Once we were all inside, I stood near the epitaphion so that I could admire its beauty during the two-hour-long liturgy, which is a full funeral service that ends with a procession through the village. Father Prokopi circled the epitaphion three times, splashing it with myrrh. Toward the end of the service, my six-year-old friend Popi came and slipped her small hand into mine. We watched as four men acting as pallbearers attempted to lift the epitaphion to bring it outside. There was brief but heated controversy: Should they use the long wooden sticks to carry the epitaphion? It turned out to be impossible to maneuver through the church doors with the carrying sticks, so they grasped the funeral bier with their bare hands and heaved it off the table into the air, shaking under its weight. The whole congregation followed, holding their lit candles, with Popi and me right behind the epitaphion.

As we made our way down to the church of Agia Triada, the entire extended village fell in line behind us; I wondered if there were any Liotes left in Athens. At every crossroads the procession would stop for a short prayer, and at Agia Triada we turned to retrace our steps. Families whose homes we had passed on the way down had splintered off and were now standing in front of their doors, glowing in the candlelight, as the procession made its way back. Once we reached the neighborhood of Agia Paraskevi, Father Prokopi stopped in front of Marianthe's house, which had a large black bow tied around its gatepost to indicate a household in mourning. There we sang the mourning hymn, praying that her husband and son—who had been there the previous Easter, died within two weeks of each other, and were now lost to Lia—would live in everlasting memory. As I stood among the candle-bearing worshippers, I realized how deeply everyone felt their loss. Lia was such a small community that everyone in it mattered to you, whether you liked them or not. The absence of two vital neighbors left the village a little hollower that Easter. Then we continued the few steps to Agia Paraskevi. At the outer gate of the churchyard, the pallbearers raised the epitaphion onto their shoulders so that the rest of us could pass under it for luck before it was placed back inside the church.

I stayed in the courtyard, watching people's faces illuminated by their candles as they passed by, wishing one another <<Και του χρόνου>> ("And next year"). I had always assumed that this phrase, uttered on every special occasion, meant "May we be together again this time next year." After singing the mourning hymn, I realized it also means "May we be alive, safe, and healthy enough to celebrate again next year." It wasn't just being together that mattered. It was being able to come together, and lucky enough to find your loved ones waiting for you when you arrived.

Then I noticed that everyone was clutching flowers. The *filakta!* I ran into the church. The epitaphion had been transformed, almost back to its pre–Good Friday wooden shell. Still, I managed to snag a few wildflowers and one rose to place behind the icons in the house. Next year, I'd have to keep an eye out for some daphne.

The rest of Greece went to church on Saturday morning for the First Resurrection. But there was no service in Lia—Father Prokopi needed to rest up for the evening. Most of us took this as a special dispensation to throw ourselves into pre-Easter preparations. Five different women visited my house, bringing me Easter cookies, bread, and the local version of *mageiritsa*, the soup used to break the Lenten fast after the Resurrection service. *Mageiritsa* is a medley of greens, herbs, and sweetbreads, which means that I've never indulged in more than a taste of the real thing; I draw the line at offal. Since you're never supposed to return someone's plate empty, I gave back the visitors' china filled with my decorated eggs, which were an especially big hit with people who were in mourning and therefore weren't supposed to dye their own.

In between visits, I fielded phone calls from three of the four *thitsas*. "Where you eating tonight?" Thitsa Lilia asked. "I been making *mageiritsa* all day."

"What you wearing to church?" Thitsa Olga wanted to know. "And how does the icon I donated look? Take me some pictures of that."

"You help with the epitaphion?" Thitsa Kanta demanded. "That's good luck. Maybe this year you meet a boy. Now tell your *thitsa*, who's in the village? Lotta people?"

I dutifully recited the names of all the villagers I recognized, then told each aunt which of her childhood friends had asked about her or wanted me to pass on a joke that, since it was rooted in ancient village slang, I couldn't really understand. And then, when I got tired of being the *thitsas'* live feed to Easter in Lia, I'd ask my own question. "Easter here is really fun—everyone gets totally into it," I said, three separate times. "Why don't you come next year?"

"I'm too old to fly that far!" Thitsa Olga shrieked. "But I would like to see that icon. Maybe . . . no, your uncle, Thio Dino, he can't make that long trip."

"The planes so expensive now—and so uncomfortable. Wooh!"

complained Thitsa Lilia. "Besides, since Thio Prokopi die, I don't wanna go back without him."

"This year I got the new granddaughter, maybe next year," Thitsa Kanta sighed. "But don't forget, Easter here nice, too!"

By eleven P.M. on Holy Saturday all of Lia except those in mourning had gathered in Agia Triada, waiting for the climactic service of Holy Week. We were all dressed in our best and carrying our Easter *lambades* (plain white for us grown-ups). Popi had new red shoes, and eleven-year-old Leonidas was devastated at having forgotten his soccer-themed *lambada* in Athens. Father Prokopi was there, having arrived out of breath, dashing over from Babouri, where he had completed an artificially early Resurrection service. We would have the real thing, climaxing at midnight. The interior of Agia Triada glowed as light from the heavy gold chandelier reflected off the ornate wooden 'iconostasis shielding the altar and the new icons of saints on the wall, which replaced those that had been damaged during the war. Wherever you glanced, eyes stared back at you, whether it was the ceiling fresco of Jesus looking down, saints peering from every angle, or villagers winking hello. Not to mention all the dead Liotans who were watching.

That night the church interior was even more impressive—garlands of Greek flags hung from the church ceiling, crisscrossing one another, and the icons were ringed with flowers. Father Prokopi chanted and we stood, sat, and stood again, praying and chanting in response, until he suddenly noticed that it was almost midnight and signaled to the cantors to jump ahead in their songbooks.

Just before twelve the lights were turned off. As the midnight bell began to toll and we stood in the darkness, Father Prokopi emerged from the altar, carrying a single candle. Several boys holding candles rushed forward to be the first to receive the flame; soon it had been passed on throughout the church and we were all illuminated by candlelight. Everyone's faces glowed and I was surprised that these expressions had become so familiar. Our church in Worcester had thousands of parishioners; it was easy to look around at Easter and see strangers. In Lia, without many other faces to distract me, I quickly memorized the lines on my neighbors' foreheads, the swell of their cheekbones.

Together we sang the Resurrection hymn, and outside people shot guns in celebration, causing all children under three to burst into tears. Father Prokopi tried to continue the service, but everyone was too overjoyed to stay. So the cantor flipped the switch that makes the bells ring their most jubilant chime, and we all streamed into the courtyard to shake hands, say, "Christ is risen," and answer, "Truly he has risen."

There was a sense of disbelief in the churchyard. It had actually happened—we had a priest, we were all healthy and together, and once again, at midnight, Christ had risen. All week when something good had happened, like Father Prokopi's recovering or my getting my ID number, I would joke, "Look, it's an Easter miracle." But Easter itself was the miracle.

I headed home just as my elderly next-door neighbors were making their tenuous way on foot down the sloping road to our houses. The husband of the frail couple, Barba Prokopis, had been ill recently, so after exchanging "Christ is risen" greetings, I asked, "How are you doing?"

"Fine," replied Barba Prokopis. "It does my soul good to see the church full."

"He had to go, even though he was sick," his wife piped up.

"I would have gone even if I was dead!" he said. Which, considering that the souls of the dead had been among us since Thursday, would have been entirely possible.

By now it was almost two A.M. and I was invited to break the fast at Dina and Andreas's house, where we cracked eggs together to see who had the lucky strongest one, ate *mageiritsa*, drank wine, and laughed. Andreas won the egg game, either because his egg was the. strongest or because he was especially skilled in egg-cracking technique after decades of practice. But I was feeling lucky myself, because despite everyone's urging, I had successfully managed to avoid eating the intestines being served two ways: *kokoretsi* (lamb's entrails wrapped in its long intestine and roasted on a spit) and *gardoumbes* (said entrails wrapped in said long intestine, cut into bite-size chunks and oven-roasted).

One of the pro-intestine guests at the table was Andreas's sister-in-law, an elderly widow who had been friends with my grandmother when they were both young mothers, but had survived the war, then moved to the big city. "The last time I spent Easter in that church was over sixty years ago, and I was holding my daughter, who was a newborn," she told me. "She started crying and your grandmother came up to me and said, 'Let me take the baby outside so you can stay.'" The old woman sighed. "Tonight, I saw you standing next to my daughter, who is a grandmother herself now, and I remembered that Easter. See where life brings us?"

Another, somewhat younger woman told me, "Your grandmother was like a mother to me and my sister after ours died. Even with five children of her own, she always had something extra—a loaf of bread, a few eggs—for us."

At the mention of my father and aunts, Andreas grinned. "One year when we kids played on this makeshift seesaw during Easter vacation, we wouldn't let your father join because he was too small," he said. "Your aunt Tina, who was holding his hand, said, 'What about me?' She was only a year older, still pretty little. But she was a girl, so we let her play."

"Tina still remembered that when she visited here a few years ago," Dina said. "We had so much fun that spring. When are the girls coming again?"

After everyone else had eaten his or her offal, and I sipped some token spoonfuls of *mageiritsa*, I returned across the way and immediately fell asleep. When I first arrived, each night I had lain awake worrying that since I spent time at the house site every day, my nightmare about the ruins would return. But during Holy Week, I'd been so busy by day and exhausted at night that I'd forgotten to worry at all.

That night I dreamed of the first time I ever saw a dragonfly, in the courtyard of the Haidis house on a visit when I was three or four.

I remembered the wonder I felt watching it dart around, a flash of jewel-like blue. But I hadn't actually followed it when I was a child, and I didn't in this dream, either. When I woke up, I had a vivid recollection of the experience in my childhood, and I realized that I hadn't been scared at all, just intrigued, as I let the dragonfly go on its way. Both of us had belonged in Lia, then and now. And at times like Easter, it seemed that there was nothing to be afraid of here, that life in Lia offered a series of beautiful surprises.

The next morning, the follow-up Easter Sunday service was held in Babouri. As a Liote, and one who had stayed up late listening to reminiscences, I felt entitled to skip it. I woke up late, then strolled to the *kafenion* to watch Stella roasting lamb for people who didn't have their own spits. Back in Motsala, Andreas and Dina's spit was empty, because roasting on a spit is a sign of great celebration that is not appropriate for people in mourning. Instead, Dina roasted the lamb in the oven, with spices and potatoes, which was just as delicious. I gorged myself on wine, lamb, and mountain views. In the evening, when I finally rose from the table, Dina warned me not to fold my napkin—it would mean that I wasn't coming back again. So I left my napkin in a heap on my chair and headed home to nap. When I had recovered from my celebratory gluttony, Thomas, the contractor, came over. With the passing of time and the intervention of Foti, Thomas and I had reached a compromise and settled on a price for the house's construction. Now he had arrived to sign the agreements.

An engineer friend of my father's had drawn up a contract, filling it with clauses meant to satisfy the innate Greek suspicion that everyone is out to cheat you. I wasn't really suspicious of Thomas, and I don't think he was wary of me, but there were other, less-reliable parties involved. For example, when it came to the steel rods for the frame of the house, Thomas had to go to the steelyard to oversee delivery himself. We might fall victim to a common steelyard trick of passing off cheap Bulgarian steel as good Greek steel. The document was also very clear on the dates so that there would be as little delay as possible. The walls of the house were to be done by the festival of the Prophet Elias, July 20; the roof, by the end of August; and the interior by Saint Nicholas's Day, December 6.

Once the contracts were signed, we celebrated by drinking *tsipouro*. I would like to be the kind of girl who downs a shot of moonshine without blinking, but I think it looks, smells, and tastes like rubbing alcohol. I dumped mine into the sink once Thomas left. Then I picked up *Greek Calendar Customs* to finish reading about Easter. I turned the page to the Festival of Saint George. "St. George's Day marks the beginning of the summer semester, and it is virtually the beginning of the year as far as working contracts are concerned," the author writes. "All agreements used to be signed on St. George's Day." Normally, it is celebrated on April 23, but since festivals can't be celebrated during Lent, which extended into May 2002, Saint George's Day was to be observed the day after Easter. Tomorrow.

I had been worried about our delays in getting approvals. First, the Building Department rejected Zervas's plans because they were in pencil, not regulation blue pen. Then the engineer submitting our proposal was informed that it was missing some newly required documents. He had to drive from Igoumenitsa to Ioannina and back again to get them, only to be told, "You should have known to submit them in the first place—you're a civil engineer, aren't you?" But by now he had given me both the approval from the Forestry Service and a project number that proved we had submitted the proposal. I still needed the okay from the Archaeological Services, but we could keep working in the meantime. And thanks to Saint George, spiritually speaking, we were one day ahead of schedule.

I made some tea and brought the contract out to the veranda, to admire it while watching the sunset. I had vowed to my aunts that I would become a part of everyday life in Lia, but secretly I worried that without a job, my family, or people my age around me, I would be bored and lonely. In the beginning, I was. But during Easter, I had been so busy with matters both spiritual and mundane that I hadn't even had time to notice that I was none of those things.

Having participated in the ritual of Easter, I felt reborn as a member of the village, on my way to being a bona fide Liote. I had been thinking of my year in Lia as a worthy digression from my real life, but I was beginning to realize that "real life" exists wherever you are. And I was there.

I had a house about to be under construction. I had made friends. And the Haidis house finally had a working computer and stove, a kitchen floor that no longer flooded, and a noticeable lack of squirrels and scorpions. I was starting to belong in Lia. Soon I might even learn to like spoon sweets.

FOUR

PLAYING WITH FIRE

<<Η φτώχια θέλει καλοπέραση.>>

"POVERTY NEEDS A GOOD TIME."

May 18

I am sitting on my terrace, drinking tea and watching the veils of morning mist drift up from the valley below. The mountaintops rising above the clouds look like a Japanese painting. I didn't sleep much again last night, listening to the squirrels roll walnuts around in the ceiling and the more troubling, unidentifiable thumps, creaks, and sighs the Haidis house makes. Now I am enjoying the peace morning always brings, and a farm-fresh egg courtesy of Foti's hens.

"Eleni!" a piercing voice calls. It's Dina, inviting me over for breakfast.

"Guess what I have for you today," Dina boasts once I am installed at her kitchen table. "It's milk, fresh from the goat!" She places a full eight-ounce glass of creamy liquid in front of me. "I told Iphigenia, the shepherdess, that you've never had fresh goat's milk and she gave me this for you—it's so healthy!"

And so disgusting-looking. The most milk I can handle is a little 1 percent in a bowl of cereal. But this is a gift, two times over, both from Dina and from Iphigenia. Apparently, in Lia, goat's milk is a delicacy. I pick it up and drink. It's gamey, like liquid lamb. I force down half a glass.

"Thanks!" I say. "I feel healthier already. I'll save the rest for later."

That afternoon, when Dina and Andreas are taking their siesta, I pour the goat's milk onto a paper plate, where it pools like an oily blob of eggshell paint, and leave it for Scrappy, the stray dog who frequents my yard. His tale wags in rapture. In Lia there is always enough of a good thing to share.

Epiros is the poorest region in the European Union, a fact I often heard cited by Epirotes bemoaning the indifference of their politicians. It's a dramatic statement and is meant to be startling. But my neighbors didn't look poverty-stricken, not like the people I'd seen in New York, anyway, where a lady begs near Lincoln Center wearing only a trash bag. Instead, the region's poverty manifested itself in more subtle ways—such as the lack of jobs, driving young people out of the area, emptying villages of all but pensioners and migrant workers, including Vlad and Net. No one in town was rich. Our village was rural, but we had plumbing and electricity, which had arrived in the village in 1967. Everyone else had TV, and I had Internet access. What more could a community want?

On the first Friday of every month the *kafenion* filled with Liotes eager to meet the mailman and pick up the Greek version of Social Security checks (many Liotes, having worked in the United States, happily collected those, too). But my neighbors were so generous with their food, drink, and company that I felt we were living large. Then the folk saying "Poverty needs a good time" made me realize that, in Greece, sometimes you live large *because* you're poor. Which explains why once the solemnity of Lent and Easter ended and summer began, Lia's social calendar kicked into high gear. Having seen how Easter brought the village together, I was determined not to miss any uniquely Epirotic event, anything that my aunts and grandmother might have attended when they lived there. So with ninety-one major saints' days and eleven national holidays to celebrate, life became a nonstop party.

In Manhattan a party meant brightly colored "signature" cocktails, faux comfort-food hors d'oeuvres, and goodie bags filled with freebies that rich urbanites fought over when leaving. In Lia a good time consisted of homemade wine in recycled water bottles, hunks of roast lamb, and a band that really wailed. And I do mean wailed. I saw this firsthand the night of Easter Sunday at the opening festival of the season, in the village of Glousta. Dancing was about to begin and the clarinetist struck up what I considered to be a rather mournful tune, the traditional Epirotic music that Patrick Leigh-Fermor wrote in *Roumeli* was "exactly the kind of long-drawn-out and wailing song in a minor key, whose waverings . . . bewildered and irritated Byron's western acquaintances." I was neither bewildered nor irritated, but I wasn't exactly humming along. So I was shocked when I noticed the young woman sitting next to me gyrating in her chair, drumming her fingers in front of her mouth, playing "air clarinet." She leaned over to me, sighed, and said, "It just wouldn't be Easter without the clarinet."

I found more to celebrate after Easter when my mother, Joanie, called from Worcester with a news bulletin. I had mailed her an enlarged photo of the coin Net found on the cornerstone of the Gatzoyiannis house, and she took it on a fact-finding mission to Bahnan's Market, a Mediterranean grocery where my aunts stock up on phyllo dough, olive oil, and other imported products. A Lebanese clerk scrutinized the Arabic letters in the image, ignoring the line of irate shoppers forming behind Joanie, to inform her that it read, "One *arsa*, Constantinople," and the date 1277. Explaining that Muslims date the year from Muhammad's journey to Mecca and that the current year was 1423, he figured the coin was minted in 1856. Sometime after that, but before my grandfather's elder brother was born in the 1870s, the Gatzoyiannis house had been built by one of my unknown, unrecorded ancestors, who placed this coin on the cornerstone to give the house strength and wealth. And inadvertently left something for me to find one day.

With the Worcester grocery research, the excavation of the foundation had become a transcontinental endeavor. And it was certainly transcultural. The coin had been minted by Turks, used by Greeks, found by Albanians, and identified by a Lebanese man working from a blown-up photo clutched by an inquisitive midwesterner who had married a Greek and gotten sucked into the mysteries of reconstructing his ancestral home. All roads now seemed to lead to Lia.

Even without archaeological breakthroughs, I fielded at least one phone call from Worcester a day, whether it was my parents or one of the *thitsas*. But on May 21 each *thitsa* called separately to wish me happy nameday and to make sure that I had stocked up on enough foil-wrapped chocolates to offer those villagers who would stop by to wish me many happy returns. Traditionally, birthdays aren't celebrated in Greece; you receive gifts and good wishes on the festival of the saint you're named after, without anyone ever mentioning how good you look for your age. My saint, Eleni, was the mother of Saint Constantine, the emperor who put the *holy* in Holy Roman Empire, converting his subjects to Christianity in the fourth century A.D. Both saints are celebrated on May 21.

Eleni is one of the most popular Greek names for women, as Constantine is for men. Listening to the news over lunch at Dina and Andreas's, I felt that half of Greece was paying nameday calls on the other half, with the government at a standstill because the president, prime minister, and several ministers named Constantine had to take time off to be adored by friends and family. Then the radio station started playing twenty-four hours of songs that had the names Eleni or Constantine in them.

"I didn't realize that my nameday was such a big deal," I said to Dina. "In America no one even notices."

"See that!" Dina exclaimed, amazed at how different people are all over the world. "And here people walk into the fire!"

"What?" I must have misunderstood; I still had trouble with some village idioms.

"Outside of Thessaloniki there's a religious group called the Anastenarides that dances on hot coals holding icons of Saint Constantine and Saint Eleni," she explained.

I raised my left eyebrow.

"And no one ever gets burned!" she concluded triumphantly.

"It's a miracle," Andreas added, raising his glass of *tsipouro*. "Scientists come from all over to study it, but no one knows why they aren't burned."

"I do," Dina answered, refilling Andreas's glass. "It's because the saint protects them. You have to wait for the saint to call you before you step on the fire."

"Those people are crazy," Vangelis said, spearing his lamb chop with a fork. "And God protects the crazies."

It may take a certain craziness to fox-trot over hot coals. But I admired the way the Anastenarides tested their faith on the most basic level, their willingness to walk into the fire, certain they would be transformed, better off for having faced the flames.

After a postprandial nap I went for a walk to work off the foil-wrapped sweets I had been forced to eat while keeping my neighbors company. The landscape of Lia seemed totally transformed, as if it, too, had shuffled over hot coals. In April and early May the village had a subtler beauty, with sage green mountains, slate blue skies, and woodsmoke in the air. Now everything was sharp, spotlit by the sun, and the lizards running across the road had turned the bright green of a Maybelline mascara wand to blend into the mountain. It was suddenly summer; everything was vivid and pungent, with the air smelling like plants, manure, and an occasional strong hit of star jasmine. Spanish broom exploded out of the side of the road in great yellow masses, and smoke bushes, which resemble fragile old ladies' lavender-tinted hair, were starting to bloom in lacy bunches. The magenta flowers of the Judas trees had disappeared, and a white-blossomed tree called *fraxos* clamored for attention in their place.

Once again I was astonished by how beautiful the village was, overflowing with plants and animals. It seemed we had now entered tortoise season; they crossed the road slowly, deliberately, occasionally turning their necks just a little to stare, annoyed, at my shoes. There were infant animals everywhere. When I stopped at the Xenona, a fleet of baby bats learning to fly kept springing unsteadily from the cracks in the stone walls of the inn, unable to swoop artfully like their parents. At Spiridoula's house, Thomas had undertaken a smaller-scale construction project, stringing wire along the corners of the veranda in front of the swallows' nests so that the youngsters had a swing on which to practice their takeoffs. As I walked toward the Haidis house, I found that it was the first night of firefly season; floating bursts of light surrounded me.

I arrived in Motsala as darkness was beginning to fall. This was my favorite part of the day in Lia, the long hours of the afternoon and early evening when the workday was done and people woke up from their post-lunch naps to do exactly what they wanted, whether that meant strolling through town or sitting to drink moonshine. Vlad, Net, and Xalime were chattering in Albanian; old Barba Prokopis and his wife, my next-door neighbors, were sitting on their veranda; and the house at the top of our path was now inhabited by Athina and Grigoris Ganas. Athina, stocky with short brown hair and wide glasses magnifying big green eyes that watched over everyone's business, was tending her hydrangeas when I said hello. She told me they'd be staying through September but had to return to Athens once a month for Grigoris's chemotherapy treatments. He had lung cancer, and although he was bald and swollen, his baseball cap and booming voice when he strode into the yard to greet me made it seem as if there was nothing wrong.

I sat on my veranda until it was too dark to see anymore, admiring the huge green squash leaves that were now filling my garden, then went inside to make some tea. As the hot water gushed out of the faucet, something skittered across the sink—another scorpion! I thought about calling Net to kill it for me. But he'd think I was ridiculous, not to mention helpless. Ever since Dina told me about the tomato-stake incident, Net's way of smiling made me uncomfortable—I couldn't tell if it meant "I'm a shy Greek-as-a-second-language fifteen-year-old and you're a foxy American adult" or "How come I have to work all day clearing the ruins of your house while a capitalist pig like you sits on her butt, playing on a computer?" So I picked up my shoe, bashed the scalded scorpion, and scooped it up with a paper plate.

Exhausted after the slaughter, I climbed into bed. That's when I heard it . . . a tap, tap, tap sound coming from nowhere in particular. I had been annoyed that my aunts kept calling to check if I was *sure* I still wasn't scared, alone at night in the house. Now I wished they were there with me. It was three in the morning, but only eight P.M. in Boston, so I dialed my sister, Marina. She wasn't home, but her roommate's visiting sister was.

"Would you mind just staying on the phone while I look outside to see who's tapping?" I said to the stranger on the other line.

"No problem," she replied. "I made my mom stay on the phone last week when the cable guy came unexpectedly—how did I know he was really a cable guy?"

In New York I, too, had worried about crafty thieves and rapists posing as cable guys. Now I was in a Greek village at 3:15 A.M., begging a stranger to stay on the line as I checked for wolves, ghosts, or psycho killers in the dark. I was clearly going crazy.

When I stepped onto the terrace, the yard was peaceful, glowing under a bright moon. So I thanked the stranger in Boston, hung up, and managed to fall asleep by four. At ten-thirty the next morning I was blasted awake by a car honking on the road above the house. Then I heard a man screaming, "Eleni! Elenaki!"

Some kind of emergency, I thought. Rabid wolves? War with Albania? I pulled a sweater on over my blue daisy-print pajamas, ran up the path, and saw the postman, smiling in his red hatchback. He had a letter for me and the guys at the *kafenion* had told him I was home, so he thought he'd bring it over. I took the envelope, which turned out to contain a comic strip from one of my former colleagues, and said, "Thanks so much!" But what I really meant was "Great, now the entire neighborhood thinks I lie around in my pajamas all day while they cook, clean, and build houses." I made a mental note: *Get a grip. Sleep more. Start waking up at eight.*

My nameday had me thinking even more of my namesake. I longed to see some progress at the Gatzoyiannis house, some sign that my grandmother's home would, in fact, stand again. But every day I hiked up there, although Vlad, Net, Xalime, and Thomas were industriously hauling stones from here to there, the site looked as if it had gone from bad to worse. While the Anastenarides were dancing on coals, the Gatzoyiannis house had undergone its own trial by fire. The Albanian family had disassembled the ruins into individual rocks to use in the rebuilding and had torn down the outer door to the courtyard, carefully saving the arched stones. Now the place looked less spooky, but more forlorn—an empty lot instead of a ruined home. There were new trenches for the foundation, following the footprint of the original building. Vlad and his family had cut back the bushes and vines that consumed the ruins, and I could clearly see the outline of the original dark basement. When my aunt, Thitsa Tina, returned to Lia for the first time, thirteen years after her mother's death, she had discovered a last message from her mother tucked into one of the walls of the Good Room—a small paper icon of the Panagia on which my grandmother had written her name, a prayer to the Virgin, and the words "Don't be upset, I am all right. Mana."

The house yielded that treasure to my aunt, and the Ottoman coin to Vlad. I had told Net I'd give him five euros for each item he found, and so far I'd paid for a broken coffee cup, a clay pipe, and two horseshoes. Now I looked around to see if the house had a message for me hidden somewhere, but all I saw were piles of rocks and churned-up dirt. The mulberry tree stood like a skeletal sentinel, watching over the workers digging up the yard. The setting depressed me. I wasn't sure it could ever be a place that made me happy instead of anxious, a home instead of a pile of memories.

At night I often wondered whether rebuilding the house was just a waste of money and energy or, worst of all, something that would alienate the villagers. When my aunts called, they asked about my wardrobe, my weight, my activities, and every person in the village, but never about the house or its progress. And I didn't bring it up, because I knew they cried every time I mentioned their old home. At lunches and dinners and over strong cups of coffee, my neighbors and I discussed politics, religion, and gossip ranging from marital troubles to sheep-stealing shepherds. But none of the villagers except Vlad, Net, Xalime, and Thomas ever offered advice on the rebuilding or even visited the site. So although the Liotes seemed to enjoy attending festivals or sharing meals with me, a rare young person, I couldn't tell if they supported my project. And I was too afraid of the answer to ask. If these people didn't want the house rebuilt, there was no point to my being there. To them it seemed natural that I would hang out in the village where my family originated. But with no job and most of my family opposed to my presence there, I felt I needed a project, a reason, an excuse to stay. And I wanted some visible proof that I was somehow making the village whole again, a less scary place for the people I loved.

A week later I was in the *kafenion*, trying to imagine what the house would look like finished, when impassioned shouting jolted me to attention. An argument had erupted over who makes the better sausages, Greeks or Germans. In one corner, representing Germany, was a Liotan lady who had married a German, settled in Munich, and was in Lia on vacation. In the other corner was everyone else, loudly protesting on behalf of the Greeks and particularly the Ifantis sausage dynasty, whose patriarch had been born in Lia. I slipped out before the heated argument could intensify into overturned chairs and flying beer bottles. But I felt a little better. Maybe my house project was misguided, but at least I wasn't the most obnoxious foreigner in town.

That night, over dinner at Dina's, I told everyone about the Great Sausage Debate, the newcomers at the *kafenion*, and how inflamed they all were by culinary chauvinism.

"It's exciting to have lots of people around," Vangelis Panagiotou said, brushing the sleeves of his houndstooth sport coat. "But the village is really best in spring and fall, when it's just a few of us."

"What are you talking about?" Dina retorted, setting baked feta on the table. "You'll hang out with anyone who strolls into the *kafenion* and buys you a beer."

"That's true," Vangelis answered. "But you know what they say: With the shepherd wanting it and the artist not wanting it, even Jesus wears mountain boots."

Everyone laughed, dug into the cheese, and began listing the merits of Ifantis sausages. I knew I had missed something. "What was that about Jesus and the boots?"

Vangelis, never one to ignore an audience, started to explain. "Well, there's this shepherd, see, but he's made some money, maybe he sells his goats' milk to the Dodonis factory to make feta or something." I was with him so far.

"Anyway, he commissions this artist to make him an icon of Jesus, but he wants Jesus portrayed as a shepherd. The artist says that's fine, and then the shepherd answers, 'And he has to be wearing mountain boots like mine.' The artist says, 'Hold on. In all the icons of Jesus I've seen, none show him wearing mountain boots.' The shepherd says, 'The one *I'm* paying for will!' So with the shepherd wanting it and the artist not, even Jesus wears mountain boots. You've gotta do what you've gotta do."

I wished I had some guidance as to what it was I had to do—continue rebuilding the house or respect my aunts' reluctance ever to see it again. The ground was ready for the foundation of the Gatzoyiannis house to be laid once more, approximately 150 years after the Ottoman coin was placed on the first cornerstone. But I wasn't sure of the wisdom of my mission.

And then I received a mini-miracle, or at least the kind of divine protection afforded to the firewalkers in their quest. George Zervas appeared in Lia to supervise the pouring of the foundation. I had called him several times to let him know we were ready, all in vain because of his scorn for telecommunications. But one morning I hiked up to the Gatzoyiannis house and there he was, looking around in a daze. I realized that he was following the jagged path of a metallic-hued June bug buzzing drunkenly through the air.

"Look, *chrysomiges* [gold flies]," Zervas said. "When I was a kid, we would catch one, tie a string around it, and watch it fly, like a kite. If you get a few, you can have races." I considered the bronze bugs, which always struck me as being disgusting little aliens. Somehow they now looked beautiful as they darted around, sparkling, like flying hard candies wrapped in shiny paper. But I had no time for childhood reminiscences or even seeing nature in a

new light. Zervas was going to wax philosophical no matter what;
I had to keep my eye on the prize. There was business to take care
of; a gaping square trench waited in the ground for the foundation
to be poured. Neat piles of stones that would once again join together to form walls ringed the excavation. I was determined to get
the foundation poured that day while Zervas was there—no one
knew when he would return. I needed to see the cement in place, a
concrete result that proved my stay had a good purpose and that I
was making progress.

"We're all ready to go," I told Zervas proudly.

"Great." He snapped out of his bug-induced daydream. "Where's
the rooster?"

"What rooster?"

"The rooster for the foundation. You know, when you build a
house, traditionally, you kill a rooster over the cement, leave the
head in the foundation, cook the body, and have a feast for the
workers."

"But why?" I asked, wondering why my aunts, in all their voluminous advice, had never told me this apparently essential bit of
information.

"Well, all traditions have a practical and a spiritual basis," Zervas explained. "Practically, in the old days, people didn't eat meat
often, so a rooster feast was good incentive for the workers. And
spiritually, the sacrifice makes the house stronger."

"I don't want a weak house!" I shrieked. I turned to Foti, who
was helping me supervise. "Foti, do you have a rooster?"

"Sure," he said. "But just one, and I don't want all my hens to be
widows."

"Don't worry," Thomas said, not about to let a poultry shortage
make him late for lunch. "We'll kill a rooster when we lay the foundation for the second floor."

Zervas nodded. "Let's get started, then. Where's the priest?"

Oh yeah. The priest. I called Father Prokopi from my cell phone
to let him know we had a spiritual emergency. He was available.
Within fifteen minutes Thomas had incised a cross into a slab that
would serve as the first stone, and Father Prokopi was standing at

the edge of the trench in his long black robe, red-and-white ceremonial alb, and stovepipe hat. He instructed me to write the names of all the people who would live in the house on a piece of paper, then shook his censer, filling the air with sweet smoke, and began chanting blessings for the house and its inhabitants.

As I wrote the names of my family, as well as my aunts and their children—the descendants of the original Eleni Gatzoyiannis—I wondered if she was watching and if she approved. Was she glad that we were putting the tumbled rocks of her house back together, or was the house itself, the scene of so much of her suffering, a source of bad luck? Was I setting things right, or reopening and deepening old wounds?

A drop of holy water hit me in the eye, knocking me out of my reverie. Dipping a bunch of herbs into a bowl of holy water, Father Prokopi splashed the four corners of the foundation, then said, "May you all live happily in this blessed home." Looking at Father Prokopi silhouetted against the green trees and the purple mountain in the distance, I prayed that the souls of all the people who had suffered and died there might finally be released from the grim confines of the ruins. Then Father Prokopi dipped a metal cross into the water for all of us to kiss. Thomas, Foti, George Zervas, and I all took a turn, and so did Vlad, Net, and Xalime, apparently untroubled by the fact that they were Muslims. I dropped the first stone into the wet cement and everyone clapped. There was no rooster, but it was still a beautiful ceremony.

In lieu of a rooster feast, I invited everyone to lunch at the Xenona Inn, which Zervas had also designed in the traditional style, a large stone building with wooden balconies upstairs and a huge dining room and sitting area around an open fireplace downstairs. But it was now warm enough to sit outside under the plane tree in the stone-paved *plateia* in front of the inn. Over lunch Foti promised me he'd look for a rooster with a big coxcomb for the foundation of the second story, because when it comes to lucky roosters, the bigger their coxcombs the better. Having brought my family's sheep back to the Gatzoyiannis house so many times as a boy, Foti seemed to have a strong desire to conquer the house's past and wrap it up in a safe cocoon of blessings and rituals.

"Yeah, we need a freakishly big coxcomb on our rooster, since we're throwing him in there late," I replied, grateful to have an accomplice.

"You know, I didn't give you a good answer when you asked about killing the bird," Zervas interrupted thoughtfully. "I should have told you it's an ancient Greek ritual that has survived, a sacrifice to appease the gods so they'll allow you to raise the house."

Having lived there for three months now, I had sort of figured that out.

"So many things in Epiros have survived from ancient Greece, like the folk songs," he continued. "In *The Odyssey*, Odysseus returns to find his father an old man, plowing. He says 'I'm your son,' and his father wants proof. So Odysseus says, 'I know these are our fields,' and the father responds, 'Anyone could have told you that.' Odysseus says, 'Here's the scar from when Penelope's father's dog bit me,' and the father says, 'We all have scars on our ankles from something.' Finally, Odysseus describes the day they planted the crops together, and his father embraces him."

"We have a song about that?" I asked. This was news to me.

"Not about Odysseus, but about a woman whose husband returns after years of working abroad. She wants proof that he is her beloved. He says, 'In our yard an apple tree grows.' She says, 'That's true of most yards.' He says, 'By our door a fig tree grows.' She responds, 'The neighbors could have told you that.' So he says, 'On your breast, an olive grows'—meaning a beauty mark—and she embraces him."

"That's racy!" I said.

"That's Homer," he answered. "Some people say all of Homer is just a series of folk songs strung together. I've collected three hundred songs from my grandmother and I want to turn them into a poem. Of course, it depends on my abilities whether anything good will come out of it. But I think it's a possibility."

Zervas's life seemed full of possibilities, even at seventy-seven.

He was so full of optimism, I suddenly felt positive as well. My life there in that ancient place would be epic poetry in motion, the house would be rebuilt beautifully, and when we found a rooster to sacrifice, it would have the largest coxcomb on record.

By late June the village was full of visitors looking for a good time. School had ended, and Liotes who had emigrated poured back into town to join in the summer fun. My social calendar was full. Andreas took me to pick oregano, teaching me to choose stems that had white buds on them so they looked like lilies of the valley and smelled like a well-grilled steak. Dina showed me how to "open" handmade phyllo dough using a broomstick-like rolling pin, a talent that is the apotheosis of every village wife's cooking career. (Even the *thitsas* in Worcester don't have the patience to make their own phyllo dough.) And everywhere I went, I met people who knew me, although I didn't know them. After church one Sunday an old woman in a black kerchief came up and planted a moist kiss on my cheek, explaining, "Your father is my cousin." I smiled and nodded. "I'm so glad you're rebuilding the Gatzoyiannis house," she continued. "That was my neighborhood, too." Tears spilled out of the crimped corners of her eyes. "May the Virgin Mary assist you!"

I was thrilled to have someone mention the house to me, especially someone in favor of my rebuilding it. At the same time, I always felt uncomfortable when old women I didn't recognize saw me and started to cry. It had happened before, on a visit to Lia, when one of my grandmother's neighbors, now dead, burst into tears, saying I looked so much like my grandmother that it was like having Eleni standing before her again. I never knew how to comfort these women, and I felt guilty that my very appearance brought them pain. As the tearful crone walked away, a middle-aged man in a well-tailored suit tugged at my arm to introduce himself. "I was the boy whose umbilical cord your grandmother ate so she could have a son," he said. I nodded, pretending I knew what he meant. Apparently, my poker face needed practice. "That's what they did in those days," he explained. "She had your aunt Tina afterward, but then your father, so it worked eventually."

He smiled; a literature professor, he knew that genetics did not support the theory that he played a role in the conception of my father. But he was explaining that we were related, however mystically and illogically. I was used to living in a city of strangers, who knew only what we told one another about our personal histories. Now I felt naked, not because of my lack of kerchief or my strappy sundress, but laid bare emotionally, when strangers came up and told me things about my relatives that those family members did not even know themselves. I missed my anonymity, but I knew that this is what I had come for—to have my family's past greet me at every turn, with no escape, and to let our past inform my future. It was unnerving to talk to strangers who seemed to know my family history better than I did, but each morsel of information they offered made me feel more at home in Lia and in my place in the world.

I came to Lia to uncover my family history and transform my feelings about the village until it came to seem like a place I belonged. Everyone else had come because it was *panegyri* season, a nonstop succession of festivals that would climax with the Virgin Mary's holiday on August 15. *Panegyria* are held all over Greece, although the songs played by the bands and the food served from spits and communal pots differ from place to place. But everywhere, a *panegyri* is fun for the whole family: little kids run around, teenagers show off their dance moves, and old people gossip about everyone else. My own, unsubstantiated theory is that the word *panegyri* comes from the word *gyro*, for circles, and the god Pan, because Pan liked to party hard and kick up his little goat heels in circles.

I was kicking up my own little heels all over the mountain range. I threw my donation into the basket at the *panegyri* for Agios Prokopi in Lista. (It's pay-by-donation, Foti explained, because the Listans figured out they make more money than by charging for food—everyone wants to be seen tossing in an impressive amount.) In the village of Agia Marina, I listened to old men harmonize as they squatted in a circle, recalling words to a forgotten Epirotic tune. I even supervised ten-year-old boys running a race from the churchyard to the cemetery in Glousta during the festival of Saint John the Baptist.

But my favorite celebration occurred at the *panegyri* of Agia Triada, right in Lia, when I joined my fellow villagers in a parade to show off our icon of the Holy Trinity, which was framed by pink and fuchsia hydrangeas for the occasion. At the end of the evening service in Agia Triada, Antonis Makos, the church council president, picked up the icon and took the lead, followed by Father Prokopi wielding his censer, Spiro the cantor, Sofia the lady cantor, and several boys who had come for vacation with their families and been given the important task of carrying the gold standards used in church parades. We proceeded toward the church of Agia Paraskevi, in front of the men drinking coffee or moonshine at the *kafenion* who rose to cross themselves as we passed by singing hymns devoted to particular saints.

In the middle of one hymn, Costa, the eight-year-old son of the *kafenion* owners, yelled, "A car's coming!" We stayed put, singing, figuring that any car could wait for the Father, Son, and Holy Ghost. That's the risk you take driving the one road through the Mourgana mountains; sheep or saints could stop you at any turn. I was flushed with the thrill of power. Lia may be small, poor, and remote, but when we got together to make a joyful noise unto the Agia Triada, we stopped traffic.

There were a few secular celebrations as well. Net turned sixteen, and we marked the occasion with souvlaki and fries around Andreas's homemade swimming pool. Net and his parents had been working on the house's basement for over a month now, and they had a system all worked out: Net poured water into the concrete mixer, Xalime carried concrete and stones to the foundation in a wheelbarrow, and Vlad laid rocks and concrete on top of each other. I was surprised that Xalime did the heavy lifting, but, given that she probably weighed more than Vlad and certainly outweighed Net, she was probably the strongest of the three. In any case, I wasn't about to volunteer to replace her, so I kept my mouth shut.

By the first week in July, the basement was finished and we were ready to pour the foundation for the ground floor. I knew what this meant: it was time for a rooster to meet its maker. Part of me found the idea of a sacrifice disgusting and barbaric. But I knew you didn't raise a house in Lia without decapitating a rooster, and as a new villager I had to play by the rules. Besides, this was a free-range rooster that had inseminated lots of hens and lived to a ripe old age, and I planned to put every part of him to good use, cooking his body so it would nourish citizens of three different nations (Greece, America, and Albania) and immortalizing his head in a building. What more could a rooster ask for?

For all my rhetoric, I still felt guilty when Foti pulled a struggling rooster out of his truck by its legs, which were tied together. An old black rooster with an impressive coxcomb, he was less than feisty. Maybe I was saving him from a long, slow death from disease, giving him a glorious martyr's end. I had almost convinced myself we were doing him a favor when Foti handed me an ax and said, "Here you go."

"No way!" I said, dropping the ax. "I mean, I think the chief builder should do the honors—besides, I need to take pictures to document the ceremony."

No one argued with me. With his bandy-legged walk and high puff of curly black hair, Thomas somewhat resembled a rooster. But he didn't seem to feel any sympathy with the bird and acted pleased to do the honors. So I stood in the semicircle of spectators around Thomas and the rooster: Net, Xalime, Vlad, and Foti. Even Grigoris Ganas had insisted on coming up to the house, although his wife said he should rest, since he was weak from chemotherapy. But Grigoris had been in construction himself and loved a good rooster ceremony, so he stood next to me as I gripped my camera.

Thomas put a board on the edge of the wet cement, laid the rooster's neck on top of it, raised the ax, and let it fall. It took a few hacks to sever the head, and the rooster jerked a bit. But he didn't jump up and run around with blood spurting from his neck stump, which is what I expected. As I snapped photos of the severed head before Thomas covered it with more cement, Net walked over to

Thomas and asked, "Why did we kill a rooster? Isn't there enough blood in this house already?"

The villagers had told him that after the civil war, they uncovered the bodies of thirty-seven people who were killed by the Communist soldiers and buried in the yard of the house. It was a gruesome statistic, and Net was just a clever boy making an observation. But I still felt heat rise to the tips of my ears. Did he think I was being ridiculous and callous rebuilding this house? Did all the villagers, who could be counted on not only to know my business but also to have an opinion on it, agree?

If they do, what is it to me? I thought, striding angrily toward the car. I didn't need Net's approval, or my aunts'. All old houses have ghosts and tragedies. A home is a place where people's lives take place, and life includes pain and suffering. I wanted a rooster sacrificed *because* there was blood in this house, and I refused to let the house languish as a former cemetery. I was going to turn it into a home again, and I needed all the help I could get. If three thousand years of Greek tradition told me that that meant killing a rooster, so be it. Anger pulsed through my body; I whipped myself into five feet of indignation so that I wouldn't realize how hurt I was. I thought we had all become a team to perform this ceremony: Foti finding a spare rooster, Thomas rising to the occasion as executioner. Now Net's comment had me feeling like a bumbling outsider again. I was a joke to these people, and one in poor taste at that.

Grigoris caught up with me, wheezing from the exertion. "Wear the white dress you wore last night," he said. I looked up, cross and confused.

"To the rooster dinner," he continued. "You look pretty in that." He smiled, and my anger dissipated. Grigoris and Foti had come to see my building site, and we all had rooster blood on our hands (just figuratively speaking, thank God). At least now we were in this together.

Net wasn't complaining about the rooster when we gathered at Foti's house that night to eat it. Normally, the task of preparing the rooster fell to the *noikokyra*, the lady of the house. But I had never even imagined cooking one, so Spiridoula, as wife of the contractor and all-around expert, took over, transforming the scrawny bird into a delicious wine-flavored stew over spaghetti. Foti, having donated the rooster, allowed me to hold the event at his place, since I didn't have enough chairs. My contributions were an apple pie and a toast: "To the rooster! May his memory be eternal!"

Lia was down one rooster. But she was gaining inhabitants daily as people streamed in for the high point of Lia's social calendar: the festival of the Prophet Elias. Most Greek villages have a chapel to the Prophet Elias on one of the highest peaks in the area, where the temple to Helios used to be in pagan times. Helios was the sun god and needed to be high up so he could ride his golden chariot to the sun. The Prophet Elias never actually died, he just rode up to heaven on *his* golden chariot, so he likes a sky-high chapel himself. (Father Prokopi once told me that before the end of the world, God is going to send the Prophet Elias down to Jerusalem to be martyred so he can leave his physical remains on Earth like the rest of the saints. "We won't know who he is," Father Prokopi added thoughtfully. "But maybe we'll see it happen on TV.")

In Lia the saint's day of the Prophet Elias is an even bigger to-do because he is the patron saint of the village. Ever since his church has existed (and probably back when it was a temple to Helios), Liotes have climbed the mountain to pay their respects on the day of the festival and have celebrated on the nights before and after. It was during the festival in 1939 that my grandmother sent for the *mami* (midwife) to come down from the dancing and help her give birth to the baby who would become my father. Since the Germans had burned the village's records, the only way my father could establish his birth date—July 23—was, as an adult, by learning from a Lia crone that he was born on the third day of the festival.

So when my parents heard how many Liotes were returning for the *panegyri*, they decided to come spend my father's birthday in Lia. I was excited to see them. I could force Joanie to help battle the killer mold that had invaded my closets, with two other people in the house I would definitely sleep better, and it might be fun to celebrate as a family. After all, how much trouble could a couple of parents cause?

We were in happy-family-reunion mode on July 19 when we headed to church for the service and litany of the Prophet Elias. Only two of us actually made it to Agia Triada, however; my father felt the call of the *kafenion* as profoundly as Joanie and I felt the call of the saint, so he was drinking *tsipouro* with his cronies when we streamed out with the congregation, following Father Prokopi in the procession of the prophet's icon around the village.

Later that night we reunited in the churchyard, ready to party. A woodcarver from Metsovo was selling his wares, another peddler hawked roasted corn, and Stella the *kafenion* owner sliced pieces off a lamb revolving on a spit. Local dignitaries arrived; members of Parliament, a deputy mayor, and two mayoral candidates in upcoming elections. Soon, four hundred people from nearby villages had poured in—a good showing, considering that many Liotes could not attend because they were in mourning, and bereaved Greeks don't participate in celebrations.

The president of the Liote Brotherhood invited Father Prokopi to lead the first dance. At first Father Prokopi demurred—he had a sore foot after the icon parade. But it is a tradition in Lia for the priest to kick off the *panegyri*, so he removed his hat and led four consecutive dances. The first song was an Epirotic tune about a handsome priest (a nod to Father P., whose cassock was flying out behind him as he kicked and twirled). I danced, my father danced, and proving the adage that poverty needs a good time, Vlad and Net danced more vigorously than anyone else. As the clarinet wailed, they leaped and stamped and flicked their wrists like aristocrats.

The following morning we were up at 6:45 to participate in the centuries-old ritual of climbing to the mountain peak. My father drove me and Joanie to the old border guard post, handed us two walking sticks, and said, "Have a good time." He couldn't climb, he said, because of his heart condition. So Joanie and I hiked up the dirt paths, passing friends on the way. Everyone was in high festival spirits, despite the early hour. Everyone except me. I've never been a

morning person, so when we finally made it to the jam-packed chapel
the size of the freight elevator in my building in New York, I sat outside on the edge of the cliff, baking in the sun like a salamander.
Father Prokopi would occasionally step outside to waft the
sweet smoke of incense over those of us who were worshipping al
fresco. In between censes, I listened in on my fellow villagers.
"Kyrie Vassili, I haven't seen you here in years," said one old man
to another. "It was the occupation, 1944? I was nine years old."
"That's the last time I made it up," Kyrio Vassili agreed. "I wasn't
sure I'd be able to again. But here I am." He turned to admire the
view, leaning on a cane.

Eventually, even we bystanders were swept up in the service as
two efficient women carried a table out from the church, unwrapped several huge, round, frosted breads, and sliced them into
hunks. They passed around pieces as Father Prokopi emerged,
smiling, carrying a metal cross for us to kiss, and waving a clump
of basil to splash holy water on us. <<Χρόνια πολλά παιδία>> he
said. ("Many years, children.") <<Και του χρόνου>> ("And next
year!")

"Next year, God willing," responded Kyrio Vassili.

"Now if you'll hold on a bit, I'm going to do a brief memorial service for Elias," Father Prokopi continued, referring to Marianthe's
forty-year-old son, whose wife had taken the kids shopping one
morning and returned to find him slumped in his chair, dead from
a heart defect he didn't know he had. Suddenly, in the middle of a
blessing, Father Prokopi stopped chanting. His thin frame started
shaking and he sobbed quietly for several minutes as the rest of Lia
stared. Soon we were all crying, too, remembering this lost member
of the village, a man whose life we should have been celebrating
that day, on his nameday, instead of mourning his death.

Eventually, Father Prokopi composed himself and finished the
service, and everyone kissed one another good-bye and started
climbing down, some to pick oregano, others heading straight
home, scattering across the mountainside like the holy water Father Prokopi had splashed over us. Joanie and I started down and

bumped into Thomas driving his pickup, the only four-wheel-drive vehicle that had made it up to the top, ferrying several loads of people too old or too citified to climb.

"Hop in," said Spiridoula. "There's room." There were nine of us squeezed into the back of the pickup, eight women and one old man. Father Prokopi, striding by with a gym bag full of holy articles, declined a ride. As we bumped over rocks and dirt clots down the mountain, villagers waved at us and Thomas yelled, in his best Gypsy grocer voice, "Nice, fresh women. Take your pick."

Halfway down to the center of the village, we got out at the Gatzoyiannis site, where the growing gray walls were just beginning to take on the outline of a house. Vlad and his family had skipped the service and, with the basement done, were now starting to pile stones and grout on top of each other to form the very beginnings of the second-story walls. My father was also there, toying with an old hand grenade Net had found on the job site. People passing by on their way down from the Prophet Elias glanced at the work in progress, but it was still just the suggestion of a house, not a finished home, and they had nameday calls to pay on all the local men named Elias, so they kept moving. At least, I hoped that was why they kept walking, that it wasn't because they feared the house or that seeing it brought back awful memories.

Back at the Haidis house, as Joanie and I lay down to rest from the morning's exertions, I said, "It's only one P.M. and it's already been a great day."

At one-thirty my father walked into the house, blocking the light coming into the bedroom door. "Get up," he said. Joanie did. I didn't. I needed my rest.

"The bad news is I totaled the car," he said. "The good news is I'm alive."

I sat up in bed, trying to understand. He had taken the car to go visit some friends, he explained. "Right, you took *my* car, and then?" I asked.

Well, these friends had a long narrow driveway, and instead of making them move their car so he could turn around, he thought he'd back out of the driveway. Except that he backed *off* the driveway—the car rolled over once and landed on the road below. I was in shock. So was he. I stood up. He went to lie down. "Your pants are torn," I said. I went into the living room to collect my thoughts, and Joanie came in to the bedroom to investigate. My father had scraped his legs and butt, she reported. I heard the gate slam. Foti rushed in, tears welling in his eyes. "What happened?" he cried. "I saw the wrecked car near the Xenona."

"He drove off the road," I answered. "The car flipped over, but he's okay."

"It was a miracle," Foti said, sighing. "The saint saved him." He walked to the bed, kissed my father on the cheek, and made the sign of the cross. My father was alive because the Prophet Elias had given us a miracle.

"It was the evil eye that drove you off the cliff," Foti continued, putting everything into perspective. "Everyone passed by the house today, saw how quickly it was being built, and felt jealous. They praised it and they gave you the evil eye."

Foti was losing me. I thought the careless brain was more at fault here than the evil eye; my father should have known better than to back off a cliff. Besides, I refused to believe that the house could be responsible for my father's accident, even indirectly.

"He's bleeding," Joanie said. "Nick, take off your pants to show Foti."

Everyone paused. Foti turned to me. "Do you want me to take you to see the car?"

I did indeed. Looking at the mashed hunk of metal, I realized that when the Prophet Elias performs a miracle, he does not mess around. Each window was broken and the windshield had buckled. If Joanie or I had been in the passenger seat instead of sleeping off our trek, we'd be dead. If the car hadn't hit the huge rock that held it in place, it could have rolled right on down the mountainside. We were shaky with gratitude and disbelief.

By the time Foti drove us home, my father's calf had swollen to the size of a honeydew. Foti offered to drive him to the hospital in Ioannina to get checked out while I waited for a tow truck to retrieve

Asymina's crushed carcass. I thought back to the moment in Athens when the Avis clerk told me that insurance cost an extra six dollars a day. "That's a hundred and eighty dollars a month!" I said, outraged. But I could hear NickGage's voice saying, "Get the insurance." So I did. The Prophet Elias plans ahead.

That afternoon a tow truck driver in red overalls arrived, attached a huge cord to Asymina's earthly remains and pulled them onto his truck. Seeing my shock and separation anxiety, he handed me a clipboard and said gently, "Fill this out. I'll need twenty-four euro for the ferry to Athens."

I knew we were incredibly lucky that my father was alive. At the same time I was rather annoyed at not having a car—and even angry that I had been a responsible driver for months and that within one week of arriving in Greece, my esteemed father had trashed my car joyriding around the village. But as Asymina receded into the distance on the back of the tow truck, I knew steel can be fixed and humans can't. The Prophet Elias had made the right choice.

Back at the house, I was just starting to calm down when the phone rang. "Lenitsa!" a voice screeched so loudly that I had to hold the receiver a foot away from my ear to prevent hearing loss. "What happened? I have to know the truth! If you lie to me, I curse you so you marry a man who lies, lies, lies all the time."

"Hi, Thitsa Kanta," I said, amazed at how quickly news had spread from Lia to Worcester. "NickGage is fine. Foti took him to the hospital just to be safe."

"Oh, the shepherd's with him, good." She calmed down. "Why didn't you go?"

"I had to stay because the tow truck was coming to pick up the car—it's totaled and smoke was coming from the engine," I explained.

"Oh, *Panagia mou!*" Thitsa Kanta keened. "You don't need to tell me that. You just like the doctors today, they tell you everything. I tell my doctor, if something wrong, I don't need to know, but someone got to make plans. If I'm gonna die, you call my son."

"Well, no one's going to die today, Thitsa Kanta," I assured her.

"You better be telling me the truth," she repeated before hanging up. "Otherwise, someone else in the village will, and you know my curses work. God loves your *thitsa!*"

In the end, I didn't need to worry about curses. We knew my father was fine when he returned from the hospital, beaming, and reported that even without insurance, the bill for all his tests and X-rays came to less than sixteen dollars.

We were all exhausted from the long, dramatic day. But the only way Thitsa Kanta and assorted other Liotes of Lia and Worcester would believe that NickGage was all right was if they heard he danced at the *panegyri* as he had the night before. That was what it meant to live in Lia; the entire village became your meddling extended family, relatives who love you too much to leave you in peace. As I watched my father dance opposite the clarinetist, I realized that I knew what the skeptics who had studied the Anastenarides hadn't been able to figure out. Life is risky, and people get burned. So you'd better pray you have saints—or even civilians—looking out for you.

FIVE

MOTHER TONGUES

<<Πολλοί άνθρωποι, πολλές γνώσεις.>>

"MANY PEOPLE, MANY OPINIONS."

July 29

"Look what I found!" Net yells, striding toward me with a heap of tangled metal.

"Thanks!" I grab the rusted lyre-shaped object, which has a hook hanging from it. "So, what is it?"

"You don't know?" Net asks. He turns it around, holding it by the hook so the lyre now hangs upside down, like the letter Π, *with two curved legs. I shrug.*

"It's a tsellinge*!" he bursts out. "You put it on a rod in the fire, for to hang the meat and roast." Now Net is laughing so hard that he snorts.*

How could I have known that? I'm not exactly in the habit of roasting meat on a hook above a roaring fire. I give him his five-euro finder's fee and thank him again.

"No say thank you," Net protests. "Not mine. Tsellinge *belong to your family."*

He's right. I rub the rusted metal and think that the last person who touched it may have been my grandmother, who did roast meat above the fire on the rare occasions she could get some. The coin had been an interesting artifact, a clue to the history of the house. But this hook is something more: direct contact with the grandmother I had never met. As the house yields more clues, I am starting to consider my grandmother's life more than her death. Holding the tsellinge, *I see her for a moment, bending over the fire in the space where the fireplace once was and soon will be again.*

I turn to thank Net again. He and Xalime are mixing concrete for Vlad to spread between the stones of the slowly growing walls, chatting in Albanian.

If I came to Greece to "find myself," when I got there I found everyone else. And they all spoke their own language. I had traveled enough to know that "Greek culture" is not one concrete, monolithic category: there are resorts, islands, mountain villages, hectic cities. Even the language has several different registers, levels of formality, and dialects. But I thought that by moving to the remote province my family came from, I was narrowing my options to one cohesive cultural milieu, characterized by an oatmeal-mouthed village accent. By midsummer, however, I realized there are almost as many obscure cultural groups in Epiros as in any liberal arts university that touts its "diversity."

Even in Lia, which in late July was nearing its full capacity of three hundred or so inhabitants, only about half were native Liotes. There were several Northern Epirotes—the Christian, ethnic Greeks from Albania—including a family of three master stonemasons I had hired at great expense to do the really difficult stonework Vlad wasn't skilled enough to handle, and to speed up the lagging building process. Then there were the mostly Muslim Albanians, like Vlad, Net, and Xalime, who were starting, under the master stonemasons' supervision, to build the second-story walls. And a number of widows and widowers there for the summer had acquired caretakers from Ukraine to cook, clean, and, in at least one case, boss them around like army generals. (A seventy-year-old, diaphanous-blouse-wearing Ukrainian vamp hired Vlad and Net to rid the house of her employer's old junk by dumping it into the ravine, creating a grotesque landfill of beds, bureaus, olive oil tins, and bedspreads.)

I wasn't happy about the newly created trash slide, but on the whole I liked the formerly Communist-bloc new arrivals in Lia. All except the Yugoslavian-made Skoda we had been given by Avis to replace Asymina. A squat blue vehicle with upholstery that featured lady robots in triangular miniskirts dancing a kick line, the Skoda's main drawback was its stick shift, which I could not drive. Avis said automatic cars were impossible to find now that it was high tourist season and all the other isolationist honkies who were too lazy to learn to drive a stick had already rented them. (They didn't say that exactly, but it *was* implied.) Since I was not the one who had committed vehicular homicide on Asymina, I reasoned, it was not my responsibility to find myself another automatic, it was my father's. But he didn't seem quite as troubled by my lack of wheels as I did; there was plenty of excitement right there in town, he said, now that Lia was full of old friends to visit. Who needed a car?

My father was in denial about his accident; I had moved on to anger. But Thitsa Kanta was more interested in blame, calling from Worcester to lay it directly at my feet. "You didn't believe the curse, and look what happened," she boomed into the phone.

"The curse?" I asked.

"When my mother say good-bye to me and your father, she make us throw black stones behind us and promise not to come back to Greece to live, or we would have her curse," she explained. "It's okay to go for vacation like I do, one, two months, but not to live like you. That's why NickGage had the accident; it was a warning he should go home, take care of his family, not worry about that cursed place."

Just what I needed—another reason to feel guilty about my presence in Lia. Of course, I didn't really believe that my father's dead mother had crashed my rental car with him in it as a subtle warning. Thitsa Kanta was just using the curse to make her point: her way of visiting Greece was right and my way of living there was wrong. On the other hand, Thitsa Kanta knew more about curses than I did.

A few days after Asymina's untimely demise, we went to lunch at the home of a woman everyone called the *papadia*—the priest's wife—although her husband, the village's former priest, had been dead for several years. (Actually, *presvytera* is the correct term for a priest's wife; *papadia* is a village nickname, as some Athenian girls I met once were kind enough to point out. They were the same girls who clued me in that fireflies should be referred to as *pygolambides*, the ancient word for "firefly" instead of the village term my aunts taught me to call them, *kolofoties*, or "ass-on-fires.") As we ate, the *papadia* asked about my travels. I told her about visiting Metsovo at Easter, how surprised I was to see ladies in native costume, hear them chattering away in Vlachiko.

"Did you see any Sarakatsanis in Metsovo?" the *papadia* asked. "There used to be a family with a summer place in the mountain there."

"Like a vacation house?" I asked.

"No!" her nephew burst out, laughing. "Sarakatsanis are nomadic shepherds, who graze their sheep in the mountains in summer and in the lowlands in winter. You used to see their straw huts in the countryside. There are probably only about five nomadic Sarakatsanis left now. The rest are doctors, lawyers, whatever. But they're proud of their history, organized into federations all over Greece. A friend who was president of the Epirote federation told me they gather the first weekend in August at a museum of huts."

The next day, hearing that a foreigner was interested in his people, the president, Christos Raptis, drove up from Ioannina just to tell me all about the Sarakatsanis. He and his family had been nomadic until he was twelve, erecting round straw huts to live in as they traveled around with their sheep. "My wife's family was nomadic until she was eight," he said, showing me a photo of a brunette in a peach pantsuit, who looked as though she never went anywhere without a travel iron.

"So, what happened?" I asked. "Why did you stop living that way?"

"Well, in the sixties, Greece was modernizing and our parents wanted to educate us, give us more opportunities," he replied. "It's a hard life, being a nomad. So now I bring my daughters to the museum to show them how Sarakatsanis used to live, the whole family sleeping on the floor of the hut around the central fire." He smiled. "Everything happened in that same space—sleeping, meals, sex."

It all sounded so . . . unsanitary. But Mr. Raptis seemed lost in a happy reverie about simpler times. As he left, I realized that if I kept coming back to Lia once the house was finished, I'd be choosing a seminomadic life myself. At first I'd been shocked that this middle-aged man who was younger than my father remembered such a primitive lifestyle. But I might be re-creating a twenty-first-century version of the same existence, as though I was moving backward in terms of cultural evolution.

I pushed any thoughts of my future aside, telling myself to concentrate on the present, but even then I couldn't stop empathizing with the Sarakatsanis. Since they were no longer nomadic, the only way for Sarakatsanis to preserve their identity as a community was by celebrating together, gathering a few times a year at their museum to recall the past. It's an elusive balance but perhaps is what we all want—the romance of the virgin forest and straw hut, but with the hygiene of a bathroom and separate bedrooms. I was doing the same thing to a degree; living my family's past for a bit, trying to preserve what's important from our history and incorporate it into a more comfortable future.

By the end of the week my parents and the Skoda were gone—they had dropped it off in Ioannina on their way to the airport and reserved another Hyundai for me, a twin of Asymina's, except that she was gold instead of silver. I decided I'd name her Chrysanthi, "Golden Flower." She wasn't available for pickup until a week after they had to return to the United States, so my father arranged for me to hitch a ride to Ioannina with his friend Babis, who would pass through Lia on his way from Albania to Athens.

Babis looked like Billy Bob Thornton: bald and thin, with an insane gleam in his eye. He already had three passengers in his car, so I squeezed in between two strangers as rain started to fall. Pressed thigh to thigh, we were making uncomfortable small talk as Billy Babis sped along the curving road to Ioannina. On one hairpin turn, the car began to skid. The woman on my right screamed and Billy Babis swore as his car slammed into a copse of trees that blocked us from rolling down the cliff. No one spoke. Billy Babis got out, checked his BMW for damage, then got in, backed out of the grove, and sped on without a word. The woman on my left spent the rest of the ride hunched over, her head in her hands. I no longer had to make small talk, which was good because I didn't think I'd be able to; I was too painfully aware that now two members of my family had almost died driving off the mountain, fulfilling a curse I claimed not to believe.

But if the curse existed, I managed to elude it one more time; I made it to Ioannina in one piece, and Chrysanthi and I returned safely. As if to replace my parents, a new foreigner had arrived in Lia, Vlad's eighteen-year-old daughter, Dorina, whose boarding school in Tirana was closed for summer. We met over dinner at Dina's; Dorina had adorable dimples and a compulsion to chat. She didn't speak Greek, but her school was run by Italian nuns and I had studied Italian for a year in college, so we got by. As we dug into our lamb chops, she described her home (Albania is beautiful but poor), her fiancé (a twenty-two-year-old soldier who wanted to move to America), and both her grandmothers (one was Catholic, the other Orthodox Christian, but both converted to Islam at some point, then gave up religion under communism). She told me lots of other things, too, but I couldn't quite make them out. "You speak Italian like a Spanish person," she said, grinning.

I did understand when she said, wide-eyed, "I can't believe we're all in one room. I told my father this is no way for a family to live! There's no room for any more people over here." I looked around. Dina and Andreas's courtyard was cluttered with tubes and rocks; Andreas was building an artificial waterfall, fed by mountain water rushing into his pool. Ever since his son had died, he dreamed up one home improvement project after another to keep busy. He reminded me of sharks, who die if they don't keep moving.

"You can stay with me until my sister comes to visit," I told Dorina.

She smiled, then ran next door to get her toothbrush. The next morning I took her on a walk up to the Gatzoyiannis house to visit her family at work. Vlad, Net, and Xalime thought it hilarious that we had walked up in the hot sun by choice. It didn't seem to make Dorina uncomfortable that her family was lifting stones and mixing cement while we strolled, doing nothing useful, but I felt awkward, so I continued on to a house above. To the left of its new white aluminum front door was an old wooden one with broken hinges and coats of variegated blue paint that looked like the different depths of the ocean. It was an ancient lye-based paint, worn and faded by time.

"Hey, Net," I called. "Do you know what they're doing with this door?"

"Throwing it out."

"Really?" I said. "Can you bring it to me in the truck when you come home?"

Net stopped spreading concrete on a block of stone and looked up at me, shielding his eyes from the sun. "What do you want that old door for?"

"I just like the color," I replied. He kept staring at me, expecting a more reasonable answer. "Maybe I'll make it into a table," I improvised.

He laughed and said something to Dorina in Albanian that made her dimple.

That afternoon Dorina and I were eating at Dina's when her family came home from work. "Dina, can we have some buckets of hot water, please?" Net called.

"I keep telling you, just use our shower," Dina yelled back. But she brought him his bucket anyway. "Sometimes Vlad and Net use the shower, but Xalime never does," she whispered to me. "I think they're not used to showers. But because the girl lives at a school, she is. That's why she's so glad to stay with you; you have one." I was happy to promote good hygiene. And Dorina came over only to shower and sleep. I didn't feel obliged to entertain her, so I would occasionally hop into Chrysanthi and drive off in search of adventure. One night, at a dinner in the harbor city of Igoumenitsa, I met Georgia Vaya, a brunette in a smart navy suit who was married to the mayor of Arta.

"On Saturday I'm going to be the *koumbara* at a Gypsy wedding in

Arta," I heard her say to the hostess. (The *koumbara* and *koumbaros* are the wedding equivalent of godparents.) "I can invite anyone I want. Do you want to see the Gypsy neighborhood?"

"I do!" I jumped at the chance, although the invitation hadn't exactly been issued to me specifically. Even when they lived in pickup trucks and walked around barefoot, all the Gypsies I'd seen had gold jewelry, working TVs, and a unique fashion sense—they fascinated me. But most of my fellow Liotes were less entranced by the peddlers who drove through town daily, hawking tables, sheets, and live poultry. The Liotes warned me that Gypsies would try to cheat me and were known to steal babies, so it was a good thing I didn't have any.

"How come the Gypsies are still so poor, nomadic?" Nikki the innkeeper asked one night over dinner in the Xenona. "Look at the Albanians; they came here and in ten years they've built homes, gotten jobs, lives. But the Gypsies are cursed to roam. I'll tell you why. It's because a Gypsy smith made the nails used to crucify Christ."

"That's funny," Antonis Makos replied. "In the army, a Gypsy soldier told me that the Romans were going to use many nails to crucify Christ, but a Gypsy stole a few, sparing him some pain. So Christ *blessed* the Gypsies with permission to steal forever."

Despite the warnings, I was determined to see the Gypsies up close and personal myself. So three days later I was in Arta, standing outside the Byzantine church of Agia Theodora with Georgia; her husband, the mayor; a nervous nineteen-year-old groom in a gray suit; and several of his sisters, who were ululating and gyrating their hips while holding large trays of *boubounierres*, traditional Jordan-almond wedding favors, high above their heads. The church, one of many important monuments from Arta's Byzantine past, was dedicated to Queen Theodora of Arta, whose husband killed her after he took up with a prostitute. Then he felt bad, and built several churches in her honor. This one, right across the highway from the Gypsy neighborhood, was the Gypsies' church of choice. Georgia and her husband had baptized the bride, Efstathia, there eighteen years before. Now nineteen, Efstathia was the eldest of six children of the Panagiotopoulos clan, a Gypsy family that always voted for Mayor Vaya. The groom was one of eleven offspring of the Karafatalos family, a clan that voted for the opposition despite Georgia's best efforts. "You would not believe the number of coffees I've made for old man Karafatalos!" she told me.

Now Arta's two most powerful Gypsy clans were merging; a month earlier Mr. Karafatalos had called Mr. Panagiotopoulos to ask for his daughter's hand on behalf of his son. While we awaited the bride, Georgia pointed out the major players to me and her other guest, a matron in a pearl gray suit. "See that girl, the groom's sister? She's twenty and has four kids! But two of his other sisters married Greek guys," she said. "In a few generations Gypsies will be completely absorbed into Greek culture. Look how the younger girls have started to dress like us." She indicated some Gypsy lasses in flowing gowns with spaghetti straps.

"No, dear," replied her friend, raising an eyebrow. "We've started to dress like them."

The gray lady was right—this was a particularly Stevie Nicks moment in Greek fashion, replete with lace, gauze, and handkerchief hems. Disregarding the trend, the Gypsy women over thirty favored brightly patterned long skirts and voluminous tops that hid a pouch of valuables secured at the waist. All females older than five wore makeup and jewelry; even the toddlers had hennaed hair. Overall, the Karafatalos clan was very good-looking, including the groom, whose only flaw was a little teenage acne.

I was knocked out of my reverie by the sound of a tambourine, a clarinet, and rhythmic shouts of "Heh, heh, heh, heh!" The bride was arriving! A J. Lo look-alike in hennaed ringlets and a white, sequined, full-skirted confection, she was escorted by a retinue of dancing women and one effeminate male relative with long hair and a hologram shirt that glinted in the sunlight. The gyrating crowd parted so the bride could do a little shimmy of her own, arms raised above her head, wrists twisting, gold bracelets gleaming. Then her father, debonair in a pinstripe suit and black mustache, led her to the church door where her groom awaited, holding a bouquet. He handed it to her as the onlookers shouted for a kiss. The couple shyly complied, then entered the church. The ceremony was like other Orthodox weddings I've attended, but with even more throngs of children running around, some topless, others in Pokémon T-shirts. But once it was over, the drummer started drumming, the clarinet began wailing, and we danced out of the familiar, fragrant world of the Greek church, gyrating en masse across the highway, into the Gypsy enclave of dirt roads and whitewashed cottages. I snapped photos on the way and was soon besieged by requests from the multitude of children. "Miss, take my picture with the baby," said a nine-year-old, hoisting up a one-year-old sibling. "Miss, you're pretty. Take me in front of our truck." Flattery *will* get you everywhere, my young Gypsy friend. "Miss, I'm the brother of the bride—take me with this girl." They may not have cameras, but one thing Gypsies do not lack is self-esteem. I was the lone paparazzo in a neighborhood full of superstars.

We swarmed over to the designated honeymoon suite, the house of one of the older Karafatalos brothers. Before crossing the threshold, the bride stepped on a plate to break any bad luck and drive away evil spirits. Then everyone sat on the porch, drinking *tsipouro* while the newlyweds' siblings shimmied to a tape of what must be numbers one and two on the Gypsies' Top 40: a Greek song that complains, "You snuff me out like a cigarette, toss me away like ashes," and the Australian pop tune "Daddy Cool." Although their relatives from ages five to seventy-five danced energetically, the newlyweds remained seated. The groom beamed in relief that the ceremony was over, but the bride was somber.

Mrs. Karafatalos, a grandchild on her hip, offered to give Georgia and me a house tour. The large living room was consumed by the bride's dowry and gifts (except the gold items she was currently wearing on her wrists, neck, fingers, and thumbs). Columns of folded comforters and blankets rose from floor to ceiling, and waterfalls of china and cutlery cascaded down the tables. The next stop was the bedroom, dominated by a king-size bed whose pink silk comforter was strewn with rose petals. Mrs. Karafatalos waved her hand over the bed like Vanna White, then pointed to the bedside table. "That basket is where we'll put the virginity," she said.

My eyebrows shot up. Seeing my expression, Mrs. Karafatalos explained, speaking slowly, as if to a small child. "After the dancing, the couple comes here to make love, and the woman bleeds." (Here she indicated her groin to make sure I understood.) "We take the bloody sheet and put it in this basket to bring to the party. The relatives throw money on it—fifty euros, one hundred, whatever. It's a Gypsy tradition."

No wonder the bride looked nervous. Georgia, ever the gracious guest, said, "How lovely!" Looking closely at our hostess, she added, "You're not a Gypsy, are you?"

"No," Mrs. Karafatalos admitted. "My mother, she threw me away when I was born." Suddenly she grinned, exposing two missing teeth. "But an old Gypsy lady took me in, so I became a Gypsy. I even learned the language."

As a Gypsy, she was an overachiever, what with eleven kids and twenty-eight grandkids. We followed her to the porch to find the mayor, a stocky seventy-year-old, boogying to "Daddy Cool" in the heat. The man would risk a heart attack to secure those Karafatalos votes.

Luckily, Mr. Karafatalos arrived to put an end to Mayor Vaya's high-risk hoedown and lead us to the reception in the main square of the neighborhood. There, on a flatbed truck with one open side, a Gypsy band from Athens was blasting the endlessly requested "you snuff me out like a cigarette" song as tables were set around three sides of the square and relatives of the newlyweds carried the laden dinner plates, using as trays the tops of the plastic tables Gypsy merchants sold door-to-door. Gypsies from all over Epiros ate spit-roasted goat, drank wine, danced to the Cigarette Song, and had an all-out fabulous time—even Efstathia was smiling as she and her husband led several circle dances. But I couldn't stop worrying about the sheet. The anthropologist in me wanted to see the ritual, but the rest of me was nervous for the bride.

At two A.M. the bandleader tapped on the microphone. "Okay,

folks, that was the last dance, because we Gypsies have our traditions to uphold," he boomed. "I need a child from the bride's family and one from the groom's to come up here and receive the couple's money. Let's see which one of them raises the most for their new life together!"

People streamed up with cash and envelopes. Money poured in and the couple sat there smiling; this seemed to be the stress-free part of the evening. I hadn't brought a gift, so I beckoned an eleven-year-old and handed her fifty euros for the bride "from Eleni"—no last name, please. She strolled up as the announcer bellowed, "Yiorgos Karafatalos is busy with his watermelon business on Corfu, so he can't be here, but he gives eight hundred euros to the groom and two hundred to the bride." My fifty came next. Everyone clapped politely, but after the Watermelon King of Corfu, it was anticlimactic.

Then I felt it—a drop of rain. "That's it, folks, good luck to the happy couple," the announcer said, ducking under the truck/stage. The band put a tape in the sound system and started packing their instruments as rain fell more steadily. Georgia stood up. "Looks like the party's over," she said. "We'll take you to the hotel."

"What about the sheet?" I asked.

"It got rained out." She shrugged. "Don't worry; I'll call if there's a scandal!"

Both relieved and disappointed, I said good-bye to the smiling bride and left as the groom's sister, the twenty-year-old mother of four, continued to dance, twirling in the rain.

Driving to Lia, I wondered what life would be like for the newlywed Gypsies' children. Would they assimilate into the Greek mainstream, as Georgia predicted? Two of the groom's sisters had. One, a chef's assistant in Athens, told me, "I could never come back to live here; I'm used to another way of life." But that left nine siblings who were still entrenched in the community. When you have eleven kids, chances are that a few will follow in your footsteps. But Efstathia planned on having only three, she told Georgia, so she could educate them all. The Gypsies were masters at choosing their own identity: were they thieves or chosen people, kidnappers or rescuers of orphans, Gypsies or Greeks, or both? I started to wonder about my own children. Would they learn Greek? Would they even be interested in visiting their grandparents' home, which I was now rebuilding?

By the time I entered Lia, I had stopped mulling over my potential progeny and started worrying about Dorina's immediate future. In a few days Marina, my sister, would arrive, and I needed the bed for her. I'd have to send Dorina back to the crowded room with no shower. As I passed the Xenona Inn, Vlad flagged me down.

"Eleni, I have something for you," he said. I pulled up to the side of the road.

"Come see new house," he insisted. I had no idea what he was talking about, but I often had a hard time understanding Vlad's broken Greek, so I followed orders. He led me to a house belonging to a Liote family who lived in Athens. Xalime, who was working in the garden, rushed inside to get me some cherry juice while Vlad indicated that I should sit on the couch. Dorina and Net appeared from back rooms. Vlad handed me a silver coin he had found in the ruins of the Gatzoyiannis house; it had a hole at the top, so it had been worn as part of a woman's dowry. Later, after some Internet research, I learned it was a six-*kreuzer* Austrian coin bearing the grotesque profile of Leopold the Hogmouth. But at first all I could make out was the date, 1685. I wondered how this foreign coin had reached my grandmother's house—did it serve as jewelry on her wedding day?—only to be discovered by Vlad 317 years after it was minted.

"Thanks," I said. "This is great. But what are you all doing here?"

Net explained that the owners of the house came for a visit and agreed to let Vlad and his family live in it in exchange for taking care of the place. Dorina broke in, saying in Italian that the house had two bedrooms, a living room, kitchen, bathroom, garden, and washing machine. I realized that I had just sunk to the lowest rung on Lia's socioeconomic ladder; I was now the only Liote I knew without a TV *or* washing machine. But I was glad for the family; this was a step up from one room.

"Congratulations!" I said. "That's wonderful."

Vlad sat down across the table, dejected. "Dina and Andreas very mad," he said. "She spoke to me angry, said not take anything she give us, even TV, which I pay seventy-five euro to fix in Igoumenitsa. They not good people I thought."

I had forgotten; Dina and Andreas let the Albanians live rent-free in their one-room shack so Vlad and Xalime would watch *their* house when they went on dowry-selling trips. Mourning two dead sons, they had started to think of Net as family.

Back in Motsala, my neighbors were abuzz with the news of the Albanian defection. "Vladimiros had to take this opportunity," Athina reasoned. "He told me he hadn't been able to go to his wife for four months because they were all sleeping in one room." You could always count on Athina, who had a squirrel's cheeks but a hawk's eyes, to disseminate crucial information.

"You're right," her husband, Grigoris, said, nodding his bald head. "But he should have told Dina that they might leave as soon as he knew, instead of springing it on her just after Andreas's son's memorial service, on the day they moved. She feels abandoned."

"Look, everyone got mad at that moment," Vangeli Panagiotou chimed in. "But Vladimiros should apologize now, say he appreciates all they've done for them, feeding them, housing them, introducing them to you, Eleni, who gave them the jobs on the house and let the girl sleep in your own home. Albanians are ungrateful people." He shook his head definitively. "They're not like us."

I wasn't taking a racial-profiling view of the situation; it made sense for the family to move on up to a bigger place. But I felt bad for Dina and Andreas. They hadn't discussed the incident with me, I suspect, because I employed the family. But Dina complained that the neighborhood was so quiet, it depressed her. And Andreas started expanding the kitchen, the latest in his self-prescribed course of movement therapy.

We had all gotten along so well for so long, eaten so much *pita* together in the courtyard. It was sobering to see how easily our community could fall apart, how quickly prejudices arose, hostility between those who left and those who were left behind. But as my neighbors bickered, I was about to inject more international flavor into our local mix of nationalities; my sister was on her way to visit me.

I drove to Ioannina to pick Marina up, leaving a day early to check on my own internal drama: it was time for the sonogram that I'd promised my doctors in America I'd have every few months in Greece. When I made the appointment, it seemed routine. Now, having learned about my grandmother's curse, I was nervous. My appointment was a crushing reminder of my lack of control over my fate. I was able to decide where I would live, what language I would speak, even my citizenship. My identity was up to me, but I couldn't choose to be tumor-free.

At Ioannina's University Hospital Dr. Tsamboulis, a soft-spoken man who had been recommended by a friend, led me into the ultrasound room, where a young female doctor stood wearing jeans and a crop top under a lab coat. Normally, I don't like to be examined by anyone with an exposed midriff, but I was new there, so I didn't protest.

"My patient is in the bathroom right now, so wait a moment, we'll be right with you," said Dr. Britney, as I liked to think of her. An old man shuffled out of the bathroom, boxer shorts visible above his unbuttoned pants, and lay on the exam table.

"Turn to the wall," Dr. Britney commanded. I did, understanding that the gentleman wanted his privacy. "Not you!" the sexy doctor said as she burst out laughing. "Him."

Grandpa rolled over so she could X-ray his back. He seemed untroubled by my presence; if he wasn't embarrassed, I wasn't going to be, either. The exam ended, the old man left, and Dr. Tsamboulis locked the door; my sonogram would have no studio audience, thank God.

Fifteen minutes later he handed me my X-rays and a letter in English to send to my oncologist in America. My tumors had shrunk slightly, he said. That was the good news. The bad news was that they were still there; I'd have to return for a follow-up sonogram in three months. I was just happy that nothing was horribly wrong with my reproductive health and that my grandmother wasn't cursing me for breaking my family's vow. I could ignore the whole thing for a few more months and take my sister on vacation!

Marina's ten-day visit was perfect, except that, as a French professor who had spent the past two years in Paris, she was frustrated to discover that her Greek was nowhere near as good as her French. One night at the Xenona, Foti Tsandinis bought us drinks. As we chatted, he turned to Marina and said, "Honey, how come you don't speak Greek as well as your sister?" She muttered, "I concentrated on French and haven't been here in a while. But I understand it all." Everyone was satisfied until Vangelis joined us and asked Marina the same question. This time she just glared.

On the walk home, we developed a plan. Later, at dinner at Dina's, Marina hadn't taken her first bite of *pita* when Grigoris said to her, "You don't speak Greek as well as Eleni, sweetheart."

Marina swallowed. "My Greek's not that great," she said. "But *vozono alafiatika.*" (I speak tinker language.) There was a moment of stunned silence. Then a roar of laughter rose up around the table. Marina was now the most popular girl in Lia. She might not know perfect Greek, but she was fluent in the mother tongue.

After her triumph, Marina and I walked home. Looking out at the lights of a village on the mountaintop across the ravine, she whispered, "It looks like a constellation!" I had been there for so long, I had stopped noticing how striking my surroundings were; Marina had to remind me not to take Lia for granted. We stared at the glittering night sky and chatted for hours, then finally went to bed.

At three-thirty I awoke to someone stroking my hair. Then I realized the hand patting me was an awfully tiny one.

"Turn on the light!" I yelled. Marina did, and then screamed, "There he is!"

And there he was; a squirrel scampered across my bed and up the chimney. He kept popping his head out of the fireplace, waiting for us to leave his house alone. At last, Marina chased him into the hall and shut the bedroom door as I sat there cowering.

I tried to persuade Marina to stay, to improve her Greek and protect me from amorous rodents. But she had a summer course waiting. "Look on the bright side," she consoled me. "With the squirrel around, you never have to sleep alone."

I didn't have a chance to get lonely, because soon after Marina left, my father called to say a friend of his was bringing a tour group for lunch in Lia on their way from Corfu to Ioannina. I decided to stop by the Xenona to ask the group, who were mostly New Yorkers, what was new back in the city. I found thirty people in jeans, shorts, and fanny packs streaming off a bus; twenty-five of them appeared to be over sixty-five.

"Where's the bathroom?" said one gray-permed lady by way of introduction.

"Right down there," I chirped, pointing toward the inn's basement.

"You mean there's stairs? Good Lord!" she groaned, hobbling off.

"Miss, is there cheese in this pie?" a tall man in glasses asked, beckoning me. "I have to take pills if I eat cheese. I'm lactose."

Lactose! It had been five months since I'd heard the phrase *lactose intolerant.* In Lia, old people climbed everywhere and ate everything—the memory of years of starvation had inspired many of them to cultivate Santa-like paunches and force food on me. I was ready for some frivolous, fanny-pack-wearing picky eaters. My fellow Americans!

The leader of the group introduced himself. An athletic middle-aged man with a gray beard and the voice of an NPR announcer, Isaac looked like the head of a progressive private school, the kind of guy who would lead the entire student body on a hike to the top of a mountain, where they would then sit in a circle and "share."

"So, tell me what you all have done already," I said to him as the innkeepers Fanis and Nikki served *tiropita* and *moussaka.* "How was Corfu?"

"Corfu was a wonderful, emotional experience," Isaac intoned.
"I took everyone on the route the Corfiot Jews walked when they
were deported, and asked them to be silent so that we could hear
our footsteps on the cobblestones the way our relatives did as they
were led to the boats headed for Auschwitz."

Suddenly the fanny-pack wearers seemed a lot less frivolous.
My fellow Americans, it appeared, were also my fellow Greek
Americans. Except that they were descendants of the communities
of Greek Jews that had thrived before World War II.

"Now we go to Ioannina, where our relatives came from," Isaac
continued.

"I've passed by the synagogue tons of times, but it's never open,"
I told him.

"Well, the community is so small and elderly now, they don't
usually have a *minyan*, the ten men required to hold a service," he
responded. "But we're holding one on Friday. You're welcome to
come."

Over lunch, I learned that the New Yorkers were members of a
Jewish community I'd never heard of, the Romaniote Jews, who had
settled in Greece by the first century A.D. and had lived there ever
since, speaking Greek and conducting their services in Greek.
When a large number of Ioanniote Romaniotes immigrated to New
York at the turn of the twentieth century, they founded the Kehila
Kedosha Janina Synagogue on the Lower East Side, "the only Romaniote synagogue in the entire Western Hemisphere," Isaac told
me. Most of the people traveling with him worshipped there.

Over lunch I got to know the group: three had been born in
Greece; the rest had parents or grandparents who were born there.
David's mother was from Ioannina, but he was born in 1919 in
Egypt, where he learned eight languages, including Greek, which
his family spoke at home. Markella, whose father was from Ioannina, was born in Athens under a fake name while her family lived
across from the German commanders' post during the war. "My
father said that it was the safest place to be," she recalled. "No one
would suspect a Jew living under the Germans' nose." Belle was
there because Ioannina was her father's birthplace, although he

moved when he was two. "For the descendants of Romaniotes in New York, Ioannina is a very big thing," she explained. "Growing up, you heard 'Ioannina' all the time.' So I had to see it." By the end of the meal, I had decided to join them in Ioannina. I went to pack, leaving just in time to hear a lady tell Fanis, "But you're even better-looking than Anthony Quinn!"

In Ioannina we pulled weeds, branches, and dirt off of the graves in the Jewish cemetery, where a new wall to deter vandals had been built with funds from the Kehila Kedosha Janina Synagogue in New York. Ninety percent of the graves were overgrown, and the dense brush made it impossible for most of the New Yorkers to find the tombs of their ancestors, but many were happy just to be on hallowed ground. "I always promised my mother I'd come visit the grave of my grandfather," said eighty-three-year-old David. "Now I've done it."

The next day we met at the headquarters of Ioannina's Jewish community on Joseph Elia Street, where the second synagogue had been located before the war. The Germans used it as a stable, so when 163 Jews returned from the Holocaust—all that survived of Ioannina's 1,950 Jews—they tore down the ruins to create apartments and offices. Inside the office, New Yorkers in shorts and Nikes hugged tiny Ioanniote men and women in suits. Then they pored over the archives for their relatives' names. Occasionally their murmured questions would be interrupted by a joyous outburst. "I found him! I found my uncle Mordecai!" yelled a woman in a tracksuit.

As I left, a forty-year-old man with the kind of bushy mustache that identified him as Greek stopped me, pushing a shy thirteen-year-old boy ahead of him. "You speak Greek, don't you?" he said to me. "Well, this is my son, Zachariah, and we were in there just now watching old people greet other old people. No one even introduced him. Tell your friends the community needs to do more to encourage young people's involvement. Zachariah's mother is Christian, but he chose to be Jewish."

The next day as we sat outside the synagogue in the *kastro*, Ioannina's old walled city, waiting for services to start, I told Marcia, the other tour leader and the head of the American Friends of

Greek Jewry, about the agitated man. She frowned. "That's a big question for the Central Board of Jewish Communities in Greece, which holds free summer camps in Thessaloniki for Jewish children," she said. "Do they accept kids of mixed marriages, or not? Technically, a child with a Christian mother, like Zachariah, is not a Jew unless he converts. But because the communities are so small and assimilated, intermarriage and emigration are the norm."

"And soon these old people will die and the community probably won't exist anymore," said Judy, one of the younger New Yorkers. "In the end, Hitler won."

Her statement shocked me. I thought the fact that we were waiting to attend a service in the centuries-old synagogue meant that Hitler hadn't won. But the story of Ioannina's Jews is a tragic one. Rae Dalvin's book *The Jews of Ioannina*, describes how, after 48,674 Jews from Thessaloniki were deported between March and August 1943, the Ioanniote Jews considered taking refuge with resistance groups in the mountains. But a prominent local businessman, Sabethai Cabilli, visited the occupying German commander, who assured him that his community would not be harmed. Cabilli urged total cooperation, only realizing his fatal error on March 25, 1944, when the Jews were rounded up on the lakefront for deportation. "I have sinned!" he cried. The elderly Cabilli was among the first killed on arrival at Auschwitz.

Elsewhere in Greece, some Jews did escape the Holocaust. Archbishop Damaskinos and Evangelos Evert, the chief of police, issued false identity cards to Athenian Jews, saving two-thirds of the community, including Markella and her family. And the 275 Jews on Zakynthos were unharmed after the Germans requested a list of Jews and the mayor and bishop gave him only two names: their own.

Most Greek Jews were not so lucky: about 87 percent died in the Holocaust. Before the war, there were 78,000 Jews in Greece. Today, Marcia said, there are about 5,000. Life wasn't easy for the survivors once they returned. Markella's aunt Estir, who still lived in Ioannina, said that when her husband came to reclaim his property from squatters just after the war, as was his right according to Greek law, a woman living in his sister's home said she would not let a Jew in the house. "So he sued, and got it back," Estir said. "But the lady in his parents' house said, 'Mr. Laganas, this is your home. Let me make you a cup of coffee.' Because of that act of kindness we let her live with us rent-free."

As darkness fell, the owlish community leader, Moises Eliah, arrived to lead us in to services. The restored synagogue was breathtaking, with high arched ceilings, a wide central area, and an *ieron*, a cabinet that houses the *tikkim*, the ornate wood-and-iron cases in which Romaniotes keep the Torah scrolls. These *tikkim* were 200–400 years old, Marcia explained, and were saved from the Germans by Ioannina's mayor during the war. I sat next to Rose, the president of the Sisterhood of the KKJ in New York. Tears filled her eyes as Samuel, a white-haired Ioanniote, began the service. "I can hear my grandfather chanting this," she said. I asked if Samuel was a rabbi or a cantor.

"He's just an elder," answered Rose. "His daughter lives in Israel, and his wife wanted to move there. But he said if he does, who will lead the services in Ioannina?"

The service ended and at the farewell dinner afterward, people found relatives they didn't know they had, identified mystery family members in old photos, hugged, kissed, cried, and exchanged information. Then, as president of the sisterhood, Rose stood up to present an award to the Ioanniote community "for keeping Judaism alive in Ioannina." She wept once more as she said, "We consider Ioannina our home. It means so much to all of us to spend time with you, our family."

I tried to leave the family gathering unnoticed. But David stopped me on the way out. "I have a nephew," he began. "A doctor. He's thirty-three and he lives in Great Neck. When I get back to New York, you call me and I'll put you in touch. He wants a girl like you, an old-fashioned girl. You're like us." I appreciated the thought. But I lived in Lia now and was not about to start looking for long-distance love. Instead, I was searching for the same thing these senior citizens sought: a link to my past.

A few days later, as I drove out of Ioannina along a cobbled back street, I realized everyone was staring at my car. A boy on a bike rode up and yelled, "You have a flat!"

I pulled over, got out, and looked at the boy, a pudgy ten-year-old in a T-shirt that bore a picture of a tiger and the phrase "Wild Thing!"

"I'll change it," he offered. "My father owns a garage and I help out."

"But I don't have a spare tire," I cried.

Wild Thing looked at me as if *I* were the one wearing a stupid T-shirt. Then he walked to the trunk, opened it, and lifted the false bottom to reveal a tire. Several older boys offered to help, but Wild Thing brushed them all off. Then the sound of laughter and gum snapping alerted me to the presence of four teenaged Gypsy girls, giggling at us.

"Is that your kid?" the ringleader asked me.

"No!" I yelled. "He's helping me!" Did I look like I could have a ten-year-old? The girls doubled over in laughter. Wild Thing was not amused.

Seeing Chrysanthi cured, I was so thrilled that I slipped Wild Thing forty euros in my farewell handshake. Actually, I tried to slip it, suavely, as if he were a maître d', but Wild Thing held the bills in front of his face. "Thanks, lady," he said.

It was worth it. Wild Thing gave me back my mobility, but he also revealed to me a part of my identity that I couldn't escape. I did have a place in this community in which I lived. I was there to amuse everyone: the Gypsy girls, Net by asking for the old door, and the computer guy who, when I brought my expensive machine for repair, chuckled, "Where you are, there's the worst electricity, worst phone lines, worst everything. What are you doing up there?" I was a regional punch line. That was good enough for me.

Back in Lia I discovered that while the Romaniotes were searching for their roots, Vlad and Net had been literally digging up mine. Clearing the courtyard around the house, they unearthed a massive, rusted lock for the front door; one bullet (unexploded); one *chibouk* (a ceramic pipe); one *lichnari* (a metal lantern); one enamel dish with a green-vine-and-red-berry design; assorted forks, spoons, and broken *flitjania* (coffee cups); and a glass oil lamp. I never knew how to read Net's attitude toward me, but both he and Vlad were very industrious in bringing me these knick-knacks, and sensitive, too—once Vlad found a pile of bones that he hid discreetly under a stone slab, in case they were human, until local experts identified them as goat.

I displayed the nonskeletal findings on the veranda. My favorite was a plastic medallion showing the Mother and Child on the front, and in back, a crown above the letter φ, ringed by the phrase "the Soldier's Undershirt." It must have belonged to a nationalist soldier stationed in the house after the civil war. People would knit socks and undershirts for the army, so any donation to the soldiers was called "the Soldier's Undershirt." The crown and the φ meant this was a gift from Frederika, Greece's queen during the civil war and mother of the last king before the monarchy was abolished.

I don't care much about Queen Frederika. But I have a definite fondness for the Virgin Mary. Greeks are big on patron saints; islands, people, even boats have them, and I've considered the Panagia mine since I wrote my senior thesis on the festival of the Dormition of the Virgin Mary on Corfu, an experience that made me yearn to live in Greece someday. Judging by the note my grandmother had left on the back of a paper icon of the Panagia before she was killed, the original Eleni Gatzoyiannis felt a special bond with the Virgin Mary as well. So when Vlad handed me the piece of plastic, I felt it was a message from my patron saint, or perhaps even my grandmother, indicating approval of what I was doing, or at least negating her curse.

If it was a sign from above, it was the only family encouragement I was going to get for rebuilding the house. Shortly after finding the medallion, I picked up Thitsa Kanta, and her husband, affable Thio Angelo, who had come to spend two months in Greece, partly because, despite her complaints, Thitsa Kanta could never stay away for too long. My bulletins from Lia made her so jealous that she decided to visit. But I knew that Thitsa Kanta and her husband were there mainly to keep an eye on me.

Thio Angelo had his own family house in Lia, so we wouldn't be living together. This was for the best; there might not have been room at the Haidis house for the three of us. Thio Angelo is trim and mild-mannered; Thitsa Kanta and I are both only five feet tall, and she's slim, with a blond bouffant and round glasses. But although she may be small physically, she has a huge personality. Thitsa Kanta is the only person I know whose self-esteem rivals the Gypsies'. The minute she boarded the plane to Greece, she told the man sitting next to her that she was "arch-right-wing, pro-junta," identifying herself as a fan of the military dictatorship that ruled Greece in the late 1960s and early 1970s, perhaps the colonels' only remaining fan. Then she admonished the customs agent in Athens for not doing a more thorough check of her bags, telling him, "In America, a man hid a *bomba* in his sneaks!" Thio Angelo, standing by in his black-rimmed glasses and driving cap, tried futilely to mediate the argument, but eventually Thitsa Kanta placated the agent by showing him the nonstick Teflon pan she had brought so she could cook without butter. It turns out he had high cholesterol, too. This was all a clever diversionary tactic; if he had checked her gigantic bags more carefully, he might have confiscated her two tins of Maxwell House coffee. "I love American coffee!" said Thitsa Kanta. "God bless America!"

Marina and I felt self-conscious about mistakes we make speaking Greek, and my cousins from Corfu were shy about their imperfect English. But Thitsa Kanta happily spoke a hybrid mix of the two, confident that people would understand her Kanta-ese. In Ioannina, a waitress refilled her water glass, and she said, <<ευχαριστώ>>, honey!" At first I thought this phrase encapsulated the lifelong dilemma of the immigrant, a nonnative who never belongs but remains an outsider in not one but two different cultures; in America Thitsa Kanta's accent gave her away as Greek, but in Greece she couldn't stop using American words like *honey, sweetheart,* and *relax.* But I soon realized that Thitsa Kanta doesn't feel like an outsider; on the contrary, she belongs everywhere. Her unique syntax represents exactly what she is: a Greek who moved to America, made it there, and now, with her Easy Spirit pumps and Maxwell House coffee in tow, is welcome anywhere, as far as she is concerned. And so was her vociferous opinion.

Shortly after they arrived, I took Thitsa Kanta and Thio Angelo to see the Gatzoyiannis house in progress. "I told NickGage, 'Why waste your money? Give it to me instead!'" Thitsa Kanta joked as we drove up. "No, I don't want the money. But I don't want the house, either!"

I was hoping the sight of her resurrected childhood home might change her mind. But when we got there, she just wandered around, crying quietly while Thio Angelo patted her. I realized how, to her, it could be a depressing sight; everything was now erected except for the roof, doors, and windows. I hadn't known how much a house that is rising up would look like one that is falling down. "All right," Thitsa Kanta said, walking to the car. "I saw it. I don't need to come back."

As I drove her home, I wondered whether it was curiosity that compelled Thitsa Kanta to return to the site of a past she clearly wished had never occurred. Or whether it was nostalgia for a place she secretly loved as much as she openly hated. I couldn't tell; she didn't discuss what drew her to Lia—she was too busy complaining about what she found there.

Over the next week as I chauffeured her from my house to hers, to visit this old crone or that one, to Filiates to get her hair done, and to church, church, and more church, I kept hearing her same litany of sorrows. "When I saw the basement, where my mother was a prisoner for twenty-five days, I could hear her moaning," she told people. "It was like she was there in front of me."

One night over dinner at the Xenona, Thitsa Kanta told friends she had a pain in her arm; used to equating mental suffering with physical pain, she decided she must be having a heart attack brought on by the emotion. The arm wasn't sore because she'd slept wrong on the plane or was tired from her journey. No, she was dying because I had shown her the house; I was responsible for yet another family member's near-death experience.

I felt bad that my aunt was upset. But I was starting to get angry. I was devoting a year of my life to rebuilding the house, taking a sharp detour off my career path, and relinquishing another of my reproductive years to live as the only young, single person in Lia, all to watch it rise. If Thitsa Kanta was right about the curse, I was even risking my life. It was something I chose to do, but still, I wished she could have appreciated my efforts to reconstruct her childhood home, even a little.

Foti ambled in and treated us all to another round. "Not for me, Foti," Thitsa Kanta said. "I don't feel too good; I'm sick from seeing the house. I told NickGage he shouldn't waste his money. I don't know why he's letting her do this."

This was more than I could handle. "Because, Thitsa Kanta, if the house stays a ruin, then the people who ruined it have the last word," I burst out, my patience exhausted. "They tried to destroy our family like they destroyed the house, but our family was not torn down, it's still strong."

"I know," she said. "But I got bad memories."

"You do," I replied, a bit more quietly. "But what about Sydney, your new granddaughter? If she wants to come here in thirty years to see where you were born, why should she see rubble? She should see a strong, surviving symbol of the family."

Thitsa Kanta drank her orange soda thoughtfully. "Okay, for that, for other people, it's good," she said. "Just not for me."

Thitsa Kanta and I had very different relationships with Lia; she couldn't fully escape it, and I couldn't get enough of it. Our differences of opinion were probably inevitable; the generation that emigrates often adapts to and adores its new home. Their children are the ones who have the luxury and the burden of considering their identity, whether they belong to the country they were born in or their family's homeland, which nation they can claim as their home. But we were both yanked back to the village where our family had suffered by a similar impulse, however difficult it was to define. Perhaps we were drawn by a desire to revisit a place that embodied our shared history. If I felt this way, I reasoned, so would future generations. I can't say for sure if Thitsa Kanta agreed with my hypothesis. But at least she didn't argue with it; she never complained about the house again.

Instead, she stuck to her other favorite topics: how she would never change her religion or political affiliation even if you held a knife to her neck; how since she stepped one foot on the Blessed Land she has never known a moment of suffering; and how she loves American coffee, God bless America. As she talked, I would sit back and relax and Thio Angelo would nod and sometimes wink at me.

A week after Thitsa Kanta and Thio Angelo arrived, I got an e-mail from one of the New York Romaniotes. "I just picked up my film and was thinking about what a wonderful trip we had, and how much I admire what you are doing in your village to honor your own family," she wrote. "It reminds me of what Elie Wiesel said, 'We must remember the past, but we must not be prisoners of it.'"

As I tried to turn a prison back into a home, I had at least one supporter. I thought about my visit to Ioannina's *kastro*, how two mosques, one church, and one synagogue coexisted in a small, ancient place. When I was young and watching Saturday morning cartoons, I was so proud during the *Schoolhouse Rock* segment about "America's melting pot" when a cartoon of a Greek immigrant with a handlebar mustache walked across the screen holding a sign that said "*Yiasou!*" Then Reagan abolished the law requiring a minute of educational programming for each minute of advertising on morning TV, I grew up, and the "melting pot" theory fell out of favor. It became more politically correct to describe America as a casserole, a combination of slightly mushy, somewhat soggy separate entities joined together into one delicious taste treat that can be reheated again and again. Epiros was also a casserole, just with different ingredients and sprinkled with a layer of feta.

I had met so many different ethnic groups that were as native to Epiros as the Liotes around me. They weren't always humble or cooperative or even tolerant of one another. But they had all been there, together, for eons. I shouldn't have been surprised that so many cultures lived in Epiros; look at the different opinions, lifestyles, and even languages that existed within my own family: Greek, English, French, Kanta-ese, and of course *alafiatika*. Thitsa Kanta had the right attitude; each of us is our own civilization, no matter where we happen to be at the time.

SIX

HOME SWEET HOMELAND

<<Παπούτσι από τον τόπο σου, και ας είναι μπαλωμένο.>>

"WEAR A SHOE FROM YOUR HOMETOWN, EVEN IF IT'S PATCHED."

August 10

I'm shading my eyes from the sun, to get a better look at the yellow earth-mover tearing up huge chunks of ground in front of the Gatzoyiannis house. The masons from Northern Epiros, working with Vlad, Net, and Xalime, have erected the stone walls of the house in just two weeks. Yanni, the master builder, taught Vlad how to chip at the old stones with a pick, turning them into squares for the house's corners and curves for the graceful arches above the gaping holes that will be windows and doors.

Vlad, Net, and Xalime will now build a low wall around the property to define the courtyard. Before that happens, the earthmover has to remove all the gnarled tree stumps, overgrown bushes, and massive boulders that have accumulated for over the past fifty years. As the masons admire their work, Vlad examines the uphill side of the house, where he'll use his new skills to build a small stone room that will be one of two modern spaces in the home, a kitchenette with a stove and running water. Before the war the same space was the plistario, *the washroom.*

"Eleni, come see," Vlad calls.

I climb up. The spot he's looking at has yielded a number of treasures—my family's broken spoons, an inkwell, and medicine bottles. It must have been used as a dump by soldiers during the civil war. But once I hike up there, Vlad hasn't found anything. He's just pointing at a large boulder.

"That's a big rock," I say. "It must have rolled down the hill."

"No, this," Vlad insists, pointing to an iron rod curving up from under the stone.

"What is it?" I ask.

"Who knows?" says Vlad. "Must move rock for to build kitchen."

I have a quick consultation with the man driving the earthmover. A few minutes later Vlad, Xalime, Net, and I watch as the swinging, grasping metal claw reaches for the rock, wedges under it, and lifts it in one swooping arc. While the rock is being dumped into the empty lot across the way, Net darts forward to pick up the curved metal. He holds it up—a tangle of intricate art nouveau curves joined in places by rusted metal flowers. As my eyes adjust, I solve the puzzle.

He has unearthed the iron bed that my aunts used to jump on, a piece of furniture that helped condemn my grandmother. My grandfather Christos had ferried the iron bedstead up the mountain on a donkey during a visit to Lia because in America he learned that "sophisticated" people sleep in beds, not on pallets on the floor. Although she seldom slept in it except when her husband was home, my grandmother's iron bed, along with her Singer sewing machine and wind-up gramophone, were seen as fancy American innovations, envied by her neighbors. Jealous of my grandmother's relative prosperity, and eager to curry favor with the ruling guerillas, a few villagers testified against her at her trial, insisting that the "Amerikana" had buried her riches somewhere to hide them from the invading Communist army. The testimony led directly to my grandmother's torture and execution.

Before the civil war, the headboard was a source of pride, a family showpiece. I look at its tangled remains and pick up the curving frame, ignoring Vlad's warning that I'll get dirty. I hand Vlad a twenty-euro finder's fee, a bonus for such a valuable artifact, and for working so hard in the hot sun. In August 1948 Eleni Gatzoyiannis was a prisoner in her own cellar. It's August of 2002 when we find her cherished iron bed.

August in Greece means one thing: the *panegyri* of the Virgin Mary, a festival focal point that falls smack in the middle of the month. On August 15, Greeks celebrate the anniversary of Virgin Mary's Dormition, the day she "slept" and her soul ascended to heaven. The event isn't just observed or commemorated; it is truly celebrated with feasting, music, and dancing because it is considered a happy occasion. After all, when various apostles crowded around her deathbed, crying and keening, the Panagia, knowing she was about to be reunited with her son, commanded them, "Don't turn the moment of my joy into a time of sorrow." Greeks have followed those instructions ever since, by partying hearty on August 15 at hundreds of *panegyria* held throughout the country. And virtually everyone takes part in the other traditional August ritual: taking a vacation, whether it's the two weeks leading up to the holiday, the two weeks following it, or the whole damn month. In August even Lia becomes a tourist boomtown. "Last night, I counted three hundred and twenty people in town," reported Foti, stopping by for coffee early in the month. Before the civil war, Lia's population numbered more than 1,000, but now 320 meant packed to capacity. I worried we might be breaking some fire code.

All over the country, my Greek friends were getting awkward tan lines on sunny beaches and dancing at open-air clubs until early morning, then sleeping in until afternoon, when they'd get up to drink iced coffee that would give them enough energy to repeat this vicious cycle of diving, dancing, and drinking. But in Lia I went to bed at midnight, rose at eight, and spent the day chauffeuring Thitsa Kanta and Thio Angelo around or cooking with my friends. Occasionally I'd check my e-mail and turn down invitations to various summer homes. Everyone else was on vacation, but in Lia I was constantly on duty. I couldn't leave now—who would take Thitsa Kanta to Filiates to get her hair done every week? Even without my driving duties, I had to stay to make sure the masons resisted the many temptations that could draw them away from building walls in the hot sun.

My latest native guide was Andoni, the Papadia's son and the self-appointed keeper of Lia's flame. When he was four years old, Andoni was one of the many Liote children taken by the retreating Communist forces at the end of the civil war to be relocated across the border to Albania, then Hungary. The plan failed in his case; he was not reeducated to be a good Communist. But he was left with a yearning for his lost home in Lia that could not be satisfied, even when his family returned to the poverty-stricken village in 1954 and his parents had to put ten-year-old Andoni and his sister in an orphanage until they could grow enough food to provide for them. Andoni, who is tall, gaunt, and mustachioed, a millennial Don Quixote, has lived his whole adult life as a lawyer in Athens. But he has spent the past ten years writing a vast history of Lia. Andoni saw me as the latest-model Lia fan, a younger, female, less hirsute version of himself. Naturally, he was committed to passing his lifetime of knowledge on to me. Now in town for the holiday, he was determined to show me Maleshovo, or what I liked to call the Lost Continent of Lia. In the 1750s, Maleshovo was abandoned by villagers, who moved up the mountain to found Lia in its current position. No one's sure why; Andoni suspects a plague hit, forcing the survivors to move onward and upward. His cousin, the shepherdess Iphigenia, sometimes grazed her sheep near the ruined village, and first took him there fifteen years before. Now suffering from foot trouble, she had sent her son, an orthodontist named Gregory, to guide us to the abandoned village in her place.

The three of us started down a sloping path, armed with canes, water bottles, and *pita* the Papadia had packed for the journey. The last time the men saw Maleshovo, Andoni said, they found two ruined churches, one dedicated to the Lifegiving Well and the other to Agios Giorgos. Gregory said you could still see painted wall icons inside the shells of the ruined churches; Andoni wanted me to photograph them for his book on Lia.

"It may be the last time someone photographs them before they deteriorate completely," he said, outlining the historical importance of our mission. *It may be the first time anyone photographs them, too,* I thought as we descended deeper into the brush. We passed an irrigation pipe and a number of large cowpies, then the area became increasingly thorny and isolated. Not even Gregory was sure we were going the right way. He offered to go on a fact-finding expedition to see what was ahead, using the carved oak *bastouni* he had borrowed from his mother to clear the brush in his path.

"We'd have to slide down on our butts," he reported, climbing back toward us. "We could get to the next valley, but I'm not sure how we'd get back up." I could tell that Andoni wanted to keep going, but he looked tired already. He was sixty now, fifteen years older than the last time he made the trek. And Gregory didn't want to be responsible for our lives if one of us twisted an ankle. Defeated by the topography, we agreed to turn back. "Maleshovo is lost forever." Andoni sighed. "Forget her." He sounded so sad that I imagined our village disappearing forever into the gray mountain mists.

"Come on, Andoni," Gregory responded. "We lost the battle, not the war."

We trudged back uphill to the road as Andoni and Gregory remembered other landscapes of their childhood that had been abandoned by people and devoured by the wilderness. "Everywhere else there is deforestation," Gregory said. "In Lia we have the opposite problem." I wondered if our entire village might one day be a huge, vertical vacant lot, a lost continent of its own.

"I'm too old to get to Maleshovo," Andoni lamented. "But maybe you'll try again next year, Eleni." The continent might be lost, but Andoni wanted to resurrect the possibility of rediscovering it. And with the Gatzoyiannis house progressing rapidly, it was no secret in Lia that rediscovering the past was my business.

Andoni returned to Athens, leaving strict instructions with his sister and mother to invite me when they made *trahana*, a cream-of-wheat-type substance that kept the Liotes from starvation during the German occupation, World War II, the civil war, and all the lean years that followed. For many Liotes it represented a difficult but purer past, when men were men and women spent three days cooking homemade mush. A Proustian breakfast cereal, it is traditionally made in August when the weather is hot and dry. *Trahana* preparation is a three-step process. On day one, the Papadia and Vasso, Andoni's sister, made the dough, taking large quantities of milk that had soured into a yogurt-like substance, pouring it into a tub of flour, adding *progemisma*—yeast-starter dough saved from an earlier batch of *trahana*—and knead, knead, kneading. Then we left the dough to rise, covering each tub with a huge *pita* pan and each pan with four blankets. The tucked-in dough was set on top of the Papadia's wooden *casella*, a chest carved with a double-headed eagle that had once held her dowry.

"Ah, youth, that it would come twice and old age not even once," sighed the Papadia, admiring her *casella*.

"We had to work so hard when we were young," added a neighbor lady who had come to help. "If I had my youth again, I'd have a *wonderful* time. But I wouldn't overdo things like they do today, going on TV in their underwear. You know what I mean?" She threw a glance at the straps of my tank top.

The next morning I showed up more modestly dressed to watch step two: Vasso separated the dough—now three times its original size—into balls that she placed next to one another in large pans, which she shoved into the huge wood-burning beehive oven. Once the loaves were baked we spread a sheet over a double bed to prepare for step three. Using a *koskini*, a reversible grater-sifter made expressly for *trahana* production, we grated the loaves into hailstone-size crumbs, then flipped the *koskini* over, using the sieve side to sift the grated *trahana* onto the sheet. There it would dry in the sun for several days, until it was packed up to be boiled on cold winter mornings. Mushlicious.

When I told Thitsa Kanta about my *trahana* seminar, she said the Papadia was doing it wrong; it's cheating to bake the dough so it gets hard enough to grate. Her mother used to just leave it in the sun until it was ready. I wasn't surprised that the *trahana* didn't get her seal of approval. While I was throwing myself into village life, Thitsa Kanta was practicing her own favorite pastime: remarking on how much worse everything is there than in America. No place was sacred, not even church.

As we sat in front of the elaborately carved, worm-eaten iconostasis in Agios Demetrios, waiting for the nightly countdown to the August 15 service, Thitsa Kanta leaned over to a middle-aged blonde in a stonewashed denim dress, smiled, and informed her that "in America, the priest gives Communion *every* Sunday."

"Why would you take Communion every Sunday?" demanded the petite blonde, wrinkling her brow. "To make sure you get enough?

You need to *prepare* for Communion. These women who take it every Sunday, don't they have husbands?"

"Sure," Thitsa Kanta said. "I mean, some are widows, but most do." Father Prokopi began chanting, but he was ignored. His flock was busy following this theological debate taking place in the back of the church.

"Well, then," said the blonde triumphantly. "They must be having sex."

"But with their husbands!" Thitsa Kanta was indignant. "That's not a sin!"

"So?" The blonde paused for effect. "You're supposed to abstain from sex before getting Communion!"

I had not been taught this in Sunday school. Of course, Sunday school lasted only through eighth grade, so perhaps the administration felt sexual prohibitions were not need-to-know information. Now that the info was flowing freely, I was riveted. So were the other worshippers. I'd never seen it happen, but I think Thitsa Kanta was blushing.

"Oh, look, church started," Thitsa Kanta said, giving the blond spitfire a friendly tap on the arm. "And the men are listening to us!"

"Let them listen!" insisted Blondie, not even whispering. But both she and her worthy opponent finally quieted down and let Father Prokopi command center stage. Agios Demetrios had performed another miracle—Thitsa Kanta met her match.

In Lia we may not have had Communion every Sunday, industrial-size washing machines, reliable electricity, or really good steak (which, I have to agree with Thitsa Kanta, I missed, too). But we did have our share of high culture. The entire village had been eagerly awaiting a performance by polyphonic singing troupes who were touring the region. I wasn't sure what polyphonic singing was, but I didn't want to seem culturally illiterate, so I pretended to be excited, too. The tree-lined square near the Goura spring and the historic plane tree under which Saint Cosmas once slept was transformed into a *Midsummer Night's Dream*–like grove for the occasion.

A retired electrician siphoned power off the village lines to run a string of lights through the trees, and plastic chairs were set on the flagstones under the spreading branches. I secured seats for myself, Thio Angelo, and Thitsa Kanta. By nine-thirty a crowd of more than 250 Liotes and friends had assembled; there's nothing Epirotes love more than some good polyphonic tunes.

These turned out to be Epirotic songs in a minor key, sung a cappella, in close harmony. But of the five groups, only two were from the region I thought of as Epiros proper; the remaining three consisted of a troupe of Northern Epirotes who sang in Greek; another of Albanians who sang in Albanian; and a soulful-looking trio of Serbian women in traditional dress.

"Tonight our performance transcends borders," said the bearded, ponytailed young leader who looked like a graduate student in ethnomusicology. "We'll start the way we begin every festival in Epiros: with *moirologia* [mourning songs]!"

The crowd applauded heartily. One of the Romaniote New Yorkers had e-mailed me this joke: "Short summary of every Jewish holiday: They tried to kill us, they lost, let's eat." Similarly, the short summary for every Epirote song could be: "I'm miserable, I'm going to die in a foreign land, let's dance."

After the first two and a half hours of what seemed to me like nasal whining, I'd had just about enough polyphonic revelry, but the rest of Lia was one enthusiastic fan club. Toward the end of the performance, the leader stepped up and asked for audience participation. Despite her sore foot, Iphigenia leaped forward, as did several other Liotes. I was surprised to see Grigoris Ganas's round face smiling out from under his straw fedora as he sang along. That morning I had driven him home from the *kafenion* because his cancer medication left him too winded to walk back. But that night he smiled as he sang a love song a local man had written for his wife. Sophocles said, "None love life as much as those who are growing old." Watching Grigoris, it seemed that none sing as loudly as those who suspect they might not be able to join in the song next year.

Finally, after almost four hours of polyphonic pleasure came to

Christos and Eleni Gatzoyiannis
in a photo taken the year they got
married, 1926.

NickGage looking Byronic in front
of the original Gatzoyiannis house,
circa 1963.

The ethereal architect,
Georg Zervas.

Thitsa Kanta, Eleni Gatzoyiannis, NickGage,
Thitsa Olga, Thitsa Tina, and Thitsa Lilia in
Lia, 1946.

Vlad, Xalime, and Net, Easter 2002.

Dina, Ruda, and Andreas up at Prophet
Elias, with the village in the background.

Father Prokopi, the spiritual leader of Lia.

The Kafenion in April 2002.

Spiridoula directs Eleni and friends
in decorating the Epitaphion for
Good Friday 2002.

The gypsy wedding. The groom's sister
leads the bride and groom, the mayor's wife,
and the gypsy families from the church to
the reception.

Father Prokopi leads the
dancing at the panegyric for
the Prophet Elias.

The men of Lia:
Vangelis Panagiotou,
Vassili Karapanos, Foti,
and Vassili Deppis.

Thitsa Kanta
sees the recreation-
in-progress for
the first time,
September 2002.

Thitsa Kanta and Eleni at
dinner in Keramnitsa.

Thio Angelo drinks from the
fountain of his youth in Albania.

The hunters, including
Thomas (far left) and
Foti (in cap), show off
their kill.

Eleni's twenty-eighth birthday dinner.
From left: Thitsa Kanta, Thio Angelo,
Atheena Karapanou, Spiros Karapanos,
a friend of Foti's, Eleni, Foti, Vangelis
Panagiotou, Antonis Makos, Vassilis
Deppis. Photo taken by Fani the
innkeeper.

The fireplace decorated for the
housewarming ritual in December 2002.

The other Eleni Gatzoyiannis,
Thitsa Kanta, Eleni.

Eleni in the outer door of the almost
completed house, November 2002.
Photo taken by Nicholas Gage.

The house blessing on St. Nicholas Day. From left: Spiros Karapanos, the Gatzoyiannis wedding photo, Father Prokopi, and Antonis Makos.

Father Prokopi blesses the basement at the housewarming on St. Nicholas Day.

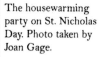

The housewarming party on St. Nicholas Day. Photo taken by Joan Gage.

Thomas and Vlad, having
climbed the roof of the
completed Gatzoyiannis
house for the housewarming
ritual, December 2002.

Eleni and a friend of her
grandmother's, as seen from the
veranda of the Gatzoyiannis house.
Photo taken by Joan Gage.

Dina and Foti catch up at the completed Gatzoyiannis house in 2003.

The ruins of the original Gatzoyiannis house, March 2002.

George Zervas and his creation, the completed Gatzoyiannis house, in December 2002.

Eleni under the keystone of the Gatzoyiannis house, May 2003. Zervas engraved the stone with the dates of the house's construction and its subsequent renovations. Photo taken by Nicholas Gage.

an end, we walked to the *kafenion* for a well-deserved drink. Thio Angelo called to a debonair gent in the Albanian troupe. *"Mer-minges,"* he said. The singer smiled and responded. "What did you say?" I asked. "Hello," Thio Angelo answered. "You didn't know your uncle speaks Albanian, did you?" No, actually I didn't. "Oh yeah, I live there for six years," Thio Angelo continued. "My father and uncles owned two tinker shops in Albania—in Leskoviki and Premeti. You ask the old-timers there; they still remember the Stratises."

Thio Angelo was seventy-six, so I wondered, just how old were these "old-timers." Instead, I asked, "You've been back and asked around recently?"

"Oh, no. We left in 1941, during World War Two, when the Italians invaded, and the government throws out all the Greek citizens. The Northern Epirotes, they stuck there, but I walk over the mountains for five days to come back here. Fifteen years old. I saw lots of dead soldiers." Thio Angelo paused to take a sip of *tsipouro.* "Then after the war the communism came, the border closed. The Northern Epirotes, they can't leave Albania, and the Greeks like me, they can't visit. I haven't been back for sixty-one years."

Thio Angelo wasn't the talker in the family, but when he did say something, he often surprised me. Maybe it was the *tsipouro,* but he teared up a little, recalling his formative years in Albania. Shouting from the next table distracted me, and I turned to see Thomas, the contractor, waving my architect's blueprint under the nose of Yanni, the head stonemason from Northern Epiros.

"Zervas wants this roof to last forever!" yelled Thomas. "That means you pour six inches of cement onto a wooden frame to create the pitched roof, then press the slate tiles into the wet cement."

"Then you'd have to wait a month for the cement to dry, before you can take the wooden supports out from under and get inside to plaster the walls!" Yanni shouted back. "I've never poured that much cement into a pitched roof; I'm not sure we can do it."

I jumped up. I didn't want to delay construction for a month only to find that the pitched cement roof had been done all wrong and was going to collapse. Besides, we were already two weeks behind schedule because of the time it took to find and transport the old traditional gray slate roof tiles. All the newfangled village houses had roofs of orange ceramic semicircles placed in neat rows.

"So Yanni, how would *you* build a slate roof?" I inquired.

"I'm glad you ask, because building a real roof is very different from creating a roof on paper," Yanni said, shooting a look at Thomas. "I would make a flat ceiling of cement to hold the walls together, then set the pitched beams for the frame of the roof. On top of that would be a layer of wood, then a layer of aluminum sheeting, corrugated tin, more wood planks, and *then* I would attach the slate tiles with mortar." He sat back with a smug smile, resting his case.

"But the other way—with the pitched cement roof—will last forever," Thomas insisted. "NickGage wants this house to be as secure as possible. He said even if someone rolled a boulder down onto the roof, it should remain standing."

I laughed, imagining one of Lia's senior citizens heaving a boulder down the hill onto the Gatzoyiannis house. But my outburst was blocked by Thitsa Kanta's yelling.

"You listen to Thomas!" she screeched. "Who knows what the Communists around here might do!"

My aunts' paranoia had infected my father as well. They remembered too clearly the old hostilities and jealousies that had led Eleni Gatzoyiannis' neighbors to testify against her at her trial. When planning her visit to Lia, Thitsa Kanta thought only of the friends she'd see and the delicacies she'd eat, enjoying the luxury of selective memory. But once she arrived, she couldn't forget how her family had been betrayed and torn apart here. Still, right now, I had no time to ponder my relatives' psychological scars. I had to make an executive decision to put a roof over our heads. I turned to Thomas.

"Do it the fast way," I said. "As long as it's safe and strong." It was better to choose a technique the workers felt comfortable with, I figured. But more than that, I wanted the house to look finished before Thitsa Kanta left. Right now it was a gray stone box with gaping holes where windows should have been; if it looked more like a home, maybe she wouldn't be so adamantly against it. In the meantime, we'd revisit Thio Angelo's childhood so I wouldn't be the only one exploring her homeland. And after all the turmoil over the roof, I too wanted to be on an August adventure. I needed a little getaway.

"Let's go to Albania," I said.

"What, now?" Thio Angelo asked.

"Sure. We can drive through customs control in Kakavia." After all, southern Albania was Northern Epiros; it was part of my heritage, too. Operation Homeland had just expanded in scope. Thitsa Kanta was on board, eager to see something new or maybe just to get farther from her unpleasant memories. And Thio Angelo was ecstatic. I could tell by the way his upper lip twitched when he said "Oh, yeah. Let's go."

"But don't tell anyone where we're going," Thitsa Kanta advised. "Better they shouldn't know our business. And what if Nick-Gage thinks it's too dangerous for you to go and gets mad at us?"

"If you believe in the curse, staying here is too dangerous," I argued.

I told my pals at the *kafenion* that I would be driving my aunt and uncle around Epiros for a few days, which wasn't really a lie. All summer I'd heard Liotes describe Albania as Anarchy Central: a place where if you parked your car, you might come back to a metal frame stripped of wheels, engines, lights, even the icon hanging from your rearview mirror. To ensure our safety, NickGage, who often traveled to Albania to do human-rights work for the oppressed Greek minority, put me in touch with Kyria Deena, a Northern Epirote politician who would pick us up at the border, along with her security guard and bulletproof SUV.

Driving toward the border control center in Kakavia, I became increasingly nervous. I was about to see a place that other Epirotes seldom visit but think about all the time. For Epirotes, Albania is the wrong side of the tracks, the really poor neighborhood next to the lower-middle-class neighborhood where you grew up. It's a place that makes Epirotes feel better about their own lot, a constant reminder of how their own lives might have turned out if not for the vagaries of fate and international politics. Which, for people living in Lia, really amount to the same thing.

Legend has it that when the great powers settled the borders between Albania and Greece at the Paris Peace Conference that ended World War I, they sent a committee headed by a German official to explore Epiros and draw up the border. The Xenona didn't exist back in 1921—no inns did—so he stayed in monasteries, including Saint George Kamitsani, which is fifteen minutes away from Lia on the road to Filiates. I had visited it myself, and was mesmerized by the naive frescoes with bright blue backgrounds, and crumbling wooden bishop's chair carved with the faces of angels. Back in 1921 it was even more impressive, and the German official, who had, it seems, an eye for design, admired one of three candlesticks that Father Demetrios had on the wall.

"Take it," the monk offered. "It's yours." The German must have missed the "Ethics: Say No to Bribery" seminar at the Paris Peace Conference. He clutched the candlestick and said. "It's lovely. But how can I repay you, Father Demetrios?"

Father Demetrios kept abreast of local politics. So he whipped out a map and said, "Actually, there is something you can do for me, mein herr. See these three villages?" He pointed to Lia, Babouri, and Tsamanta.

The German saw them all right—after all, he had a candle handy. "When you set the border," the monk said, "I'd appreciate it if they stay on the Greek side."

The official agreed and was as good as his word, although his promise caused the border to bulge awkwardly in that spot, ruining the line's otherwise graceful curve in a way that must have upset his precise German sensibility. But Lia remained Greek, and the story confirms two firmly held Greek beliefs: all is determined by fate, and it helps to have powerful people obligated to you, so a nice gift here and there never hurts.

When Greece and Albania were under Ottoman control, they

had a common enemy—the Turks—and ethnic identity didn't matter as much. But once the newly independent countries' borders were defined by the Great Powers in 1923, things got trickier. For the next decade and a half people trotted back and forth. But World War II changed everything. After the war, the Communist dictator Enver Hodja snapped Albania's border shut. Defecting was dangerous; occasionally refugees would make it across, but just as many were shot to death by Albanian border guards.

Once communism fell in 1991, many Northern Epirotes were allowed to stream into Greece. Ethnic Albanians looking for work followed, especially those who, like Vlad, had lost their humble life savings in pyramid schemes. Now I was driving in the opposite direction, with one sixty-nine-year-old auntie with perfectly coiffed hair and an emotional uncle. "Angelo's heart is flying to see his old house," Thitsa Kanta said.

At the border, long lines of Skodas waited to cross into Greece. I parked Chrysanthi under the watchful eye of a fruit peddler and we walked to the immigration building, where Kyria Deena and her Albanian driver, Benny, met us and helped us breeze through, flashing our American passports like MasterCards: "So worldly, so welcome!" (People with Greek passports have to get visas to enter Albania, and vice versa.)

Driving into the country, I peered out of the bulletproof windows of Kyria Deena's SUV. Southern Albania looked like northern Greece except much, much dirtier. The scenery was gorgeous: mountains, rivers, and gray stone villages nestled into hillsides. But there was trash everywhere. There was already too much litter along the highway in Greece for my taste. But the roads in Albania were like paved dumps.

Twenty minutes into our drive, Thio Angelo and Benny were new best friends. Benny called Thio Angelo *piako*, which means "old man" in Albanian. Oddly enough, Thio Angelo loved the geriatric nickname, maybe because the last time he was in Albania, he was calling people *piako*. We let him sit up front next to Benny for the entire drive to visit Kyria Deena's parents, who lived in the village of

Frastani, one of many Greek villages surrounding the imposingly beautiful fortress of Argyrokastro, which means "silver castle" in Greek.

With grandchildren climbing on their armchairs and an impressive garden out back, Kyria Deena's parents could have been any *yia yia* and *pappou*. But as they chatted with Thio Angelo and Thitsa Kanta, her father revealed that he was one of the Omonia 5, leaders of the Democratic Union of the Greek National Minority in Albania, which formed after the fall of communism to protest the abuses against Albania's Greek-speaking minority. The party's leaders were charged with treason by the post-Communist government in 1994 and were imprisoned for ten months until human-rights groups made it too uncomfortable for the government to keep them locked up.

"They held my friend in a closet-size room," he told us. "And they would beat one of us in front of the others to demoralize us."

"Oh, we've all suffered," Thitsa Kanta responded, patting his hand. "The poor little world! But good for you, you showed them. You're my kind of person!"

Under the new government, though such excessive oppression was rare, the assault on the ethnic Greek minority took a more insidious form. Although international human-rights law states that a person's national identity is self-determined, the Albanian government had created "minority zones," so Greek schools and churches exist only in the zones that are designated Greek. The illegal minority zones are manipulated to the government's advantage, Kyria Deena's father explained. For example, although most of the six thousand citizens of the seaside town of Cheimara say they are Greek, the city is not a minority zone and therefore cannot have a Greek school.

But the unjust policies did not concern Kyria Deena's father as much as the actions of the Northern Epirotes themselves. "The government tried to stamp out Greek culture in Albania, where it has existed since antiquity," he said wearily. "Now that the borders are open, ethnic Greeks are leaving on their own and the result could be the same. The government tried to eliminate us, but we're doing it ourselves."

I saw his point. If you abandon your home, you can't expect to have a homeland to return to someday. But as we bumped along the road to Kyria Deena's house, I understood why people moved away. In Greece we had the same striking scenery plus paved roads, fair-to-middling litter removal, and all the churches you could want. But next to me sat Thio Angelo, who enjoyed paved roads in both Greece and America and was still desperate to see the place where he grew up. I once saw a nature show that said mothers of all species are biologically programmed to love their children. Perhaps children are programmed to long for—if not love—their motherland. You can forget the language of your forebears or never see your ancestral home. But for Thio Angelo and me, anyway, the places our families came from were an inextricable part of our identity.

The next morning, leaving Kyria Deena to her work, Thitsa Kanta, Thio Angelo, Benny the driver, and I set off on the Return to Leskoviki. Thio Angelo kept talking about how beautiful Leskoviki used to be, "a second Paris." The first thing he was going to do, he vowed, was drink from the spring where he had collected water every day.

As we drove into town, past concrete bunkers and high-rise housing projects that loomed awkwardly amid the mountain scenery, it became clear that Leskoviki wasn't even comparable to Paris, Texas. Thio Angelo looked bewildered. Suddenly he pointed to a ruin. "Look, that was City Hall!" he said. "The Italians almost kill me and my father there—some locals shoot at a soldier, so they round up Greeks and Albanians to kill. But one Albanian guy speaks Italian, he convince them to let us go."

All the times I'd seen Thio Angelo—in a suit at church or wearing his jaunty paper hat at his pizza place—I'd never realized I was looking at a man who had cheated death by the age of sixteen. Now he wanted to find his old house, but with all the new streets, he didn't know where to start searching. So we headed up to the edge of town, looking for the spring he remembered, the fountain of his youth. As we approached, I noticed a shriveled crone in a housecoat and head wrap resting on her haunches in front of a brokendown Fiat. She looked like an old-timer to me; she had to be close to a hundred.

"Thio Angelo, let's ask that lady if she knew your father," I suggested. We pulled over, and Thio Angelo, too nervous to talk himself, instructed Benny to ask if she remembered Nikolas the tinker. Benny did, gesturing to Thio Angelo. The crone gave him a wide, toothless smile, pointing us in the right direction. Thio Angelo handed her five euros, and she kissed him on both cheeks. The kisses must have emboldened him, because he said something to her in Albanian and she chattered away, raising two fingers. Then he asked about the fountain, and she led us to the spring. Thio Angelo and Thitsa Kanta drank lustily as I snapped photos of them at this important site. After hugs, kisses, and more euros were exchanged, we drove on toward Thio Angelo's old street.

"What did the lady say?" I asked Thio Angelo.

"When I heard her name, I realize who she is," he said. "Her father worked for King Zog, and when the Italians come, Zog left Albania, but he don't take her dad with him. I remember she and her sister have a horse, but she say no, two horses." I would never have guessed that the shriveled crone was practically royalty, but Thio Angelo was still caught up in her lost glamour. "When she rode into the market on that horse, she look so beautiful," he mused. "I remember her much taller."

Then he spotted his house, and just as he could visualize the toothless old lady as the stunning daughter of the richest man in town, I could imagine him as a twelve-year-old tinker's son home from the spring, not an elderly American with a camcorder. The good thing about having a poverty-stricken hometown, I guess, is that it's less likely your childhood bedroom will be torn down to make room for a new multiplex.

Two young men were retiling the roof of the house, so Benny

went up and asked if we could go inside to take some videos, explaining that the *piako* used to live there. Suddenly the home-improvement specialists ran down their ladders, bolted inside, and slammed the door, yelling something in Albanian.

"They think you're here for the house," Benny explained. "According to Albanian law, if you have three witnesses who say it was yours before communism, you can take them to court to get it back."

A woman in the high-rise housing project across the way stopped hanging her laundry on the line to scream at Benny. "She says, 'Where are they supposed to live now?'" he told us, shrugging.

"Benny, tell her we don't want the house!" Thitsa Kanta laughed. "They can keep it! What we gonna do with a house here? We got one in America, one in Lia, and Eleni's building another one we don't want—that's already too many!"

To steer us away from any impending property disputes, Benny drove us out of town to a nearby hillside so we could look over into Greece.

"That's Bourazani," Thio Angelo said. "I used to go back and forth there."

I couldn't believe Bourazani was so close. A month before, I had visited the area with my cousin Areti, who took me to see the old villages, called the Mastorochoria, because the men from the towns were builders, *mastores*, who traveled Eastern Europe and Asia Minor building stone houses. Just as I was now standing in Albania, looking into Greece, we had walked to the guard post to peer down into Albania, at the border where three rivers meet. It was the same border crossing Thio Angelo had passed through often, and it was slated to reopen that winter after sixty-one years.

"It will be the largest crossing in all of Greece," the lonely Greek soldier posted there had told my cousin and me. "See the lights along the highway on our side? We put them there so that people will know they just entered Europe."

I told Thio Angelo and Thitsa Kanta about the plans for the lights and said that maybe the border crossing would revitalize Leskoviki. After all, these were historic mountains. The Italians

had invaded Greece by coming over them from Albania at the start
of World War II, and the outnumbered Greek forces beat them
back, a victory for the underdog Greek army that riveted the attention of the world. Areti had pointed out a mountain where the
word <<OXI>> (No!) is written in stones. According to popular
folklore, that is what Metaxas, the Greek prime minister, said
when the Italian ambassador asked him not to resist the occupation. (What Metaxas really said was, *"Alors c'est la guerre,"* but that
would look awfully sissy carved into a mountaintop.)

"Well, all I can say, Ange, it's a good thing the Italians come to
kick the Greek citizens out of Albania," said Thitsa Kanta, turning
away from the storied view to walk to the bulletproof SUV. "Otherwise, you'd still live here."

Aristophanes said, "Our country is the country in which we
prosper most." Having seen Leskoviki, Thitsa Kanta was feeling
particularly red, white, and blue. But Thio Angelo had six years of
Greek Albanian in him, and on the way back to Saranda he wanted
to stop in Premeti, where his family had owned a shop for two
years before moving to Leskoviki.

Premeti was built along a river, and with the housing projects,
mosque, and river view, it looked just like the East Nineties in
Manhattan. I felt right at home, but Thio Angelo's past had not
survived there as it had in Leskoviki. An airy modern town with
wide streets, Premeti now had a large main square with a new
church and school, right where the old church and Thio Angelo's
house once stood.

We wandered into the old part of town, visiting two other
churches to make sure that he correctly remembered his old neighborhood. In Agios Nikolaos a wizened old man entered the church
and lit a candle, asking Benny who we were. His name was Vangelis, too, like Thio Angelo, but he didn't know Greek beyond a few
pleasantries. Benny asked if he remembered Nikolas the tinker who
lived there in the 1920s, but Vangelis said no, he couldn't have
known him, he was born in 1941. This *piako* was the same age as
my mother, who was undoubtedly attending a power yoga class in

Worcester at that moment. Stooped and gray, he looked about twenty years older.

We shook hands good-bye, and he told us his last name, Athanassios, which means "immortal" in Greek. That seemed appropriate; he was still there after all. He didn't speak Greek, but he was lighting a candle, as his ancestors must have done for centuries. The old man made me hopeful that Kyria Deena's father might be wrong, that there would always be a Greek presence in Albania, however stooped and gray. As we drove back to Kyria Deena's house in Saranda, Thio Angelo napped. I wondered if he dreamed of the now-disappeared streets of Premeti.

The next morning we were awakened in Saranda by ringing church bells; it was August 15, the Panagia's holiday, and because Saranda is partly populated by ethnic Greeks, it was being celebrated there, too. We went to Saranda's shiny new church and attended the service, surrounded by Orthodox Christians who hadn't been allowed to practice their religion until communism fell in 1991. There were no old ladies dropping to the floor with the assurance that comes from a lifetime of frequent genuflection, like the experts in Lia, but it was still a nice ceremony.

After church, as we made our way back toward Greece, Benny suggested we stop in Klissoura, an ethnic Greek village just on the Albanian side of the border, which was hosting a huge *panegyri*. Dozens of the villagers' relatives from Greece had come for the occasion. The square was hung with a banner that read, in Greek, "We thank you for making the effort to come to our remote village to celebrate with us today and beautify the solitude with your presence."

The president of the village treated us to coffee in the *kafenion*. Today only sixty-five people live in Klissoura, he said, but before the war there were three thousand inhabitants, including traders who traveled all over Epiros. He pulled out a prewar photo of children in front of the school, and Thio Angelo identified a friend he knew from church in Worcester. "I gotta take some movie," Thio Angelo said, whipping out his camcorder. "Jimmy Bazooka gonna see where he grew up."

Once Thio Angelo finished adding to his oeuvre, we set out for Greece. Paved roads! Clean villages! Even Thitsa Kanta was happy to be back. When we reached Lia, Vangeli Panagiotou asked where we had gone. "To Albania," I said. "To see Leskoviki."

"That's right, Angelo lived there as a child, so it pains him," he responded. "The way Cheimara, where I grew up, pains me."

A place that pains you, in Greek vernacular, is somewhere you love. To love a place is to feel for it, to let it wound you so it leaves a scar, a permanent keepsake that helps you identify yourself. When I had picked up Areti for our trip to the Mastorochoria, we drove through Lia. "These mountains make me think of the war," she said as we neared the village. "Probably because of the stories my mother told us about that time."

Her mother's mother had been executed alongside my grandmother. In a way, Lia was her mother's Leskoviki, a place where she went to remember the past and realize how lucky she was that fate had carved out a different path for her, but a place that, even if it disappeared, would live on in her mind and pain her when she remembered.

That night Thio Angelo, Thitsa Kanta, and I went to Babouri, the village next to Lia. As we danced with dozens of Epirotes in Babouri and, later, hundreds in Tsamanta, I knew that all over the world, from Australia to Alexandria, Greeks were celebrating.

The next day I didn't see Thitsa Kanta or Thio Angelo anywhere in town. So I drove to their house, where I found them turning various shades of green, running back and forth to the bathroom. "We shouldn't have drunk from the fountain in the damn Albania," Thitsa Kanta whispered, clutching her abdomen.

Drinking in Thio Angelo's past, while good for his soul, had made both of them sick to their stomachs.

A few weeks later Thitsa Kanta had recovered enough to go into Ioannina and stock up on the candied chestnuts, feta, and Turkish delight she was hoarding in anticipation of her eventual return to the United States. After clearing out the Arvanitis Supermarket, we were ready to return to Lia and were cruising along when the car in front of us screeched to a halt. A matron in a jade green suit got out to stand in a parking spot while a woman with platinum hair and black roots leaned out of the driver's seat. "Go backward so I can park!" she screamed. "Can't you see my hazard lights are on?" Her snarl propelled me across a psychic border of my own, from my polite American persona to an in-your-face Greek driver. I rolled down my window. "Oh, this is my fault?" I boomed. "No, this is your fault! If you want me to do you a favor, you'd better ask nicely. I'm not going anywhere!"

I turned off the motor of the car, pulled the key out of the ignition, and raised it into the air like the fist in a Black Panther salute. The "blonde" retreated into her powder-blue Fiat hatchback as the matron in the green suit pleaded with me. "Please, Christian woman, just back up a little!" she entreated. "There's lots of traffic!"

"There's traffic, but there's also the matter of civilized behavior!" I said huffily. But they seemed appropriately cowed, so I slowly backed up just enough to let them park.

Thitsa Kanta stared at me as we waited for the Fiat to wedge itself into its newfound home. "Lenitsa, I'm shocked," she said. "I always thought you were a lamb, but you can be a goat, too. Good for you."

I normally shunned confrontation; in New York I made my roommate handle all potential confrontations with real estate brokers, plumbers, and the like, ever since the Time Warner Cable operator had reduced me to tears. After spending an hour on the phone trying to persuade the operator to give me information about my own cable bill, I started sobbing audibly. "Anything else?" she grunted into the phone. "Yes!" I gasped. "You should know [sob] that you are *not* [sob] a nice person."

Thitsa Kanta was amazed at my new alter ego, which was like the three Fates rolled into one sixty-inch *natural* blonde: fair, swift, and justifiably bitchy. We were in good spirits until, as we hit the highway, torrents of rain started lashing the windshield. I pulled over to wait out the storm, but it showed no signs of letting up and it was getting late.

"Maybe we call Kaity and George to stay with them?" Thitsa Kanta said, quavering.

It was a sensible request. But although the storm scared me, I was filled with a yearning to be home, and for me that now meant Lia. Plus, this was my chance to prove to Thitsa Kanta that there was nothing to be afraid of in Lia—no wolves, no ghosts, and no curse. So I drove off toward the mountain. I knew I was being pushy, and my behavior shocked me almost as much as it did Thitsa Kanta. I couldn't explain it. But maybe living in the village with generations of survivors, I had grown stronger as the rebuilt house grew taller.

As we drove on, I thought the weather was improving. But then it started pouring again, lightning flashed, driving rain alternated with the rattle of hailstones, and I clutched the steering wheel, terrified that I was leading my aunt to her death. I drove so slowly that a number of 18-wheelers passed me on the right-hand side. Thitsa Kanta was silent, but I noticed her crossing herself every time we turned a sharp corner.

Then, as driving rain gave way to blinding fog, she said, "My mother was right. We're going to die in this village."

Thunder crashed and I started shaking; it was the kind of storm Greeks refer to as <<δευτέρα παρουσία>>, the Apocalypse. Thitsa Kanta was there because of me. I hadn't forced her into the car physically, but I knew I was to blame if we crashed and died. Still, I tried to convince myself, I had driven through worse. And I was almost home.

Suddenly we were there. I pulled into Thitsa Kanta's driveway just as the rain stopped. "We made it," she chirped, gathering her packages. "Good job, Lenitsa." Now that we had arrived safely, it was as if she hadn't noticed the rain at all; the curse was forgotten as her selective memory kicked in again. Despite my newfound assertiveness, I was too polite to gloat. Besides, I understood why Thitsa Kanta believed in her mother's curse, which would punish any of us who returned to the village. My aunt's memories of the village were so tragic and Lia's scenery and history are so dramatic that it was natural for everything there to seem a risk, as if the compelling surroundings couldn't help but invite catastrophe. In the village, life seems tenuous, with death always close at hand. It was nerve-racking but exhilarating as well.

By mid-September the late-summer rains had produced a new crop of wildflowers, yellow fall crocuses and purple wild cyclamens, loud bursts of colors that glowed in the bright fall sunlight. The days were clear and the nights cool enough to build a fire in which Thitsa Kanta and I would roast chestnuts.

"Lenitsa, want me to tell you why I woke up at four this morning?" she asked me one evening. She was still getting over her bout of stomach trouble, so I wasn't quite sure I did want to know. But my curiosity won out.

"I had a dream," she rushed on. "I was here in Lia, filling a barrel from the Motsala, like in the old days, when I hear my mother calling, 'Oooh, Kanta.'" She slipped into the shrill tones village ladies use to yell to each other across the ravines.

"Suddenly, I was standing next to my mother above the Haidis house." Thitsa Kanta swirled her hand in the air. "She looked just like she did before the war, with two long braids. She held a loaf of bread—that's good; bread is a sign of strength."

"So, what did she want?" I prodded.

"She says, 'Kanta, I'm so glad you're here,'" Thitsa Kanta reported. "'I'm exhausted, I've been busy for so many months. Now that you're here I can go rest.'"

"Go where to rest?" I asked.

"I don't know—I'm just telling you what she said," Thitsa Kanta continued. "I ask, 'Why are you so tired?' and she says, 'I've been watching the *kopela*'—that's you—'and the *paidi*'—that's you father."

Kopela means "young lady," which is about right, but at sixty-three, my father hardly counted as a *paidi*, a child, in my opinion. Still, to my aunts and my grandmother he had been the family's youngest and I wasn't about to quibble with the dead. But Thitsa Kanta had no qualms about doing so.

"I ask, '*Mana*, what about NickGage's accident?'" Kanta continued. "'Were you watching then? He almost died!' My mother says,
'I wasn't there right away, but Nitsa stopped the car with her back
so it wouldn't roll down the mountain. Then I broke the windshield to get him out; see, I have a scar on my hand.' My aunt Nitsa
had no kids, she always like NickGage best," Thitsa Kanta mused.
"Maybe that's why she get there first."

"Wasn't Yiayia Nitsa buried at the Panagia church?" I asked. In
Lia, because of the shortage of flat, consecrated land for burials, the
dead are traditionally disinterred after five years, with their bones
stored in a box decorated with their name and sometimes a photo;
I had just seen my great-aunt's bone box in the ossuary next to
Panagia. "That's right below where my father drove off the cliff."

"Of course!" Thitsa Kanta cried. "Nitsa had her back to the accident so she stopped the car!" She smiled.

"So what happened next, you know, in the dream?" I prompted.

"Oh, nothing really," Thitsa Kanta replied. "I said I'd stay, and
my mother disappeared. But when she was gone, I could still hear
her saying, 'Watch out for the *kopela*, the *kopela*.' So I know, even
with the stomach trouble, I can't go home early. I have to stay until
October tenth, the date my ticket says, to look out for you."

"You think your mother knows the date of your ticket?" I was
skeptical.

"I don't know what she knows," Thitsa Kanta said. "She probably meant that she'll come back because she wants to see her house
finished; she's glad."

It's a good thing I was drinking iced coffee instead of hot, because I spilled it all over my hand. Two months earlier Thitsa
Kanta implied that her mother caused my father's accident because
he broke his vow not to come back. Now she thought my *yiayia* was
disrupting her eternal rest because she was so eager to watch the
reconstruction of her house? I was shocked, but I was not about to
point out the sea change in Thitsa Kanta's thinking. Thio Angelo's
joy in visiting Albania and my own desire to live in Lia had taught
me how strong the pull of home is on a living soul; why wouldn't
that yearning continue after death?

Besides, I was thrilled by Thitsa Kanta's new attitude; she now had the otherworldly approval she needed to support me—and the house. And it seemed I had something even more valuable than my aunt's encouragement: divine protection. Perhaps the near-fatal driving disasters my family and I had suffered in Lia weren't caused by my grandmother in her anger at my breaking our family's vow; instead, they were mitigated by her so that my father and I were saved. I suddenly thought of myself as lucky, not ill-fated. And although my family's history had often seemed like a curse in itself, now, as I strolled through Lia at sunset, the past seemed less a burden and more a blessing.

SEVEN

DOORWAYS TO THE DEAD

<<Ο θάνατος είναι ο μόνος θεός που δεν ικανοποιείται με δώρα.>>

"DEATH IS THE ONLY GOD WHOM GIFTS CANNOT APPEASE."

August 24

Rounding the turn just below the Gatzoyiannis house, I hear shouting.
"If that's how you feel, take your cash and go!" Zervas's normally
melodious voice bellows. I hike up to see two musclemen with crew cuts
sputtering, "But . . . but . . ."
"No! I will not work with extortionists!" Zervas throws down some
euros and turns his back to the men, who are twice his size. The cash lands
on the low stone wall that Vlad is completing while he keeps one eye on the
battle.
One of the crew cuts bends down, scoops up the cash, spits on the
ground, and storms toward a pickup parked nearby. The other follows him,
then dashes back to retrieve a red bundle that looks like a sweatshirt—only
it seems to be moving. He jumps into the truck, and the men zoom off.
I wave, as I do at every car that passes by here in Lia. Crew cut Number
Two responds by shoving his hand, palm forward, out of the window. The
ultimate hand-gesture insult! My mouth drops open—I've never had any-
one mountsos *me when I wasn't behind the wheel of a car. Zervas is pac-*
ing back and forth at the front of the site, where the outer door to the
courtyard will stand someday. But apparently not anytime soon.
"Who were those guys?" I ask him.
"Workers!" he shouts, raising both hands toward the sky. "I brought
them to make the frame for the outer door to the courtyard—the entrance
gate is a house's most noticeable adornment, and the stonework has to be
perfect."

"Why isn't Yanni doing it?" I ask.

"Yanni!" Zervas spits. *"He's another one! Once he finished the roof, he demanded an extra five hundred euros for the chimneys. I said I wouldn't even mention that to you—we had agreed on one price for the roof, and that means chimneys and all!"*

I look at the slate roof and the adorable stone chimneys with their own sloping slate mini-roofs and latticed stone vents. They look like something out of a fairy tale. But not a fairy tale worth 500 euros.

Zervas is still fuming. *"So I call this pair who are from Albania, just over the border from my village,"* he continues. *"We drive here, singing Epirotic songs. I buy us lunch at the Xenona and bring them to work. Then this one gets involved."* Zervas shakes a bony finger at Vlad.

Vlad looks up brightly. Zervas glares at him. *"They laid the cement, then sat for a break; and this one starts talking in Albanian,"* he says. *"The guys come up to me and say, 'Fifty euros each a day is not enough. We need a hundred each to finish.' So I told them to take their money for today and go. Now this one's all happy, because there's more work for him. But he doesn't have the skills to make an* exoporta. *It has to be a showpiece!"*

"Vlad already has too much to do!" I yell. *"The interior walls, the courtyard—months of work. But who's going to build the outer door?"* I stare at Zervas, this tiny man who has managed to antagonize not one but two teams of muscle-bound builders so they couldn't cheat me. Now I have my dignity, but no exoporta. When I first saw the ruined house, the outer door was the only part still standing. I thought of the stone arch each time I visualized my grandmother's home. It was the entrance to her world.

"I have to go back to Athens and find other masons," Zervas says, pulling on the natty sport coat he's wearing even though it's ninety degrees out. *"I'll be back next week."*

I groan, knowing he will be days, even weeks, late. Then I remember something. *"Kyrie, Zervas!"* I shout. *"What was the worker hiding in his jacket? It moved."*

"Ach!" He whirls around. *"They found a hedgehog and planned to kill it and make stew, but it skittered away. They must have trapped it again!"*

I shudder. Hedgehogs are adorable—that's like eating a kitten! Zervas looks at the sky in despair and repeats the expression that Greeks always turn to in times of misery: "Mother, why did you give birth to me?"

I wasn't surprised to hear a seventy-something man complaining to his dead mom. People in Lia communicate with the dead on a daily basis, lighting oil lamps at the roadside memorial shrines, adding fresh flowers to the plastic garlands that decorate the gravestones in the churchyard, and asking advice, out loud, of parents who have been dead for decades. Lia's geographic and political borders have had a long history of controversy, but one border has always been fluid—the fine, shifting line between the world of the living and the world of the dead. Everyone talks to dead loved ones, and sometimes they get an answer back. Eternity is one long conversation; just because someone dies is no reason to stop talking to him. Like any relationship, the bond between the living and the dead is one of give-and-take. The living are obligated to light candles and hold memorial services so the deceased know they're not forgotten. In return, the dearly departed keep an eye on the world below, popping in with a message or warnings, just as my grandmother visited Thitsa Kanta in a dream, asking her to protect me.

I was an absolute beginner at communicating with the dead. But in Lia, seeking their advice was a practice as old as Epiros itself. So when my sister, Marina, visited in July, I took her to hell and back, on a visit to the underworld where ancient Epirotes chatted with their deceased loved ones. In Parga we boarded a tour boat for an Epirote death trip up the Acheron, the River of Woe, to the Necromanteion, the Oracle of the Dead; in the ancient kingdom of Hades. We sailed across the cobalt sea for half an hour, then maneuvered into a narrow stream of Gatorade-colored water flanked by banks of reeds. Gliding along the river, we were surrounded by throngs of distinguished dragonflies in deep, rich blues, purples, and greens; turtles sitting on mangled stumps; and the grasping branches of overhanging willows. I tried to photograph the dragonflies, but like souls, they proved too ephemeral. The place seemed like death itself—both frightening and beautiful. "This is like the Jungle Cruise at Disney World," Marina said. "You know, only real and with ghosts."

Our enthusiasm faltered when the captain pulled up to the bank of a field and announced he would lead us on a two-kilometer walk to the Necromanteion. It seemed that the River Styx—a small tributary between the Acheron and Hades—had dried up. But there had been no mention of a hike; I assumed the ruins would rise majestically from the banks of the river so I could photograph them from the comfortable boat. Sort of like the Jungle Cruise.

After what felt like a near-death-inducing march, we reached the Necromanteion. Surrounded by green fields, it looked dead itself, a gray, postapocalyptic collection of dusty, sun-baked boulders and scattered cracked urns, with a stone chapel to Saint John the Baptist rising from the rubble. It was built above the ruins in the eighteenth century by Christian leaders eager to capitalize on the ancient holy site. Below the chapel, flimsy metal steps wound down a hole in the ground. Our tour group circled it fearfully, no doubt wishing we had Teiresias, the blind seer and ancient tour guide to Hades, in the crowd.

"Hey, Mare," I said. "You go first." In her twenty-five years as my little sister, Marina had learned her role well. She climbed down, a canary into a coal mine. I followed nobly, like Eleanor Roosevelt saluting the miners. On his journey back to Ithaka, Odysseus had visited the Oracle of the Dead to commune with his fallen comrades from Troy; I had to consult the Necromanteion on my odyssey. So I descended into the scene that Circe describes to Homer's hero, "the Great Hall of Hades and Persephone." Built in the fourth century B.C., this was where disoriented pilgrims were led through complex labyrinths to speak to their departed loved ones. A barrel-vaulted chamber with slick stone floors, slimy walls, and a powerful echo, the cavern had a slippery floor, gouged out in places to unsettle the pilgrims even further. The arched underground hall was infinitely scary and majestic, even to modern visitors. "It smells of corpses!" gasped an overexcitable tourist, shimmying down the stairs in her capri pants.

Later, as we sailed out of the swampy confines of the Acheron into the kaleidoscopic waters of the sea, a yacht's tender passed us. At the front, like a carved mermaid on a ship's prow, sat a topless blonde in black bikini bottoms. I was sweaty, tired, and disappointed, because I sat in the slimy cavern for twenty minutes and never heard a word from Persephone, Odysseus, or anyone else in the Great Beyond, just the chirping, capri-wearing Greek tourist. But the speedboat mermaid looked cool and confident, and I envied the rich-girl moxie that let her ride bare-breasted into the mouth of hell.

On our way back to Lia, Marina and I visited a monument to the fifty-six women of Zaloggo who, with their babies in their arms, danced off a cliff in 1803, choosing death over the dishonor of being captured by Ali Pasha's Turkish army. We climbed 410 steps straight up to stand at the base of the towering stylized stone figures commemorating their dance of death. When we finally reached the statues at the edge of the cliff, I looked for a place where a dissenting woman might have been able to hide. A year earlier, if I had heard the story, I might have imagined myself gracefully leaping to my doom, a heroine. After living in Lia, where the dead and the idea of death were ever present, I realized how attached I was to my own imperfect life. Now I found the story frightening, a cautionary tale about people trapped by fate and their homeland, doomed to tragedy.

My morbid mood didn't last long, because we drove on to the town of Glyki, where the narrows of the Acheron River begin. If the reedy, insect-infested length of the Acheron we sailed is the creepy part of the underworld, the narrows of the Acheron must be its Elysian fields. Marina and I hiked along the banks of the clear river, then, when the banks disappeared between rock cliffs, jumped in and waded through the narrows—a gorge that has hundred-meter-high cliffs on either side and is two meters wide at its narrowest point. The views were astounding—like being at the bottom of the Grand Canyon, looking up. Mountain-fed streams bubbled right out of the rocks, and although the river was teeth-clenchingly cold, we felt revitalized by its coolness in contrast to the oppressive heat of the day. But on our hike back we didn't see any dead men wading. Our search for a calling plan to reach the spirit world had been invigorating but, overall, was a bust. The dead apparently weren't interested in hearing from us.

Once Marina left, I gave up on communicating with the dead. With early-fall tomatoes turning red in my garden and the heady scent of ripe grapes filling my terrace, I concentrated on tending my "crops" and resurrecting the Gatzoyiannis house. But even though I stopped looking for death, he kindly kept stopping for me. While I was in Arta to shop at the fall bazaar, I visited the city's famous bridge, three asymmetrical stone arches sloping across the rushing Aracthros River. In the small folklore museum, a docent led me into a stone-paved, cryptlike room with seaweed on the walls. Pressing a button, she announced, "Now you will hear the legend of the Bridge of Arta." A familiar folk song started playing. "Forty-five bridge builders and sixty apprentices," a voice intoned, citing the men who in 1612 worked every day to build the bridge, then watched in despair as it fell down every night. In the song, a bird flies overhead, hears the men weeping, and informs them that for the bridge to stand, they must wall up the master builder's young wife in one of its columns.

The next day she arrives with her beloved husband's lunch and notices him watching her. "Why are you so sad?" she asks. A wily apprentice answers, "His wedding ring fell down that pillar, and no one will go get it." Of course, she volunteers and meets her doom as her husband's employees brick up the pillar around her. Even today, people cross it in silence, because the sound of whistling or music makes her wish she were alive, and the entire bridge trembles with her rage. I crossed the bridge quietly, thinking that the lesson here must be that it's hubris to try to subvert nature by building a bridge's arch over a river, and the gods require a sacrifice to appease their anger. After Arta, I felt much less guilty about the rooster head buried in my foundation.

In all my wandering through Greece, I found that death was regarded as something like the postman: a frequent visitor who has a job to do. And the afterlife is a nearby, familiar place. Once, in Ioannina, I asked where a bakery I remembered had gone. "The baker moved to <<Οδος Αναπαύσεος>>," the new shopkeeper told me. It was only after he laughingly described the street as being located "north of the city—very far north" that I realized the street name translated as "Avenue of Eternal Rest."

In America, death is a specter lurking in books and movies as scary or poignant entertainment. When death isn't part of a thriller or tragedy, Americans seldom seem to think about it. But Liotes hold rituals to honor death with nonchalant regularity. The villagers are so used to people leaving to work in a city or foreign country, and coming back, that the one thing they know to be eternal is a Liote's fierce homing instinct. It was only natural that people would hover around Lia after they passed on to their reward.

One Sunday, when Father Prokopi was performing the liturgy in Babouri, I arrived at church late, just in time to see him outside in the cemetery, swinging the censer over a grave, sending swirls of sweet smoke into the air. The service had ended and he was saying a *trisagion* in memory of an old woman who had died a year before. Relatives of the deceased handed me a plastic bowl of *kollyva* (boiled wheat sweetened with raisins, nuts, and powdered sugar). The wheat symbolizes the Resurrection, as it is written in John 12:24: "Except a corn of wheat fall into the ground and die, it abideth alone; but if it die, it bringeth forth much fruit." Eating the *kollyva* indicates that you've forgiven the soul of the deceased, a lady explained, handing me a packet with a plastic spoon, paper napkin, and a strip of paper printed with "We thank you for sharing in our sorrow—The Family."

She also gave me a sweet bun wrapped in wax paper embossed with a gold cross and the word *mnemosyne* (remembrance). The ancient goddess of memory was named Mnemosyne; she and Zeus conceived the Nine Muses who governed the arts, perhaps because all creative expression stems from the vivid power of memory.

After the ceremony in the graveyard, we sat in Babouri's *kafenion,* toasting the deceased with coffee and cognac. It was a sunny morning, but many people were in a reflective mood as they departed. One man opined to his elderly mother, "Life is like a watch. Time runs out and eventually it stops." She wailed, "But you can take your watch to Filiates to get it fixed. You can't do that with a person!"

The old lady was right. There I was, sitting in the sun, happily chewing what I thought of as a "death muffin," but for an elderly woman in Babouri, this was the one-year anniversary of the day she lost her own sister and was left with the insufficient consolation of memory. Although Liotes still talked to their relatives after they died, it didn't fill the black hole left by that person's absence.

When Dina made *kollyva* for Andreas's son's memorial, she explained to me that it should contain pomegranate seeds, which are desirable for more than just their tart taste and pink color. They are associated with Persephone, the goddess who became queen of the dead. She was picking flowers with her mother, Demeter, goddess of agriculture, when Hades thundered up in his horse-drawn chariot, kidnapped her, and dragged her back to his underworld kingdom, where he installed her as his queen. Devastated by Persephone's disappearance, Demeter set the whole world on an involuntary hunger strike. She froze the crops and spread famine, creating the first winter. The other gods implored Demeter to relent, but she insisted that as long as Persephone languished in the underworld, the earth would suffer as well. Meanwhile, Persephone played the martyr, refusing to eat or drink anything, rejecting Hades' hospitality and invitation to become a part of his world. Even Hades felt so awful that, according to Robert Graves's *Greek Myths*, he was "obliged to cloak his vexation, telling her mildly, 'My child, you seem to be unhappy here, and your mother weeps for you. I have therefore decided to send you home.'"

Then Hades' faithful gardener reported that he saw Persephone eat seven seeds of a juicy pomegranate, therefore tasting the food of the dead—the one thing Zeus told Demeter that Persephone must not do if she wanted to return to the world of the living. Technically, the pomegranate tasting could have condemned her to the underworld forever, leaving Demeter to mourn and the earth to starve. But Zeus negotiated a compromise: Persephone would spend nine months with her doting mother, and the remainder of the year with Hades as queen of the underworld. During those three months, Demeter was free to neglect her agricultural goddess duties, letting crops die and winter cover the earth.

Because Persephone always returns to the world of the living, the pomegranate seeds in the *kollyva* represent resurrection, and because she ate them in the underworld, they signify life after death. Today, even though pomegranate seeds are rich in significance, they're still subject to the whims of Demeter. When Dina made *kollyva* for Andreas's son in July, she sighed, "Who can get pomegranates at this time of year?"

A few days after the Babouriote memorial service, I drove Thitsa Kanta to Filiates to get her hair done, and decided to stop by the *pantopoleion*, the everything store. Ever since Holy Week when the Everything Man advised me to find someone to share my bread, I'd had a soft spot for the man, even though it took him some time to find anything in the jumble of irons, china, hunting gear, and barbecues. But once he did, he insisted on carrying my purchases to the car, despite his being old and gaunt. So I was disappointed when I walked in and saw his son at the counter. I took one look at his glazed eyes and knew I wasn't going to get any romantic advice.

"Where's the old guy?" I asked.

He blinked and stared at the gas grill in the window. "We lost him a month ago," he said. "Cancer of the liver."

I said how sorry I was, and that he had made everyone who came into the store smile. But his son said nothing as I wandered back out into the harsh sunlight. The woman in the bridge of Arta and the dancers at Zaloggo had seemed romantic, mythical. But they too had once been individuals who had given advice and done people favors and after they were gone, they must have been missed. Perhaps they welcomed death in the end because they knew how scary it is to be left behind to seek messages from oracles or to look for the fingerprint of a familiar hand on the shiny surface of a gas grill.

"What's wrong, honey?" Thitsa Kanta asked as we drove back. "You quiet."

"Nothing really," I said. "A man died. I didn't expect him to, but he was sick."

"That's the worst," Thitsa Kanta said, "To suffer before you die, like being sick, or like my mother. I'm old, I want my children to be healthy, my grandchildren, to see my niece get married. I don't care if I die. But I don't want to suffer."

"You'll live a long time," I told her. "So I have plenty of time to get married."

But she didn't answer, and I knew she was thinking about her mother. It was late August, and in a few days we would hold a memorial service to mark my grandmother's execution fifty-four years before, on August 28, 1948. Also coming for the service were the daughters of my grandmother's sister-in-law Alexandra, who was executed alongside her. And since nothing changes the fact that August is prime time to visit Greece, I had two friends from New York who would be passing through.

On the twenty-seventh I drove to Igoumenitsa to pick up a friend from New York, Elsa, at the ferry. By the time we pulled up to the Haidis house, the village was already buzzing with the news that young foreigners were in town. Anna, a Greek American friend, had arrived the night before and had spent the morning charming all my retired male pals, who were now chauffeuring her around. They pulled over and, one by one, Anna, Foti, and Vangeli stepped out of a borrowed van to hug me and Elsa.

"They're taking me to see the execution site where your grandmother was murdered," Anna said. "I've wanted to go ever since I read your dad's book, and you can only get there in a car with four-wheel drive. You guys should come."

"I'll get my camcorder," said Elsa, rifling through her bag.

I was glad I didn't have time to think about it before I smushed myself into the van with the others. I had been there for five months and had yet to see the site; in twenty-five years of visiting

Lia, I had never gone there. When I picked oregano with Dina and Andreas, I knew we were nearby, but everyone was too tactful to mention it. I did want to go, to pay my respects, but I never asked anyone to take me, although I knew they would have rustled up a truck from someplace if I had. As we bumped along to the execution site, I was embarrassed by my reluctance, considering how important a place it is in my family's history and how close I had been all this time.

My failure to go is not exactly surprising; it took me years just to summon up the courage to read the story of my grandmother's execution by firing squad, much less make my way to the isolated ravine where she and the others were given a final shot to the head, then tossed into a mass grave, their bodies covered with rocks. We invent rites of passage in an attempt to control a transition period, because changes, even happy ones such as weddings and births, are always stressful. Rituals are the sanitized celebrations of the really big, messy moments that happen off camera; there's a reason we have baptisms instead of parties in the hospital delivery room. Visiting your grandmother's grave is respectful. But I didn't know the protocol for going to the place where she was executed. And although I no longer feared her curse, I was a little wary of standing on the same spot where the original Eleni Gatzoyiannis was killed, on almost the same day.

When the van could get no closer to the execution site, we walked until Foti and Vangeli pointed out the area. The landscape of my nightmares turned out to be a lush green plateau surrounded by mountains and covered in wildflowers—wild roses, tiny blue flowers that bunched together in parasol-like shapes, and morning glory–like ground cover. There was no marker; if someone wanted to put up a plaque, he or she wouldn't know where to do so. Even the people who recovered the bodies of the prisoners wouldn't be able to differentiate this exact patch of scrub from that one. Only God knows now. The vast, craggy field wasn't telling us anything.

As Elsa videotaped Foti and Vangeli describing the area in a language she couldn't understand, I had to smile. These were the perfect men to show me this site: Vangeli, with his dramatic delivery and righteous indignation over wartime atrocities, and Foti, trying to direct us to the nearby chapel of Agios Nikolaos, to gloss over the execution itself, just as he had tried to spare me from seeing the dead mouse that had chewed through the stove's cord the night I first moved into the Haidis house.

Following his lead, we tromped along overgrown footpaths toward the tiny church of Agios Nikolaos, a comforting presence. From the outside it was just another nondescript white chapel on a mountain somewhere in Greece. But inside, it was covered with faded, cracked, but exquisite wall murals.

"This is the oldest church in Lia—they think it's from the thirteenth century," said Foti. "The outside was covered with frescoes, too, but the guerillas used them for target practice during the civil war."

I imagined those two-dimensional folk paintings of saints with gold halos and blue robes somewhere dancing with the Bamiyan Buddhas in a heaven for desecrated religious artworks. Something that expressive and powerful doesn't just disappear.

Foti led us inside, where two candles glowed in the candlestand. I wondered who had been there before us. A shepherd on his way up the mountain? Or someone like us, for whom this part of nowhere was the destination? Foti stepped through an arch to the altar, and I looked to where his candle illuminated a painting of the Dormition, with the Panagia supine and swaddled against a cobalt background, the eternal mother, nurturing even in death.

On the way out, we stopped to add our own candles to the glowing sentinels by the door. Normally when I light a candle, I make a wish, a request to the saint, usually for the health and happiness of myself, my family, or a friend or for help with a project. But that day there was no question as to the message my candle's flame should carry up to heaven; I lit it in memory of my grandmother, in gratitude for the sacrifice she made so I could live free of the suffering that made up her existence. And I was also grateful for her protection; after Thitsa Kanta's dream, I knew she had helped me avoid wolves and survive scorpions, floods, and car crashes so that

I could live in our village. In Lia, while trying to force the past into my future, I had discovered a rich present: these friends whom I now adored and this village, which I had avoided and feared but where I now felt I belonged. Like so many Epirotes from antiquity to today, I found that my deceased loved ones inspired me to love the living more.

"Let's go," Foti said, cutting short my musing. "Time for lunch." He started down the slope, then turned back. "Oh, and Eleni, I wouldn't . . ."

"I know," I interrupted. "Don't tell Thitsa Kanta we came here."

Foti laughed. "Yeah, I don't need anyone getting mad at me."

I bounded down after him, saying, "I don't need anyone getting sick!"

The next day Elsa, Anna, and I ran around, ferrying people and things up to the mountainside church of Agios Demetrios for the memorial service. It wasn't really a memorial service, Thitsa Kanta kept reminding us—that would be a big deal; we'd have to invite lots of guests and serve them food. This was just a *trisagion*, a prayer in memory of my grandmother and the four other Liotes killed along with her. Whatever it was, I thought, it was a brilliant coping mechanism: keep bereaved people so busy that they forget to be sad for a while.

When we arrived at Saint Demetrios, the church my grandmother visited almost every day of her life until the guerillas turned it into a stable, the daughters of Alexandra were there. One was already crying; the mother of my cousin Areti, she had been eleven when she visited her mother in prison and was herself beaten by the guerillas. People kept shaking her hand, saying, "It's a difficult day."

Dina, who knew how these things went, having survived memorial services for two of her children, told me and Thitsa Kanta to sit in the middle of the church, behind a table that had the memorial bread and the *kollyva* on it. Father Prokopi chanted the *trisagion*, mentioning all five Liotes killed over half a century ago on another hot August morning. Everyone held candles in memory of the dead. Afterward, we stepped out into the blinding sunshine to distribute the bread and *kollyva*. People shook hands with me, saying, "May you live to remember your grandmother." I found these ritualized expressions of condolence to be a beautiful product of Greek culture, resolving the question of what to say at such a time. In Lia everyone knew what to say: "Long life to you," "May her memory be eternal," and "May you live a long life and remember her."

The survivors of the murdered women lined up for a photograph: me, Thitsa Kanta and Thio Angelo, and three daughters of Alexandra. Their bones had been stored together in Agios Demetrios's ossuary until my grandmother's were moved to Worcester to be buried next to my grandfather after his death in 1983. In the photo we all look alike, heart-shaped faces with varying degrees of wrinkles, squinting in the sun, living to remember.

We were not the only ones keeping the dead alive in our memory. At the Xenona after the service, as we treated everyone to coffee and brandy, I overheard people mourning more recently deceased loved ones. Dina complained that the truck driver who killed Andreas's son killed four other people at the same time, and still hadn't gone to trial. "Our lawyer says he'll probably just get fined. He wasn't drunk, just a bad driver." She sighed. "It doesn't matter; nothing will bring them back."

"Nothing will, nothing," agreed the daughter of Marianthe, who had lost both her husband and her son within fifteen days this past winter. "My mother just can't cope. I tell her not to think about such things, but you think about it all the time."

A popular Greek expression says, "There are twelve apostles, and each cries for his own pain." Like most folk sayings, it is undeniably true. But as I listened to my neighbors mourning their losses, I came to understand that they didn't cry just to soften the edges of their pain but to sharpen the details of their memory. I had traveled to ancient oracles and visited lost civilizations to learn the secret of communicating with the dead, but in Lia I realized that the translator I'd needed all along was Mnemosyne. Through memory, the dead continue to live and the living to draw strength from them.

Once the blinding sun of August mellowed into the golden light of September and my visiting friends left, I focused on rebuilding the Gatzoyiannis house. The candles I lit asking Agios Demetrios for help must have been well received; one afternoon Yanni, the mason, called me to say he heard we were looking for someone else to build the outer door.

"Weren't you happy with my work?" he asked plaintively.

"Your work is great; your attitude is the problem," I said. "Zervas told me you asked for more money for the chimneys, which were included in the original deal."

"They weren't included," he said, objecting, but softly. "I never include the chimneys in the price of the roof. It was all a misunderstanding!"

He sighed. I sighed back. Finally, Yanni broke the heavy silence. "What if I come to do the outer door at my old rate?" he suggested. "Then, if you like it, you pay me half of what I asked for the chimneys: two hundred and fifty euros."

He might have been taking me for a ride. But at least it was a ride in the right direction, toward completion of the house. And Vlad liked working with him, so I knew he wouldn't try to drive him away. I agreed to his terms.

Days later I was at the house, checking on his work, which I had to admit was impressive. Slate tiles covered the sloping roof, and the expensive chimneys rose like ostrich necks. Except for the courtyard and stones covering the cement pillars of the veranda, the shell was done. It finally resembled a house more than a demolition site.

Yanni was building the two stone columns of the courtyard's *exoporta*, which would be joined by the same arched stones that had curved above the original door my grandfather built when he remodeled the house in 1936. On top of that would be a small slate roof, just for the entrance, making the gate look a bit like a pagoda.

"The house looks great, doesn't it, Yanni?" I said, trying to be friendly. "There's not much left to do now."

"Well, there's the interior walls, then the plumber has to come, the electrician, and the carpenter for the windows, doors, floors, and ceilings." Yanni paused for breath. "And of course you have to dig a septic tank, build the courtyard."

I sighed, deflated. The house was now a beautiful shell, but I worried that was all it would ever be. Vlad was building steps leading to the back door, and Thomas was sitting in the sun doing nothing. I walked over to him.

"Thomas, what's next on the agenda?" I asked, smiling in encouragement.

"Nothing," he said. "Not until I get money to pay the workers. I want twenty thousand euros, half of the remaining cost of the house."

A sit-down strike! Solving the dispute with Yanni was a stroke of luck, but I didn't really know anything about labor negotiations. I did know that hunting season was about to start, Thomas was an avid hunter, and if he got the rest of his money up front, he might not return to the house until the season was over in January. People always say honesty is the best policy, so I thought I'd give it a shot.

"Well, I'm a little worried about the house getting finished, Thomas," I said. "See, I know you like to hunt, and I'm not sure you'll have enough time to do both."

Thomas stood, drawing himself up to his full five feet five inches. "Hunting is my passion!" he shouted. "Not even Spiridoula, the wife I have fed and clothed for twelve years, can keep me from hunting, and neither can you!"

I had no answer to that. He smiled at my dumbfounded expression. "Of course, hunting is allowed only on Wednesdays, Saturdays, and Sundays. I won't go every day. I'll still work on this job . . ." he promised. "*If* I get my money."

"I need more cash transferred to my account here, but there's a law in America that you can wire only five thousand dollars a month," I answered, figuring dishonesty is the second-best policy. "If I give you five thousand, can you do the inside walls and courtyard?"

"I can start," he said, leaning back against the wall. Labor riots had been avoided. I started to walk away.

"Hey, Eleni," Thomas called. "Do you know how to cook wild boar?"

I paused, as if this were a question I was used to answering. "Not really."

"I'll get some for you, and Spiridoula can show you how," he said. "Hunting season starts tomorrow, you know."

I knew. The streets were full of trucks laden with camouflage-clad men toting guns, and barking dogs in cages in the back. That night at the Xenona, a table of hunters was laying into an early dinner. "Hunting season lasts until January first," one told me. "A lot of people go for wild boar, but they're so ugly. I shoot grouse. Have you ever seen a grouse? Beautiful bird." Once the men retired, requesting a five A.M. wake-up call, Fanis turned away from the full moon to look at me. "Poor little birdies," he said mournfully.

I was a little mournful myself. Summer was over, the house construction seemed to be stagnating, and the air was sharp with the smell of woodsmoke again. Fall is the most beautiful season in Lia, with pinkish purple wild cyclamens sprouting everywhere and trees turning rust and gold. But it is also the most poignant, as many villagers leave Lia to return to the cities. Fall fills Lia with the allure but also the sorrow of maturity, the awareness that time is passing and winter approaching, bringing loss and endings.

One day, as I gathered tomatoes from my garden, my neighbor Athina Ganas called out to me. "We're having an *efkelio* at four," she said. "Please come!"

"Of course I will!" I said. Then I called Thitsa Kanta. "What's an *efkelio?*"

"It's part of the service that happens on Holy Thursday, when the priest reads seven of the twelve Gospels and blesses everyone with holy oil," she said. "But you can have one at your house if you need blessing, and Athina is holding one for Grigoris's health. They leave tomorrow. With the lung cancer, who knows if they'll be back next year?"

By four we were assembled in Athina's dining room, surrounding a table set with a censer, some cotton swabs, and a bowl of salt with seven candles lying next to it. Father Prokopi read the Gospels as we crossed ourselves. At the end of each reading he prayed for each of us by name, and Athina lit a candle and placed it upright in the bowl of salt. Once seven candles were burning, Father Prokopi dipped a cotton swab in the holy oil and made the sign of the cross on our foreheads, cheeks, throats, and hands. I prayed for Grigoris, who seemed nervous throughout the ceremony, dashing out to get more salt. Now that it was over, he was calmer, and we all sat down to some sweet squash pita.

Father Prokopi handed me a poem about the monastery of Agios Athanassios, which he was trying to restore. While working there, he wrote the following:

> Before you speak, listen
> Before you pray, forgive
> Before you quit, try
> And before you die, prepare.

"I've never written poetry before, but the words just came to me," he said.

"It was the spirit filling you—divine inspiration," insisted Sofia, the cantor who had participated in the ceremony. "It's rare, but it happens if you believe."

By the time we left, the sky was illuminated with a pomegranate-colored sunset much deeper than the flimsy pink of the summer sunsets. Three-year-old Irini, my neighbor Spiro the cantor's granddaughter, ran up to hug me and I thought about how much I would miss her screeching once her grandparents sent her back to her parents in Athens the next week. The next morning, as I watched Grigoris and Athina's car pull out, a drop of rain fell on me. Summer was officially over. It rained all day, and poured the next. By day three of the nonstop storm, the Motsala spring, which had dried up in August, was gushing like the Hoover Dam. That afternoon Foti called with late-breaking news.

"There are waterfalls in Babouri," he said.

"Where?" I asked. "I've never seen them."

"No, they just started," he explained. "This always happens when the rains start, but it's usually not until late December. You're lucky." I drove to the bend in the road on the border between Lia and Babouri, where the tiny white chapel of Saint Charalambos the Miracle Worker stands. The saint must have been working overtime; the haze on the road parted to reveal two separate torrents of water gushing out of the side of the rocky cliff high above, falling hundreds of yards. Rain was steadily hitting my pleather raincoat, but I didn't care. The waterfalls erupting from the cliff were there for a limited time only, a miraculous—if fleeting—gift from above.

The rain continued for two more days, and every house in the village except mine and one below me lost electricity. Dina kept popping over to use my blow-dryer and marvel, "In the thirteen years since Andreas brought me to Lia, I've never seen weather like this!" The grapes were all ruined, so no one would be able to make wine. The tomatoes turned white and shriveled. Everyone was upset about the lost crops and unusually stormy fall. But although the weather was dismal, I was no longer depressed. Watching the waterfall, a sense of well-being had surged over me. My gloom over the end of my summer in Lia broke, and although I would miss my neighbors who would be leaving, I was prepared to enjoy the fall—no matter how dramatic its weather.

By the time everyone's electricity was restored, the outer doorframe of the Gatzoyiannis house was finished and Yanni was gone. In the arch he had placed the keystone that my grandfather had installed—carved with the date 1936—when he added onto the house. But on a stone on the side of the *exoporta*, Yanni had carved "2002," the date I returned to rebuild the fallen home. I was now officially a part of the physical history of the house, chipped into its entranceway for posterity.

I stood there, beaming with pride that the project had come

this far, then jumped when I heard a noise from inside the house. It was Wednesday, and although Thomas was hunting, Vlad and Xalime were there, building the interior walls, separating the house into three main rooms, divided by a hallway, just as it had been in the past.

"Can I add a brick?" I asked. I wanted to know I'd contributed to making the house stand, to try to earn the immortality conferred upon me by the carved "2002" stone.

"Sure," Vlad said. "I take your picture."

I handed him my camera, inexpertly adding a few bricks as Xalime laughed at me and at our role reversal—me building and them photographing my progress.

"How's Net?" I asked. He had started high school in Filiates, they told me, and stayed in dorms during the week, coming back on weekends to work. "Many kids live together," Vlad said. "They have time for to work, to eat, for games. But language is hard."

I made a mental note to buy Net a Greek-Albanian dictionary next time I drove to Ioannina, then left to meet Foti, Thitsa Kanta, and Thio Angelo for dinner. Foti showed up in his camouflage ensemble—he'd come from butchering a wild boar, caught after he and his cronies drove out at five A.M. to beat the other packs of hunters to the best spots.

"I want to come on a hunt," I told Foti. Fall in Lia is all about the hunt, and I wanted to be a part of it, at least as a spectator. He opened his mouth to answer, but Thitsa Kanta interrupted, waving her hands for attention to indicate we should wait for her to stop chewing. Then she turned to me.

"You cuckoo?" she screeched in English. "Those men, they go crazy in the mountains. They gonna rape you and then come back to the village and talk about it!"

I looked at Foti, who had spent years running a pizza parlor in Massachusetts. He studied his salad, doing a pretty good imitation of not understanding English.

"What would be worse?" I asked. "Them raping me or them talking about it?"

"Both are not good," Thitsa Kanta insisted. "You're not going."

We chewed our tomatoes and cucumbers in silence for a few minutes. Then Foti turned to me. "Give me your cell phone number, and I'll call you tomorrow if we catch anything good," he promised. "You can take pictures."

The next day, at 1:30 P.M., the phone rang. "Wait for me at my house," Foti's voice commanded. I was sitting in front of his gate when five trucks thundered down the road. Seven camouflage-clad men, five dogs, and one camo-clad eleven-year-old boy swarmed out of the car and around their prey.

"Bring them out so the girl can photograph them!" Foti commanded.

"Right away, Grandpa!" One of the men saluted. It took three hunters to drag the first spiky-haired boar onto the ground, a trickle of blood trailing behind her. She must have weighed 180 pounds. Then they dragged out the second sow—this one was only about 75 pounds. I had been hoping one would be a male, with tusklike curved teeth. Most of the hunters' trucks had a pair of teeth suspended from the rearview mirror to invite good luck and advertise the hunter's skill. Thomas told me that when he was little and his teeth fell out, he would throw them backward over his shoulder onto the roof of his house, saying, "Old bone, give me teeth as strong as a wild boar's!" I masked my disappointment at the lack of tusks because I knew Foti had the hunters drag the pigs there just for me. Everyone lined up and I took a commemorative group photo that I knew would be copied, laminated, and passed around for years.

We all piled into our respective vehicles and drove on to Louie's Grill, where two experts hung the boars upside down on hooks from a tree, sliced them down the middle, removed gobs of intestines, made incisions at the hooves, and started peeling the skin. I had to photograph the process; I'd probably never see another boar being skinned. But I couldn't stay close without gagging because of the stench.

"Do all animals smell that bad when they're skinned?" I asked Foti. I was starting to consider vegetarianism as a viable lifestyle.

"All animals smell," Foti answered. "But only pig entrails smell that bad."

I tried to adopt the hunters' nonchalant attitude. But when they started hacking the heads off the boars, I knew I wasn't man enough for this crowd.

Back in Lia, I saw Thitsa Kanta on the road outside my house. "Where you been?" she asked.

"With Foti, skinning some pigs," I said. "I left the guys in Agioi Pantoi, waiting for the liver to be grilled so they can eat it. Where you been?"

"I start walking here to find you, and I see some Germans looking at the sign that says, "Eleni Gatzoyiannis Road." They speak a little English, so I say, 'What you looking for?' and the lady answer, 'Eleni's house.' So I take them up to see it."

"You did?" I asked. "Did you cry?"

"Me?" Thitsa Kanta was shocked. "No! But the German lady did. I put them in the basement and I show them how the soldiers used to come and stand in the door and scare the prisoners. I tell them there was fifty people in there, and she start crying."

There were actually thirty-one prisoners in the basement, which was already so crowded that they had to sleep sitting up. But I didn't correct Thitsa Kanta. She'd gone from fleeing the house in tears to leading guided tours to it; if a few details got mixed up along the way, I didn't care. Now that the building looked more like a home, apparently it no longer made her sick. It might have been making her well.

On the last Sunday of September, all tour guiding and most hunting were suspended for the day. We had not one but two memorial services to attend. Sunday morning found all of Lia in church, chanting to the memory of Angeliki Bartzokis. She had died in the hospital in Filiates over a month ago, and according to Orthodox belief, spent the forty days after death wandering the earth, saying good-bye. Angeliki had been one of the few women left in Lia approximately the age of my grandmother. While most villagers recalled Eleni Gatzoyiannis from a child's point of view, Angeliki remembered her as a friend she lost long ago. On the festival of the

Prophet Elias, a few weeks before Angeliki had the stroke that killed her, we stopped by her house on our way down from the chapel. Angeliki had been slim in her black housedress, but she seemed in perfect health. I kissed her hello and she touched my face as tears filled her eyes.

"Eleni in name and in person," she said, noting my resemblance to my grandmother. "The same smile, same eyes." She turned toward the tray she had set out on the veranda in anticipation of guests, muttering *"Eleni mou,* where are you now?"

Now Angeliki was about to find out, I thought, as I blew out her memorial candle at the end of the service. Her family was hosting lunch at the Xenona, but since it was only ten-thirty and lunch wouldn't start before one, most villagers joined me and Thitsa Kanta and Thio Angelo at the next memorial service, seven kilometers away in Tsamanta. A flyer on the *kafenion* door advertised the annual ceremony, on the last Sunday of September, honoring ALL those killed during the civil war fighting in the Mourgana mountains from 1946 to 1949. "ALL" was capitalized to indicate that the memorial, organized by the veterans group of Filiates, would honor those who died fighting for *either* the nationalist or Communist side, as well as nonpartisan bystanders like my grandmother who simply got caught in the middle and died because of it.

The service was held on a mountaintop where a white marble obelisk rises from a series of marble slabs. Originally the slabs bore the names of most of a battalion of 160 nationalist soldiers who were captured by the Communists. After being told that they had the choice of joining the guerillas or returning to their homes, 120 of them opted to leave. The guerillas explained that they would lead them to the next village at night, to keep from being spotted and shot at by the nationalist forces stationed on the Great Ridge above. But when darkness came, they tied the prisoners together with wire and shot them. Because the men had removed their uniforms—the guerillas said they wouldn't need them if they were returning home—their mothers were unable to identify their bodies when the bones were found in lime pits below the spot where the monument now stands. So they left their sons' bones buried there, tangled together. The author Sotiris Dimitriou wrote, "Today, during the festival of the Dormition of the Virgin Mary in Tsamanta, you can hear their cries. It seems they're awakened by our songs, as if they're calling to their unlucky mothers to come find their bones and bring them home." Recently, plaques with the names of the women and children who were also murdered were added to the monument, including Eleni Gatzoyiannis.

Descendants and friends of the deceased had gathered for the service, presided over by a white-bearded Archimandrite swathed in black robes and gold jewelry, as well as five priests, including Father Prokopi. After the priests led us in chanting "Everlasting be their memory," the head of the War Veterans of Filiates introduced various veterans, who lined up to lay wreaths at the base of the monument, each saying a silent prayer. Then a fellow Liote stepped up. Vassili Deppis had lived in Germany for years, and now spent most of his retirement in Lia. He had an admirable paunch, hair that managed to remain jet black despite his age, and the booming voice of a man who doesn't hear very well.

"Brothers," he began, looking up at the monument. "We fought for freedom together, and you fell and died for freedom. The cursed ones who slaughtered you also murdered women and children. They weren't worthy of killing men!"

Everyone around me applauded except the master of ceremonies, who reminded Vassili this was a memorial for ALL the war dead. It felt strange to hear a political statement at a ceremony that, for me, marked a personal tragedy. Yet I knew that my grandmother's death was politically motivated. After *Eleni* was published, the Greek Communist Party sent a reporter to the Mourgana mountains to research the story of her execution and expose any inaccuracies. Instead, he learned that her murder was one of a cluster of killings in villages across the mountain range that were organized to terrorize locals. A leak had been discovered, and officials realized that locals must have assisted in spreading covert information to enemies of the party. Show trials and killings were ordered throughout the region to frighten the locals into silence and submission.

The reporter told my father this, but I didn't learn about it until he told me as we drove past the memorial on his visit earlier that year. But it was still difficult to see my grandmother's death as a political act. I appreciated that her name was on this monument. But my grandmother wasn't a soldier—she was a mother. I believed that the Gatzoyiannis house, where she raised her children and which was growing to look more like a home every day, was the real monument to her, the place where I could talk to her and feel she was most likely to hear me.

The last wreath bearer stepped forward, snapping my thoughts from the house in Perivoli back to the monument in Tsamanta. A slim bald man with a white rose in his lapel and a black mourning band on his arm, he saluted the monument, placed his wreath against it, and stepped back next to Thitsa Kanta, who was crying almost as much as he was. After a moment of silence, the master of ceremonies led us in the national anthem. By the time we reached the end, I was as teary as the old man. I pulled out a tissue as Thitsa Kanta tugged on my arm. "Lenitsa," she said, "we got to get to Angeliki's lunch."

All of Lia was in the Xenona, feasting on lamb and orzo in Angeliki's memory. There was another Eleni Gatzoyiannis there, my great-uncle Foti's third wife, whom he married after his second wife, Alexandra, was executed. I kissed the other Eleni's crepey cheek, thinking there were three Eleni Gatzoyiannises in the village: me, this reclusive crone, and the spirit of my grandmother. It could get confusing. A few days earlier, I had bumped into an old woman who said, "Some foreigners are looking for you—they were in Perivoli asking for Eleni's house." The visitors weren't looking for me but for my grandmother's home. Soon she would have one again.

I wasn't the only one at the memorial service with the house on my mind. An energetic little man next to Thitsa Kanta called to me over the table. "Hey, Eleni," he said. "Your aunt and I were neighbors before the war. Did you know that? I went by the house you're building and burst into tears; I was born in a house right below it!"

"It's a beautiful house," Thitsa Kanta agreed. "Just like the old days."

Apparently, once the house has made you cry, it grows on you. We were almost done eating when Father Prokopi came up. "Before you leave for America, could you videotape the inside of the Panagia church in Babouri, so the Babouriotes in Worcester can see it?" he asked Thio Angelo.

At the church of the Panagia, Father Prokopi showed us a carved metal box that held some of Agios Athanassios's bones. Thitsa Kanta recognized the metal reliquary as one the villagers used to bring to sick children to kiss. "They brought it for your father once," she told me. "It always works, but it only cures kids, not grown-ups."

The sight that fascinated me most was an icon of a winged soldier. Dressed in armor against a sky-blue background, he stood on the shrouded body of an old man, pulling a tiny, gold nude young man out of the corpse's mouth. "These are from 1819," Father Prokopi said. "That's Archangel Michael; he collects the souls of the dead." Apparently our souls are small, gold, naked, and portable, like an Oscar statuette.

I drove back to the Haidis house so I could record my latest discovery in my journal and Thitsa Kanta could call her sisters to tell them all about Vassili Deppis's speech, which thrilled her as much as learning what a soul looks like excited me.

"You should have heard him, he really told it like it is," Thitsa Kanta said, laughing into the phone. " 'The cursed ones!' Isn't that what he said, Lenitsa?"

I confirmed that it was and asked her to tell Thitsa Olga hello for me.

"She says hi, too, honey, she misses you. Next year we all got to come together, for the inauguration of the house," she said. There was a pause and then Thitsa Kanta snorted into the phone. "Of course I'd stay there! I saw the house, had my fright, and got over it. I've been there dozens of times now."

"Tell her she has to come," I yelled to Thitsa Kanta. I knew that, as the eldest, Thitsa Olga would find it painful to see the recreation of the house she had grown up in, where she had loved a family that was divided too soon. Thitsa Kanta had shown me just how hard it was to relive that sorrow. But I liked to think I had helped her overcome a fraction of her pain in order to reclaim a little of the joy she had felt in that house. We had both learned a lot recently, from people we had lost who sent messages we had to be perceptive enough to hear: my grandmother as she appeared to Thitsa Kanta in her dream, and Angeliki as she sprang to my mind at her memorial service.

I don't know exactly what happened to Angeliki or the women at Zaloggo or the Everything Man once they died. But I suspect that when Archangel Michael steps on our corpses, the golden part of each of us that he extracts is the love we have for one another. It's like Father Prokopi read from Saint Paul's letter to the Corinthians during Grigoris's *efkelio:* "Love never ends." And people who love you never stop talking to you. You just have to know how to listen.

EIGHT

POWER POLITICS

<<Ας με λένε δημαρχήνα και ας ψοφάω από την πείνα.>>
"IF THEY CALL ME THE MAYOR'S WIFE, I DON'T CARE IF
I STARVE ALL MY LIFE."

October 1

I'm sitting in an empty window opening on the main floor of the Gat-
zoyiannis house, staring at the gray, spackled interior walls, which look
much the same as they did last week and the week before. The weather
outside is just as gray and unsatisfying: a heavy mist surrounds me for the
third day in a row. Vlad and Xalime have stopped stuccoing the walls; be-
fore they can be whitewashed, the plaster needs to dry. But in this weather,
that may never happen. A stray dog that makes it his business to guard the
site barks; someone's rounding the bend, walking toward me. The hem of
a long black dress kicks into view through the mist. It's Father Prokopi,
trudging up, gasping for breath.

"Eleni!" he calls when he notices me. "I was at Agios Demetrios, saying a
trisagion *over a few graves, and I thought I'd come see the house." He stops*
below my window, hands on his hips, looking up. "It's really moving along!"

I'm glad somebody thinks so. "We've still got a ways to go," I say.

"Well, I wish the renovations at Agios Athanassios were moving as
quickly," he sighs. "Yesterday I got into a fight with the prefect in
Igoumenitsa about it."

The prefect had managed to rouse gentle Father Prokopi to anger?
Somebody in Igoumenitsa is going straight to hell!

"I asked for funds to restore the monastery, since it has historic signif-
icance," Father P. continues. "He yelled, 'Get out of my office, zourlopa-
pas *[crazy priest]! If you wanted help, your wife wouldn't run on the*
New Democracy ticket in Babouri!' "

I gasp like an actress in a Greek soap opera. I know the prefect is a member of PASOK, the ruling Socialist party. It seems that Father Prokopi's wife is on the centrist New Democracy slate in Babouri, and the prefect is holding it against him.

"I said, 'Is that my fault? Women do whatever they want these days!' " Father Prokopi sputters. "But he kicked me out of his office anyway, as if I were a criminal." Father P. shakes his head, his obsession with restoring the monastery stymied by the prefect's political chauvinism. My contractor hunts all day, my architect won't answer the phone, and even the weather seems to be conspiring against me. But at least I don't need to depend on the kindness of strangers to fund the rebuilding of our house—or the kindness of politicians, which may be an oxymoron.

It didn't surprise me that the priest's wife was running for office. One thing I learned in Lia is that *everyone* in Greece is involved in politics—or, at the very least, everyone considers himself an important political commentator. In New York I read the newspaper out of a sense of obligation, to "keep up." In Greece people glued themselves obsessively to nightly news broadcasts, which were often as bloody and sensationalized as an American cable TV series. Aristotle urged his fellow Greeks to be "political animals," interested in the workings of society. The Greeks I met were more like political zookeepers, carefully observing the workings of society, always ready with advice.

By mid-fall I was as much of a political voyeur as my fellow Liotes. It was time for local elections, and even Lia was suddenly full of political animals who were ready to roar. On October 13, all of Greece would be voting for mayors and prefects. I didn't think that anyone would take the election in Lia, with its hundred-odd voters, too seriously. We'd had the same president for the past eight years, Nikolas Skevis, a cherub-faced grandfather with a halo of curly white hair. I hadn't seen any of my elderly friends marching around with picket signs, demanding a change in power. All in all, it seemed that it would be a calm election, as low-key as it gets.

Then, one night in late September, my cell phone rang. "Lenitsa,

I'm at Foti's," Thitsa Kanta stage-whispered. "We can't make it to dinner. You better come here."

When I arrived, Foti was pacing and Thitsa Kanta was watching him, wide-eyed and white-faced. I knew there was an emergency—I just couldn't tell what it was. I turned to Thio Angelo, who looked relatively calm. "How are you?" I asked.

"Lousy," he said.

"He got constipation, but he took two Correctal, so he should be fine," Thitsa Kanta informed me. That was unfortunate, but not unusual. Why was everyone so high-strung? The door opened and in strode Spiro Karapanos, the church cantor. "She'll do it!" he announced, smiling.

"Thank God!" Foti gasped, collapsing into a chair.

"Bravo, Spiro," Thitsa Kanta added. "I'll make some coffee."

The last thing these people needed was caffeine. "What's going on?" I demanded.

"Oh, don't worry, honey," Foti said. "There was a problem, but it's okay now. Atheena Karapanos is going to run on our ballot. We needed a woman, and now we have one—and that turncoat is out on his ass!"

Apparently, Nikolas Skevis was not the teddy bear of a village president I thought, at least according to Foti. Over the past eight years, Foti claimed, the only improvements he had made in Lia were in his own neighborhood. "The road by us, where your father had his accident, is terrible, full of potholes!" Foti yelled, banging his fist on the table. "But Nikolas got the prefecture to pave the paths to his chicken coops!"

It seemed that because of his low approval rating in Lia, Nikolas had been told he wasn't welcome back on the PASOK ballot. The three-person consortium would consist of Cosmas Bokas, a former pizza parlor owner from Massachusetts with curly black hair and big dreams; Vassili Deppis, the rotund, vociferous man with an ever present cane, who had spoken at the memorial service; and Spiridoula, the token woman. She had cooked our sacrificial rooster and led me in decorating the Epitaphion, so I would have liked to vote for her. But all my other pals were on the centrist New

Democracy ticket: Foti, Vangeli, and Antonis Makos, who lived near the Gatzoyiannis house and was the church council president—and did a fine job at that.

I knew where my loyalties lay, but I was confused about the electoral procedure. "Why are there teams?" I asked. "Doesn't just one person get to be president?" Spiro, Foti, and Thitsa Kanta were muttering among themselves. So, as he waited for his Correctal to kick in, Thio Angelo stepped forward. "All this election stuff is done in groups," he explained. "Each side, PASOK and New Democracy, has to have a slate of three or four candidates for village president. This local slate is on the party's ballot, and you vote for a village president; a mayor for the municipality of Filiates, which includes Lia; and two city council members on the same ballot.

I sort of understood—you had to vote along party lines (no Socialist village president and centrist mayor), or cast a blank ballot. I wasn't used to running for office being a group effort, but life in Greece seemed to be more about the community than the individual anyway. Still, I was a little confused. "Isn't Vassili Deppis always saying he's New Democracy?" I asked.

"That's right," Spiro broke in. "He only agreed to join the PASOK ballot to keep Nikolas Skevis from running again. You have to have a minimum of three people on the ballot, so without Vassili, Nikolas could sign on to PASOK whether Cosmas wanted him as a running mate or not."

My eyes widened. Machiavellian machinations right here in Lia! "So what's Nikolas going to do now that there's no room for him on the PASOK ballot?" I asked.

"What's Nikolas going to do? I'll tell you what Nikolas already did!" Foti yelled. "Without asking us, he drove down to Filiates and signed himself up as the fourth person on our New Democracy ballot! He changed parties like it was changing underwear, pardon the expression." Foti's face was as red as a genetically engineered tomato. I worried that this added stress might give him a heart attack, given that he looks pregnant, has high cholesterol, and eats nothing but fried cheese and lamb chops.

"But there's nothing to shout about, Foti," Spiro interjected.

"My Atheena agreed to run, and each ballot is supposed to have at least one woman. Just call the New Democracy office in Filiates and tell the city councilor that Nikolas can't be on the ballot because we got a woman; she just hasn't had time to come and sign up yet."

"And I'll say that if Nikolas Skevis stays on the ticket, the rest of us are going to quit and there will be no New Democracy slate left!" Foti shouted. He stood up, knocking over his chair as he made his way to the phone. It was a good solution, I thought to myself. Atheena was a popular local matron, known mainly for her piety, boiled squash blossoms, and good skin. ND's female candidate was just as strong as PASOK's.

Foti ambled back to the table, his face slowly resuming its natural color. "It's done," he announced. "The ND chief in Filiates is going to call Nikolas and tell him we need to drop him to take Atheena." He sat down and smiled. We took this as our cue that it was safe to leave him alone. On our way out, Thitsa Kanta whispered to me: "The last time I seen Foti so upset was when a hawk kill two of his chickens!"

Foti may have calmed down, but by early October everyone else in Lia was overexcited. Since there were no debates or speeches, campaigning consisted of candidates going door-to-door, drinking Greek coffee and asking the residents whom they planned to vote for, then reconvening to whip out a list of registered voters and handicap the election like a horse race. I got to listen in on a few whispered caucuses, because in early October I acquired two roommates: Thitsa Kanta and Thio Angelo. Dina and Andreas had gone on a dowry-selling trip, and with the two other houses in downtown Motsala now empty, Thitsa Kanta insisted that I couldn't stay home alone.

"I promised my mother I'd watch out for you!" she protested when I said I wasn't scared of being by myself. "I know, you need your privacy, but Ange and I will leave during the day, and at night we'll sleep on the couches in the living room."

"You can sleep in the other bed in the bedroom," I suggested.

"Lenitsa, we old people," she insisted. "Old people snore and fart and get up at night! Better we stay in the living room." When she put it that way, I wasn't about to argue. And amazingly, having senior-citizen roommates was fun. Every night Thio Angelo would build a fire and we would sit around it, discussing the events of the day, which meant, of course, the election.

"Everyone I talk to say they going to vote for Antonis Makos," Thitsa Kanta said, throwing a tissue into the flames one night. "He's the only one going out there, talking to people. Foti and Vangeli doing nothing, they too lazy and shy to go to someone's house and ask for a vote. I bet they each get just one vote—their own."

Lia's election was shaping up to resemble a sixth-grade student-council race. Only 130 people were registered to vote, so it was easy to analyze their loyalties and figure out who was the most popular candidate. I decided I would vote the same way I had in sixth grade: for the person I thought no one else would vote for, so he wouldn't get his feelings hurt. And feelings were running high—having been frozen out of his old party, PASOK, Nikolas Skevis channeled all his icy bitterness into campaigning for the opposition, New Democracy, specifically for Antonis Makos, the one candidate who hadn't been involved in boxing him out of a spot on the ND ballot. Arguments broke out daily in the *kafenion*, and opposing candidates scrupulously avoided each other. Sometimes I could hardly handle all the tension.

So I was more than happy to take my weekly breaks from Lia to drive Thitsa Kanta down to Filiates to get her bouffant lifted. As we sat in the salon, she befriended the other ladies having *their* bouffants inflated. "Alexandra Stratis from Lia, but I live in Worcester, America," she would say, extending her hand. "Where are your people from?"

One day a matron said, "You're from America? My father-in-law lived there."

"In Worcester?" Thitsa Kanta asked eagerly.

"I don't know where," the lady responded. "He and my husband weren't close. But I do remember the day he returned after thirty years, with a suitcase full of American dresses for my mother-in-law, who was an old villager dressed in black."

"Did he manage to get her size right after thirty years?" I asked.

"I don't know." The woman smiled. "My mother-in-law opened the suitcase, took the American dresses, and threw them into the fireplace one by one. My father-in-law yelled, 'What are you doing?' And she said, 'Just like my youth went up in flames while I waited for you, so will these.'"

In America women had burned bras. In Greece they burned poly-cotton floral housedresses. This was just the kind of juicy break from political talk I needed. But it couldn't last; while Thitsa Kanta's hair set, I had to head over to the police station to secure a national ID card so I could vote in the election a week later. On the ride back, Thitsa Kanta studied my temporary ID, with its photo, my name, and birth date.

"Lenitsa!" Thitsa Kanta gasped. "That's right, today's your birthday! We gotta have a party. You tell me who you want there, and I'll arrange it."

"Okay." I smiled. "Thanks, Thitsa Kanta."

"What thanks?" she huffed. "Of course I throw a party. I love you too much!" She looked over at me. "But don't tell people you twenty-eight. You look twenty! Say you twenty."

I told Thitsa Kanta I was fine telling people I was twenty-eight. And I almost meant it. I'd never felt younger than I did in Lia, where the median age of the people I ate dinner with was probably seventy. But at the same time, as much as I was enjoying my extended childhood there, I knew that my American friends were continuing to mature. The thought of them all back in the city, racing around to exciting jobs and new relationships, suddenly made me long for the frenetic pace of New York. I was in Lia with no job, no romantic prospects, and no idea how my life would be different when the house was finished (if it was ever finished) and I returned to New York. If I thought too much about the upcoming year, it made me nervous, wondering if I would still fit into my old life. Luckily,

I had plenty of distractions. When Thitsa Kanta and I arrived home, we found Antonis Makos and Thio Angelo sitting around the coffee table with voter registration lists. "If you could stay to vote, we'd definitely win!" Antonis told Thio Angelo.

"No, we gotta leave on the tenth—the flights are full," he answered.

"I would never stay for the election!" Thitsa Kanta yelped. "Lia is gonna be crazy!" She still saw her village as a political tinderbox about to erupt into violence. And she wasn't alone. So many Greeks remember the atrocities of the civil war, just over half a century ago, that politics is still the major divisive factor in society. Modern Greek life has always been shadowed by history, not just the legends of ancient Greece but the still-fresh scars acquired by the growing Greek state in the twentieth century. Even today, some people affiliate themselves with their family's political party with a messianic fervor that approaches religious fanaticism. Still, I wasn't worried about pent-up election-related violence in our village of retirees; at this point, I had a lot more youthful aggression than any of them did.

"Oh, Lenitsa." Thio Angelo looked up. "Electrician and plumber came. They up at the Gatzoyiannis house. Electrician ask for instructions. I say, you know what to do."

I left my elders to their political strategizing and drove up to the house. The jarring blast of an electric drill meant that the plumber was still inside, hacking up the cement floors to lay pipe. And the electrician was already packing up his van. For weeks nothing had happened on the house and now, in one day, the plumbing and electricity were well under way. It was a cosmic birthday present.

"That was fast!" I said to the electrician.

"I'm not finished yet, but I've done enough for today," he replied. "The electrical box is up. The meter reader should have no problem reading that." He pointed to the front of the house. There it was, a big metal box sitting like a pimple on the face of an otherwise historically accurate re-creation of my grandmother's house.

"No!" I wailed.

"Are you all right?" the electrician asked.

"The box can't go there! Why didn't you put it under the veranda or in back?"

"I'd have to break a hole through the veranda to bring the cord down," he complained. "And it can't go on the back—the meter reader has to be able to see it."

"But I put so much effort, time, and money into making the house look like it did when my grandparents lived here," I told him. "Please, can't you at least move it to the side of the house?" He looked skeptical. It was time to bring out the big guns. "It's my birthday; I can't take a huge disappointment today," I pleaded. "It would be bad luck."

"All right." He hoisted himself into the van. "I'll move it next week, as a birthday present to you."

"Thank you so much!" I gushed.

"But I'll lose a day of work elsewhere, so I'll have to charge you two hundred euros."

"That's fine." I extended my hand. It had taken so long for Thomas to get an electrician to go up there, I was lucky this man was willing to return at all. There was nothing else I could do. I'd have to consider the 200 euros a present to myself.

That night at the Xenona, my twenty-eighth birthday dinner was attended by me and nine people over the age of sixty, making the average partygoer's age fifty-seven. Thitsa Kanta and Thio Angelo were there, of course, and so were five of Lia's seven presidential candidates: Foti, Vangeli, Antonis, Vassili, and Atheena, all trying to be civil for my sake. There was election talk, but people kept raising their glasses, wishing that I may live a hundred years, as strong as the tall mountains, and return next year as a bride, so that everyone could rejoice for me. Nikki and Fanis served a chocolate cake with MANY YEARS, ELENI on it and sparklers spitting out starbursts of light. I appreciated the sparklers, the cake, all the good wishes. But most of all, I enjoyed seeing how much fun everyone else was having. Forget twenty-eight—I had whole lifetimes of political intrigue and partying ahead of me!

The next week brought another celebration, Thitsa Kanta and

Thio Angelo's farewell meal at a *taverna* in Keramnitsa, a village down the mountain from Lia. Nestled closer to the main cities in the province, Keramnitsa had not been abandoned by young people the way many other villages had; it had a winter population of two hundred. With just four days until the election, city council candidates kept streaming through this hot spot, handing out flyers and kissing people hello. Thitsa Kanta, who loved the excitement, accepted all handouts, telling each female candidate, "You look beautiful in this photo, honey!"

Aside from being a campaign hub, Keramnitsa was also home to the man everyone said was the best carpenter in the Mourgana. I had asked him to meet us, hoping to persuade him to join my building team, but when a gent in a checked blazer and a salt-and-pepper pompadour strolled in, I assumed he was another politico. Carpenters are supposed to look like Jesus or like Harrison Ford. But ours, a smooth-talker who knew everyone in the *taverna*, turned out to be more of a Dick Clark type. He said he could have the doors, windows, and floors in place in six weeks. "What about the ceilings?" I demanded. Now that I was twenty-eight, it was time to become a savvy negotiator.

"You can't put ceilings in until spring, because wood draws moisture and swells in winter," he said, fixing his *American Bandstand* smile on me. "Everyone knows that."

Oh, right. Of course. We struck a deal; the next day he would measure the door and window frames. I wasn't sure I believed him about the ceilings, but I was glad that I now had a new deadline to give Thomas and Vlad: the carpenter was coming on November 26, so the interior walls and veranda all had to be done by then. Mission accomplished, I raised a toast to Thitsa Kanta and Thio Angelo.

"I'm going to miss you guys," I said. "Thanks for staying with me."

"Oh, we're gonna miss you, too, honey—and everybody," she said, tearing up a little. "When I get home, for a few months, all I care about is what's happening in the village. Then I forget a little, and I'm okay until the next trip."

Looking into her crinkling eyes, I saw myself a few years, and a few wrinkles, ahead. When I returned to New York, could I jump right back into my old life, or would I always be torn, as she was? The poet George Seferis wrote, "Wherever you may go, Greece wounds you." If that was true even for Thitsa Kanta, who loved Maxwell House coffee almost as much as she did me, it must be inevitable. I had gone to Lia to fill a perceived void in my mind and soul. Now I discovered that by living there, and learning to love it, I might simply be replacing the void with an even deeper longing.

Once the three of us were alone in the car on our way back up to Lia, Thitsa Kanta reported, "Vangeli Panagiotou cried. He said, 'Who knows if we'll ever see each other again?' and I tell him, 'Vangeli Panagiotou, I'm not planning on dying anytime soon!' But he still cry." She sniffed a bit herself, then added, "I think he's a little drunk."

Thitsa Kanta, Thio Angelo, and all their assorted foodstuffs left the next day, with two pounds of feta in Thitsa Kanta's suitcase to replace the two pounds of Maxwell House she had transported over. I was sad that they were gone, but I didn't have time to wallow—the election was upon us. And I was surrounded by reminders that in Lia the political is personal. The night before the election, I stopped by the *kafenion* to pick up Foti and Vangeli and drive them to the Xenona for dinner.

"Who was that woman?" I asked them in the car. "I've never seen her before."

"Which one?" Vangeli demanded. The *kafenion* was packed with Liotes in town to vote.

"The tall, skinny one with dyed black hair and the head wrap," I said. "The one who looks like death when it comes for ballerinas."

"Oh, that's Laokratia," Foti started to answer. "She—"

"You can't call her that!" Vangeli shouted from the backseat. "She'll scream at you. She wants to be called Katerina; she won't answer to Laokratia anymore."

"Laokratia?" I asked. "As in 'rule of the people'?"

"That's right," Vangeli said. "She was born when the Communists occupied the village, and her parents thought if they named her that, they might get preferential treatment—there's another Laokratia, and a Laokratis in the mountain range."

"But they got taken to Communist countries anyway, and changed their names when they returned," Foti said as we parked. "Now it's Katerina, Sophia, and Evangelos."

It seemed fitting that Ms. Rule of the People had taken the bus all the way from Athens to exercise her right to vote, but I could also see why she chose a new name; once the Iron Curtain fell, the name Laokratia became so five minutes ago.

Inside, the Xenona was packed. Election officials for nearby villages, mostly lawyers who came from Athens, were staying at the inn overnight.

"Sorry you had to travel so far," I told a middle-aged official sitting by the fire.

"Oh, no, this is a great gig—an inn, a fire, nice food," he answered. "One year I rode a donkey five hours in a downpour to get to a village in the Peloponnese. And in the end, it was all to collect twenty-eight votes!"

Compared with that, Lia was a metropolis. Especially now. Since voter registration is one way a village's population is counted and the amount of money distributed for public works is determined, many people feel obligated to return to their hometowns for elections. Schools and businesses are closed on the Friday and Monday before and after Election Sunday to facilitate the travel.

"Too bad there's not an election every few months," Fanis whispered as he passed drinks around his booming establishment. But I wasn't sure the villagers could handle all the excitement. Vangeli looked up from the list of voters that he and Foti were huddled over. "Odds are even for tomorrow," he reported.

On Election Sunday all of Greece, every mountain and islet, woke up to torrential rain. Since the topography is so varied, it's rare that it rains all over the country. When I stopped in at Dina and Andreas's for a cup of tea and a look at their TV, the storm made the national news. "With rain keeping some voters from reaching the polls, the weather is going to play a decisive role in close elections," the overly made-up news anchor chirped.

I sloshed through the downpour to church but was so eager to vote, I couldn't sit through the whole liturgy. As Father Prokopi brought out the Communion goblet, I burst out of Agia Triada and ran up the slick steps of the old schoolhouse, which now held the community offices. The polls had opened at seven A.M. and would close twelve hours later. "You can vote from sunrise to sunset," my friends told me.

Both Antonis and Cosmas were milling about the hall of the old school, in front of an antique map of ancient Greece. An old lady hobbled out of a classroom, and a brisk young woman stepped forward to bleat, "Next." I flashed my new ID as the woman checked my name off the list of registered voters. "Here are both parties' ballots and an envelope—it's self-seal, so don't lick it," she warned. "Choose a ballot, mark it, then come out and slip it into this box." It was all so official. I felt both intimidated and important as I stepped into the booth, drew the curtain, and studied the names for village president on the New Democracy ballot. Although I liked all four candidates, I had to vote for Foti—he would feel terrible if he got only his own vote. Hadn't he told me about the waterfalls in Babouri, taken me to see the skinning of a wild boar, and supplied me with fresh eggs? That made him a true patriot. I made a cross next to his name.

As I left, old men in three-piece suits and women in headscarves were hobbling out of church toward the schoolhouse. Voting is mandatory in Greece, although those who are over seventy-one are exempt from making the effort. But since the election was the most exciting thing to happen in Lia since my father's near-death experience at the Prophet Elias's festival, none of the old-timers would dream of missing it. Overstimulated by all the excitement, Costa, the eight-year-old son of the couple who owned the *kafenion*, kept running after old ladies on their way to vote, saying, "Can I pull your headscarf?" "No, don't pull it!" they'd yell, making shooing motions with their hands. He'd say, "Just a little?" They'd screech, "No!" and he'd pull it anyway.

Back at the Haidis house, I dug around in my purse for my keys, only to find that in my rush to vote, I had locked them inside the house. My eighty-three-year-old neighbor from uptown Perivoli took pity on me, hobbled down, and tried to bash the door open by ramming into it with his bony, tweed-covered butt. It didn't work. Finally Andreas jimmied the lock with a plastic square cut from a soda bottle, and I ran in to get my camera. I was the only reporter covering this election. It had to be documented.

"Can't you stay for lunch?" Dina called. I explained that I couldn't, I had to get back to election HQ, the *kafenion*. "Take some *patsavouropita* with you, then," she said, shoving a snack of still-warm pie into my hands.

The *kafenion* was crackling with election excitement. Spiridoula was making the rounds in a purple fringed miniskirt, and the older male candidates were treating everyone to coffee. All except Foti and Vangeli, who were still pursuing their no-campaigning campaign strategy and whispering election gossip to each other. Everyone else was laughing, high on the free coffee and the pride of fulfilling crucial civic duties. Lia was an important entity in the Greek state, and now we were busy nurturing the motherland that had produced us, joining together to choose our leader.

I wanted to linger, to herd with my fellow political animals, but Foti and Vangeli vetoed that, saying the *kafenion* was too crowded. We drove to the Xenona, ostensibly to watch the Athenian election in quieter surroundings, but really, I suspected, because Foti didn't want to be around when Lia's new president was announced. Cosmas was Foti's brother-in-law, and he and Foti's sister were now sitting in the *kafenion*, trying not to look nervous. No matter who won, his brother-in-law or himself, Foti would be disappointed.

At the Xenona, five border guards were engrossed in a serious game of cards. I thought they might be on riot-control duty in case the election got out of hand, but Fanis assured me that they were regulars. By eight, an hour after the polls closed, the mayoral race in Athens was officially narrowed to PASOK's Christos Papoutsis and New Democracy's Dora Bakoyiannis, since the many splinter-party candidates failed to get a significant percentage of the vote.

Neither of the two main candidates achieved 51 percent, the majority needed to win, so Athenians would be voting again in a runoff next Sunday, as in many urban mayoral races. If Dora won, she would be the first female mayor in Athens' three-thousand-year history. I was excited about the historic contest but distracted by the race at home, so I drove Foti and Vangeli to the school to check on our own results.

Outside the *kafenion*, Cosmas and Antonis were pacing nervously. Spiridoula rushed down from the schoolhouse in her knee-high boots. "They've counted only thirty of the hundred and three votes," she reported. (Apparently, 27 of the 130 registered voters had stayed away because of the weather.) "They won't be done until ten at this rate!"

That was all Vangeli needed to hear. "Let's go to Dina and Andreas's for dinner, and come back later," he suggested. I agreed—a girl's gotta eat, even when she's the only election reporter in town. Over grilled chicken, everyone revealed his voting strategy.

"What about you, Eleni?" Dina asked. "Who did you vote for?"

I looked at Foti's and Vangeli's expectant faces and answered, "It's a secret."

A surge of laughter shook the table. "How's the chicken, Eleni?" Vangeli asked. "Or is that a secret?" Everyone dissolved into hysterics again. I suppose it was laughable to think that my vote could be anonymous in such a small community. But Vangeli said I might as well keep my secret—once the results were announced he would figure out exactly how every last Liotan voted.

"How will you know for sure?" I asked.

He tapped his temple with his index finger. "I have a master's in psychology from the University of the Street."

Apparently, Vangeli was eager to get his PhD, because he kept calling the *kafenion* every five minutes for updates. On one call, at about 9:45, he jumped out of his seat, yelling, "I don't believe it!" and knocking over his *tsipouro*. (Luckily, *tsipouro* is clear, albeit flammable.) Slamming down the receiver, he reported the news: the election had ended in a tie. ND and PASOK each got forty-seven votes; there were nine votes that the election officials canceled

202 NORTH OF ITHAKA

because the self-sealed envelopes had been dropped in the wrong box, marked so they could be easily identified, or otherwise invalidated. Vangeli yanked on his coat.

"Where are you going?" Dina shouted.

"To the *kafenion*, to check things out," he said. I grabbed my camera and followed. Outside the schoolhouse, Cosmas barreled toward us, electrical charges emitting from his wiry hair. "It's forty-seven to forty-seven, with nine invalid; eight for us, and one for New Democracy!" he shouted, slapping his forehead. "The *vavves* put their votes in the wrong box!" (A *vavvo* is an old lady in villagespeak.) Voting is an intimidating process; old ladies tend to make up Greece's 5 percent illiteracy rate, and the paperwork must have confused them. Cosmas was livid, having personally ferried several *vavves* into Lia from large cities to vote. He whirled to face me. "Remember how you said in a few hours we'd know the results?" he demanded. "Well, you were wrong."

I was tempted to take a photo of Cosmas, a portrait of tension. But I refrained; I worried he might smash my camera in a Sean Penn–like rage.

The next day should have been a *panegyri* for the winning party. But there were no roasted lambs in sight. Instead, everyone was engaged in Monday-morning quarterbacking. Having garnered only six votes, Vassili Deppis left town. Cosmas and Antonis Makos got twenty-eight votes each, and the rest trickled down from there. Foti won four in the end, silencing speculation that he wasn't going to vote for himself but for his brother-in-law. If he had, Cosmas would be president today. Now Foti was moping around the *kafenion*, arguing with Cosmas's brother, who questioned his family loyalty. I had voted to prevent Foti getting his feelings hurt. But in the end, almost everyone's feelings were hurt, which *really* made it resemble a sixth-grade election. Even in Arta, Mayor Vaya had lost the race, despite his partying hearty at the Gypsy wedding. The bride's parents had lost their voting privileges as punishment for stealing, and the groom's mother had demanded 3,000 euros in exchange for her family's eleven votes, Georgia Vaya told me. "I said, '*Koumbara*, that's not done,' and she said, 'Then, unfortunately, *koumbara*, we aren't able to vote for you.'" I felt awful for my friends in Arta; after the mayor had danced so hard! And in Lia, spirits were low, although the rain had stopped and the weather was now sunny and bright, mockingly gorgeous.

By afternoon most of us had cheered up enough to start wondering what would happen next. "Won't we just vote again this Sunday?" I asked as we sat in the *kafenion*.

"No," said Vangeli. "The people have spoken." Well, we obviously weren't very good public speakers. "In a case like this, there's a drawing to find out which of the two leading candidates wins," he continued. "The municipality will schedule one for us after all the major elections are settled."

"A drawing?" I scoffed.

"That's right," Vangeli continued, assuming I didn't know this unfamiliar Greek word. "A judge will put Cosmas's and Antonis's names in a bowl, then pull one out."

But that was so . . . undemocratic! Democracy had been invented in Greece. Surely these people had a better plan B than a drawing out of a hat? Just then, Antonis strolled by the Xenona. "Mr. President!" Foti yelled.

"Not quite," Antonis responded. "The drawing is scheduled for October thirty-first."

With nothing else to do but wait, Vangeli put his degree from the University of the Street to work, divining who had voted for whom, and which two people purposefully invalidated their votes by writing in the names of soccer teams instead of making the required cross next to a name. "I'm in the *kafenion*, and Nassios comes up and says, 'How about those invalid votes, huh?'" Vangeli reported. "So I knew it was him."

"But how can you be sure?" I asked.

He looked at me sadly, pitying my naïveté. "Because," he said, "only the person who did that would talk about it. A murderer always returns to the scene of the crime."

By day two, postelection, the soccer scam was small potatoes, eclipsed by a real scandal. Vangeli had uncovered what he described as a vote-buying ring. Apparently, the PASOK candidates had visited several old people the day before the election, passing out checks for ninety euros. "What did they write on the bottom?" I asked. "Payment for vote?"

"No, the money was legal, from the government," Vangeli explained. "It's like Golf Air, like my brother says you have in the United States."

Golf Air?

"You know, money the state gives to poor people?" Oh, welfare! Of course.

"Anyway, PASOK has had the checks since August, but they gave them to their candidates to distribute the day before the election, so that the *vavves* think, 'Oh, I'll vote for him, so I'll keep getting money,'" Vangeli continued.

"But if they really did that, that's corruption!" I protested. "It's illegal!"

"I know," said Vangeli. "And they complain about *our* oily fingerprint!"

I thought this must be a folk saying I didn't know, a comment on how the heavy campaigning left "oily fingerprints" everywhere. "What does that mean?" I asked.

"It means," Vangeli said, "That one of the ND ballots that the officials approved as valid had a big oily fingerprint left on it—and PASOK somehow heard about it. Now they say that it's an identifying mark, so the ballot is invalid."

I pitched forward in my chair. "It's my fault!" I cried. "Dina gave me pita on my way to the *kafenion*, and I gave Foti some before he voted—it must be his print."

"Plug up your mouth," Vangeli whispered urgently. "Don't let anyone know it's our fault!" Damn Dina, with her delicious pitas, me with my generous ways, and Foti with his ever expanding gut!

"It wasn't us," Foti said, laughing, pulling me out of a spiral of shame. "It was the other Eleni Gatzoyiannis. She was seen eating fried dough on her way to the school."

Phew! If we lost the election, it would be my doppelgänger's fault, not mine. But that didn't change the fact that the political climate in Lia was fraught, with no chance of calming down before October 31. Luckily, we had round two of the Athenian election to distract us. On the second Sunday Dora won the race for mayor by the largest margin in Athens's history, ushering in what the TV reporters called "the Era of the Woman." Dora was the first female mayor of any major European city, so I was thrilled. But not as thrilled as her family, who celebrated at her headquarters by Cretan line-dancing in a way I couldn't imagine most American first families doing. Here in Lia, no bouzouki would strum and no clarinet wail until Halloween, which, since Greeks don't celebrate Halloween, I now thought of as Drawing Day.

In the meantime, we all tried to return to our regular pursuits and enjoy the lovely weather. The sky was a pure azure that Crayola has never quite managed to replicate, and the sun gave off the intense Greek light that overexposes the film of unsuspecting tourists every autumn. It was the phenomenon known as "the little summer of Saint Demetrios," the last blast of gorgeous weather, which occurs around the feast day of Saint Demetrios on October 26. It is also the season when sheep are led from mountain pastures to lowland winter fields, so I watched two distant cousins herd their seven hundred sheep down the mountain into the vast wilderness beneath the road to Babouri.

Foti taught me to placate their five possibly murderous sheepdogs by dropping down on my haunches and cooing, "Ella, ella," as my cousins led sheep of all sorts: woolly, shaggy, spotted. The sheep all somehow understood the shepherds' whistles and verbal cues to veer right or left. But they were discerning sheep; they wouldn't listen to just any human, and each time they sensed me walking toward them to squish their fluffy fleece, they would trot away, baaing, their bells ringing in a pastoral symphony.

Foti told me that in their trek to a village near Filiates, the sheep would cover some of the same ground as the escape route my father and aunts took when they fled Lia, sneaking off at night, barefoot, down the mountain and up to the Great Ridge, where the nationalist troops were stationed. I decided I had to hike the escape route myself. I couldn't leave Lia myself without searching out the paths my family had followed when they left the village behind. It was a trip Thitsa Kanta often referenced when she was annoyed at my father. "NickGage shouldn't yell at me," she'd complain. "I'm older, and I carried him through the minefields!"

I turned to Foti. "I know it's too late to start today," I said. "But could you maybe get someone to show me the escape route so I can hike it tomorrow?"

Foti frowned, leaning against a roadside shrine as a sea of sheep trotted by. "My friend hunts in those mountains," he admitted. "But I'm not sure it's a good idea."

"Look, if the *thitsas* could do it . . ." I objected.

"I know," Foti answered. "But there were paths then that are all overgrown now."

"They told me that they followed the streams so that they didn't step on any mines," I said. "I could follow the rivers, too, wade a little if I have to. I'd really like to see the route for myself." I looked at Foti evenly. "If your friend can't show me, maybe you can describe the route to me and I'll try to hike it on my own."

Foti sighed. "Okay, okay, I'll make sure he leads you," he said. "Just promise you won't tell Kanta about this. She'd kill me if she knew I let you hike off into the wild with only a middle-aged hunter with high blood pressure for protection."

The next day, just after sunrise, Foti introduced me to Stavros Zafeiris. We met outside Panagia church, near the starting point for the escape that my father, his sisters, and several other villagers embarked on in July 1948. Stavros, wearing head-to-toe camouflage, a red beard, and a long-barreled rifle, led me past a tree full of golden-red pomegranates onto the mountainside. We were above the timberline, and below us stood russet-colored trees and clouds as puffy as the departed sheep. With Stavros in the lead, we slid downhill, crouching under branches and stomping on brambles.

"This whole area used to be cultivated," Stavros said. The entire mountainside looked the same to me, but he could refer to patches of land by the names of the people who owned them back when Lia was bustling. Shortly after passing a ruined home whose fireplace, carved with a fleur-de-lis, rose like a watchtower above the rubble, we reached the hilly grounds of the monastery of Agios Athanassios. A bush shook and I screamed—it could be a runaway Albanian, ghost, or disgruntled saint. If I survived the impending assault, Thitsa Kanta would kill me. Suddenly Father Prokopi emerged, wrestling with the branches; he was thinning them as part of his renovation of the monastery. "Remind me, I have a hundred and fifty euros to donate from the hunters," Stavros told him. "If we shoot a pig on the grounds of the monastery, we each put in five euros for the church."

I was jealous of Father Prokopi and Stavros, for whom this landscape was a familiar retreat. The streams, trees, and hillsides belonged to them a little but were new to me. We continued on and, after three hours, approached the foot of the Great Ridge. "Only one more hour now," Stavros said cheerfully. "And it's straight up all the way." He whistled as we climbed, aided by walking sticks. But once we reached the top, the old nationalist camp, he looked down and said soberly, "There are corpses here from everywhere, Greeks, Germans, Italians." It was an awe-inspiring resting place.

I thought of my grandmother, who was forced to stay behind at the last minute to harvest wheat for the guerillas, missed the frightening, nighttime hike, and was executed for planning her family's escape. I hoped that if Thitsa Kanta's dream was right, and my *yiayia* now watched over me, she had come along that day, to see how her family had survived and how breathtaking their passage to freedom remained.

October 28 was OXI Day, the anniversary of the date during World War II when the Greek ruler, Metaxas, said no! (or *c'est la guerre!*), he would not cede the country to the Axis powers. I attended the holiday service at church and watched as veterans, policemen, and Nikolas Skevis, who was still president until January anyway, laid wreaths at the monument to Lia's fallen soldiers. Later, at the Gatzoyiannis house, a minor battle threatened to break out. Zervas, our ethereal architect, had unexpectedly arrived to check on the building. "About the stairs from the veranda: the front ones look good, but the ones leading from the door of the *plistario* have to be done carefully," he said, rolling up the sleeves of his V-necked sweater. "Vlad, let's do them now."

"No." Vlad shook his head. "First finish wall to the stairs, then do the stairs."

"But the stairs are important!" Zervas insisted. "We should handle them now, while I'm here, or else you'll do them all wrong!" Since the hedgehog incident, when Zervas was convinced that Vlad had scared off his workers, there was no love lost between the two. And now Vlad was having a little OXI Day of his own.

"I no take down scaffolding in front of door until done with wall," he insisted, shrugging. "No can do stairs until scaffolding down." With that, Vlad turned and resumed working on the upper wall of the courtyard. I glanced at Zervas, who looked as frustrated as I imagine Metaxas felt sixty-two years before. He needed to be distracted, so I volunteered to treat him to lunch. When we arrived at the Xenona, I was delighted to see Vassili Deppis, who had received a pitiful six votes after switching parties and then disappeared. "You're back!" I shouted, giving him a hug hello.

"Of course!" he boomed. "I was just on Corfu, helping my sons close their hotel for the winter."

"Oh, good!" I said. "I was worried you were feeling a little down."

"Who, me?" Vassili said, laughing as he raised his cane off the ground. "About the election? I couldn't be president even if I had won; I travel too much! I have to be in Athens for the holidays, then Germany. Last year I visited a friend in Australia. This year, who knows?"

That's the spirit, I thought, driving home. Everyone's seeing reason. Zervas returned to Athens, and I didn't see Vassili again until Sunday, when most of us gathered in the *kafenion* after church. He was sitting opposite Nikolas Skevis, complaining that he couldn't make *tsipouro* from his grapes because the church-owned still had been locked by the customs office, which now required one to get a permit before making *tsipouro*.

"A traitor in our midst tipped them off!" he yelled. Vangeli whispered to me that everyone knew he was referring to Cosmas, who allegedly was so mad when his own still got locked for the same reason that he informed the customs guy that the church had one, too.

"As president, you should go get permits for everyone," Vassili scolded Nikolas. But Nikolas was still fuming about having to give up the presidency in two short months. "Get your own permits!" he shouted. "And tell the 'traitor' what you think of him to his face, if you're a man!"

"I knew you wouldn't help us," Vassili said, sneering. "You won't do anything for the good of the village, just for your own profit!"

"No one cares about your opinion," Nikolas spat. "Hardly anyone voted for you! The village doesn't respect you! The village shits on you!"

Those were fighting words. And Vassili was ready to respond in kind. "I wouldn't have cared if I didn't even get my own vote," he blurted. "Everyone knows I'm New Democracy! I just ran to keep you off the ticket! And I achieved my goal!" With that, Vassili stormed out, as much as a heavyset man with a cane can storm.

The next day, over lunch at Dina and Andreas's, I asked if they had heard about the fight.

"Oh, that wasn't a real fight," Dina said, rolling her eyes. "Those two see arguing as a *panegyri*. This morning they went down together to Igoumenitsa and got the still unlocked. They're boiling their grapes for *tsipouro* today."

I was surprised, but delighted. See, we *can* all get along! "That's great," I said. "And tomorrow we'll know who won the election!"

"No," said Andreas, tapping his fork in resignation. "We won't know for weeks."

"But tomorrow's Halloween!" I said. "I mean, October thirty-first. Drawing Day."

"Yes, but that was before the lawsuit," Andreas explained. "Now they're going to set a court date on Corfu, because the PASOK candidate who lost the mayoral race for the region says one of the ballots is invalid."

"If PASOK wins another village, they get one more city councilor," Dina added. "So they say a ballot was marked because the sign looks more like an X than a cross!"

I sighed and helped myself to another glass of retsina. It seemed excessive to quibble over how some illiterate old lady draws a cross, but I was quickly realizing that politics is a rough game.

With the warm weather holding, I concentrated on the building site, where the Northern Epirotic master stonemason Yanni and his wife were giving the house a complete makeover, defining its features. So far, the veranda had been a skeleton frame, with two cement pillars rising to support the ground floor and continuing on from the veranda to hold up the slate roof. Yanni had now covered the pillars in front of the basement with flat, square stones and built elegant stone arches that curved underneath the cement floor of the veranda. He was starting to cover with stone the pillars of the main floor. In the mid-1930s, my grandfather had closed in the veranda with corrugated tin to create another room, but I preferred to keep it open so I could look out past the mulberry tree toward the bow-shaped mountain in the distance, the same view my grandmother gazed at over half a century ago. I was trying to imagine the house finished when Yanni stopped chipping and looked up.

"Good afternoon," he said to someone behind me. I turned and saw the sparkling blue eyes and stark white mustache of Antonis Makos, my favored presidential candidate, who lived in Perivoli.

"The pillars look great," he said. "Really make the house look like a home. Since I can't be here tomorrow, I wanted to come over and see how they turned out."

"Where are you going?" I asked.

"To Corfu—for the court case," he said. "It's for the election. The judge will rule on whether the ballots are valid, or if, as the PASOK politician says, one is marked."

"And if the judge decides they're valid?" I asked.

"If he says they're valid, I guess we'll have a drawing," he answered.

"Right then and there?"

He nodded, then shrugged. "I guess so. It's been over a month since the election—we need to find out who the new president is before he has to take up office in January." He was right. The suspense had to end. And I felt I had to watch the conclusion of this prolonged contest, almost as a monitor of justice.

"Can I come?" I called after him.

Antonis turned and smiled. "The case is going to be heard at five at the old courthouse," he said. "If you take the two o'clock ferry, you'll be there in time."

The next day at four, I found Antonis standing outside the Corfu courthouse, dressed for battle in a navy suit and leather vest stretched over his slight paunch. He tried to smile, but his face kept collapsing into a network of nervous folds. I was glad I came, because without me, Antonis would have been a lone New Democracy wolf, and Cosmas appeared to be accompanied by the PASOK politician who was bringing the lawsuit.

Antonis and I decided to grab a coffee, to pass time. "At the courthouse the guard said this is the only place open." Antonis pointed to an elegant, colonnaded Venetian building with a sign reading DIRTY DICK'S BAR. Dirty Dick's turned out to be the Algonquin Round Table of the Corfu courthouse, filled with politicians awaiting trial and poker-faced lawyers drinking ginger beer.

"Wasn't he on the ferry with you?" Antonis asked, agitated.

"Who?"

"Dr. Doumazios; he's supposed to be here." Doumazios was the New Democracy candidate who won the mayoral race for our municipality of Filiates. We had elected him, he promised to defend us, and now he was nowhere to be seen. Shades of agony passed over Antonis's face; it was like watching someone get stood up for the senior prom.

At ten to five, we filed into the courthouse, an imposing

neoclassical job crawling with cops. We found the classroom-like hall marked MUNICIPALITY OF FILIATES and managed to get seats just in time—right next to Cosmas, who looked as nervous as Antonis. The opposing candidates from Lia sat together for mutual comfort. Even I felt nervous. A raised platform loomed opposite our lowly spectators' benches, and behind this dais were seven massive chairs. Above the chairs hung a painting of Jesus, but not the Greek Jesus we knew and loved, with a middle part, ponytail, sunken cheeks, and sorrowful eyes. This was a Western Jesus with cascading locks, doe eyes, and a white robe, pointing to himself, just between his breastbones, with his left hand, and out at us with his right, as if to say, "It's not me, it's you. I died for *your* sins."

But he must have been blessing us after all, because just before the doors shut, a grim lawyer waltzed in, followed by a sharp-dressed, slick-haired man who could only have been Dr. Doumazios. Antonis sighed happily, and we were instructed to rise for the magistrates, who appeared behind the dais. It turned out that the judge was a smiling, twinkly-eyed brunette, flanked by two less-attractive and less-high-powered ladies. Lady Justice called our case, listened to our lawyers, then consulted with her colleagues behind her hot pink dossier in a highly un-Ruth-Ginsberg-like way. Satisfied, she turned to offer her decision. "I'll take a look at the motions and get back to you in a few days," she said, offering us a winning smile.

I turned to Antonis. "That was it?" I demanded.

"Yes," he said, breaking into a grin. I felt deflated, cheated, but he seemed relieved that our whole exercise in justice boiled down to a matter of five minutes. At least he didn't have to get up and defend himself, the way they do on TV.

The local PASOK candidate giving moral support to Cosmas said good-bye and set off to meet a colleague for a drink. Now Cosmas was free to hang out with us—me; his opponent, Antonis; Dr. Doumazios; and our lawyers. We settled in a maritime-themed bar opposite the harbor to await the seven o'clock ferry back to the mainland. Antonis and Cosmas sat next to each other and ordered orange sodas. Why was Antonis drinking with the enemy? I wondered. And what about Cosmas, who had been so enraged the night of the tied election? Dr. Doumazios leaned toward his lawyer. "Cosmas here wants Antonis to be president but doesn't feel he can withdraw from the race," he announced.

"I don't want to let the party down, and if I won I would serve. But I have to spend some time in America this year," Cosmas said, nodding. "And I live in Igoumenitsa. Antonis is in the village full-time. He really should be president for now."

"So," Dr. Doumazios continued, sipping his scotch. "The judge is going to uphold the ballots; if they were at all suspicious, the election officials would have thrown them out when they counted them. Once she declares the ballot valid, is there any way we can make sure that Antonis wins the drawing, since Cosmas doesn't want the job right now anyway?"

Stonefaced, the lawyer looked at Dr. Doumazios. "There's no way to control a drawing," he intoned. "If someone doesn't want to be president, he should withdraw." Cosmas shrugged and swigged his orange soda. He knew he couldn't withdraw at this point without alienating his fellow party members.

If there was a solution, we couldn't figure it out that night. Cosmas, Antonis, and I had a ferry to catch. As we hurried to the boat, Cosmas asked, "Any news from Worcester?" He always spoke to me in a mix of Greek and English. Cosmas had a facility for languages; when he and his siblings were taken across the border by the retreating Communists, he picked up Hungarian and Romanian, which came in handy when he moved to Germany and became a foreman at an auto factory, overseeing Hungarian workers. There he learned German, then English in a Massachusetts pizza parlor. If he'd been a diplomat instead of a refugee, Cosmas might be an ambassador by now.

"No, nothing new," I told him.

"I got something," he said, grimacing. "My son, he may be getting a divorce."

"I'm so sorry," I said.

214 NORTH OF ITHAKA

"That's okay—they didn't have any kids, so not such a big deal."
He shrugged. "His wife, she says she's not sure she wants to be married no more."

As we boarded the ferry, I realized that this was the reason Cosmas needed to spend time in America that year, to be near his son. A month before, the election had seemed supremely important. But now everything was different, and for the moment he didn't really care about his political future. In the ferry lounge, we sat together and Antonis brought us coffee. As we sipped, the PASOK official who had brought the suit walked in and came over to say hello. "I wanted to ask you a favor," he said, handing me a piece of paper with a name on it. "When you get to America, can you search for information about my grandmother's brother? He moved there in 1910, died in 1953 in San Bernardino, but that's all we know. Maybe he had kids. Anything you find out would be great."

I said I'd try, and he left to get his bags. "That's a good sign, that he asked you for help," Antonis said. "Maybe he thinks we're going to win, or he plans to drop the suit."

But I felt that his request was apolitical. He wanted information about a relative he'd never known, and knew that in this battle we were on the same side, both trying to learn as much as possible about our families' past as they had played themselves out between the United States and the rocky coast where the ferry was now docking.

After we disembarked, I gave Antonis a ride to Lia. On the way he told me about the August day in 1948 when he saw my grandmother being led up the mountain to execution. "I was thirteen, and had gone to collect water," he recalled. "One of the soldiers leading the prisoners asked for my canteen. I said, 'No way—what will I collect water with?' He just laughed. Now I can't believe I did that, talked back to a murderer. But I was young—and thirsty—and I didn't know any better."

Decades later, Antonis worked as a meat salesman, supplying bars and restaurants in Ioannina. In one, he recognized the decaying bartender as the once brash young soldier who had demanded his canteen. When my father returned to Greece to learn the details of his mother's death, Antonis gave him the man's name, a key piece of information that got the investigation started.

Young boys grow up to run for president, sometimes of a country, sometimes of a village as small as Lia. And children get older and can't be protected from sorrow or heartbreak. I know that politics matter. Even in Lia political differences resulted in the war that caused my grandmother's death and the kidnapping of children such as Cosmas and Antonis. Today Lia is a tiny fragment of its former self, with only 15 percent of the population it had before the war, no school, no businesses. But it has also turned into a place where a political fight is a shouting match in the *kafenion*, not a death sentence, and the man running against you for office is really just a friend in need. I couldn't explain the change. Perhaps the inhabitants of Lia have had their passions tempered by painful memories of their fractious past. Maybe history has taught them a lesson, or they simply got older or even just tired.

I knew my aunts and my father thought I was naive not to see evil or jealousy in the village. It existed there, and so did suspicion and hate, just as they do everywhere. I recognized that. But I was glad that friendship and community existed as well. Two weeks after the court date on Corfu, almost three months after Election Sunday, a cliff-hanger that had dragged on for longer than some of my romantic relationships finally ended with an anticlimactic phone call from Dr. Doumazios, informing Antonis that he was now Lia's newest representative. The first person to call and congratulate Mr. President was Cosmas.

NINE

THE FUTURE IMPERFECT

<<Άλλα σκαμπάζει ο γάϊδαρος, και άλλα ο γαϊδουρολό

"THE DONKEY HAS ONE SET OF PLANS, AND THE DONKE·

HERDER HAS ANOTHER."

November 5

I had a strange dream last night. I'm standing in the door of the Gatzoyiannis house, watching Yanni build a stone banquette between the corner of the veranda and the wall of the house itself. I'm thinking about next summer, when we'll set a table here and eat while gazing down at the mountains to watch the shadows stretch along their peaks, turning from gold to amber to purple.

"Watch out!" Yanni starts pointing at the stone steps leading up to the veranda. There's now a slobbering spotted dog bounding up them. The dog trots right up to me and opens his mouth so wide that I can see past his yellow incisors to his looming tonsils.

"So, what did the dog do then?" Kaity demanded when I told her the dream.

"I don't know," I sighed. "That's when I woke up. What does it mean?" In the village, somewhere at the Haidis house, I had the 2002 *oneirokritos* (the interpreter of dreams), a booklet with horoscopes for the year, a list of saints' days, jokes, and a handy glossary of frequent symbols seen in dreams, along with their corresponding meaning. But I couldn't find it that morning before driving to Ioannina, and I knew Kaity was such an expert at divination that she would never need to look something up.

"Well," she said, putting down her coffee cup. "What color was the dog, black or white? Because white dogs are a good sign, but black dogs are bad."

"The dog was black *and* white," I replied, fretting. "It was Scrappy, one of the strays the soldiers abandoned when they left the border post. I feed him, and he's always jumping up and knocking things out of my hand, or winding in between my legs and tripping me."

"It's your own fault for feeding him." Kaity wrinkled her nose. "You should know better. In any case, dogs in general are a sign of worry, complications, responsibilities. Maybe the dream was a warning about a problem with the house."

I wanted a second opinion. What would Freud do? "Maybe the dream doesn't mean anything about the future; it's just my subconscious reviewing things that happened that day," I suggested.

"Oh, Eleni." Kaity shook her head. "Your mind has to be more interesting than that. All dreams tell us something about the future, whether we want to listen or not. Look at me; I had a prophetic dream the night before each of my parents died."

"Really?" I asked.

"The night before my mother's death I dreamed I was walking on the beach, and I looked at the moon," she recalled. "The moon turned into my mother's face, with her hair undone, trailing into the night sky. Back then, women always had their hair up, so to me, she looked scary, wild. The next day I came home from school and she was dead."

"That's amazing," I said. "Was it the same dream with your father?"

"No. I was married and living here by then, but I dreamed I was walking down a street in my hometown and saw my mother, running in her nightgown, her hair hanging down. I called, 'Mana!' but she ignored me. Finally, I reached her and asked where she was going in such a hurry. She said, 'To your father's funeral, of course.'"

I was fascinated but terrified. If dreams are previews, are all coming attractions tearjerkers? "I'm not going to try to remember my dreams anymore," I vowed.

"It's better to know," Kaity insisted. "So when a tragedy happens, along with sorrow, you feel a tiny bit of relief, that you knew what was coming, now it's over, and you just have to get to the next surprise fate has in store. And to hope it's a good one."

I nodded, but Kaity knew I wasn't convinced. "Give me your cup, I'll read your coffee grounds," she said to placate me. "Then you should set off for Lia before dark."

Over the past eight and a half months, Kaity had read my coffee grounds dozens of times. When Thitsa Kanta was around, I had *her* read my cup, too, so I could compare one reading with the other, my system of checks and balances. Thitsa Kanta's readings were delivered with as much advice as interpretation; she'd tell me that a cross, which signifies happiness, meant that I was about to meet a man, "Because you gotta get married soon, while your *thitsa* is still strong enough to dance at your wedding!"

Perhaps because of Thitsa Kanta's less-than-subtle attempts at mind control, I didn't believe in coffee-cup readings any more than I did horoscopes in the paper. Still, I liked to watch Kaity and Thitsa Kanta point out the patterns the grounds left when they oozed down the sides of the overturned cup, and describe what they symbolized. It was kind of like code breaking. A snake, monkey, or dog was an enemy. An *e* signified *eftychia* (happiness). If the bottom of the cup was dark, coated in grounds, it indicated *stenachoria*, a word that translates as "narrow places" but means the suffocating sensation of worry. Sometimes the signs were obvious—rings meant a wedding, a cradle signified a baby. But other symbols had the opposite meaning of what you'd expect: a pile of grounds on the lip of the cup looked like a big mess but indicated a pile of money was about to come your way (just as dreaming of a pile of shit, pardon the expression, is a harbinger of riches).

In April, shortly after I arrived in Greece, Kaity had taught me a new symbol. "Look, a tree," she said. "A tree is about planting something, then waiting to see it bloom. You're about to start a project that will bear fruit long into the future, offering shade and nourishment not just for yourself but for your descendants."

Kaity knew I had taken a year out of my life to oversee the rebuilding of my grandparents' house. She could have made up the tree as encouragement. But when she pointed to the white trunk and branches spreading amid the dark coffee grounds, there it was, a tree as clear as in a drawing. I was stunned that something so inspiring could come out of mundane divination games, the grown-up Greek equivalent of the Magic 8-Ball.

Codified images like the tree had existed forever, and I suspect that they haven't just told Greek women what to expect but also have taught them how to think, shaping their emotions into culturally coded symbols, so that unbound hair indicates death, not a burning desire for a haircut. My own dreams had changed since I arrived in Lia. In New York I dreamed about walking into my office in my pajamas or discovering extra rooms to my tiny apartment. But in Lia I'd see my beloved late uncle holding an eagle in his hands before it sailed off into the sky, and I knew that flying birds meant soaring spirits—somewhere my uncle was happy. In New York my dreams were sitcoms; in Lia they were haikus.

I was starting to believe that my dreams could tip me off about future events that were preordained by fate. Luckily, at the same time I realized fate controlled me, I also learned I was able to influence it, to cheat fate, at least temporarily. When it comes to unlucky fate, it's better to be proactive than to react. So the villagers warned me to wear a blue eye amulet for protection against the evil eye, the "bad vibes" that a person who envies you, or who just adores you excessively, can cast over you with an admiring glance, sending a black fate your way.

I had gone into the city amuletless, and by the time I returned to Lia from visiting Kaity, it was too late. Now I was caught in a storm, my computer wouldn't start, and I felt nauseated and headachy. Someone had it in for me—clearly, I was *matiasmeni*, infected by the evil eye. So as soon as I arrived in Motsala, I headed to Dina's for aspirin and psychic relief. After she had children, her father had taught her an incantation to remove the evil eye, so she could cure them. But once he gave her the words, he lost the power to cure people himself, which happens when you share the secret knowledge. Before Dina could cure me, she had to confirm the diagnosis. She dropped a blob of oil into a shot glass of water. In a few seconds, the oil separated into four distinct oily eyes.

"Yup, you're *matiasmeni*," she announced. "And by a man. When you have the *mati*, the oil rises to the top of the water and forms eyes. If a woman has given it, it becomes one big eye; if it's from a man, the blobs are spread out. Take three sips of this."

I drank from the oil-and-water cocktail, sipping from three different sides of the shot glass, as instructed. Then Dina dipped her hand in the water, made the sign of the cross over my head, and left the room to repeat the incantation. I felt better already.

That night, at dinner at the Xenona with Nikki, Fanis, and our new president, Antonis Makos, I announced that I had been suffering from the evil eye. Thitsa Kanta once told me that my grandfather had a sixteen-year-old sister who died of the evil eye after a passing priest commented on how pretty she was. "Priests are the worst for giving the evil eye," she warned me. "Priests and blue-eyed people like you. They don't mean to, but they give it anyway." The pretty girl's mother took the dirt from the priest's footprint, put it in holy water, and made the afflicted girl drink it, but it was too late, she died of the evil eye anyway. Did they think it was genetic?

"Well, I hardly ever get the evil eye, but it's because of this," Nikki said, pointing to a small scar on her temple. "When I was born, parents used to burn a scar on their baby's forehead with a hot coal or poker."

"But why?" I gasped, choking on my *pita*.

"So the babies would be imperfect and less likely to get the *mati*." Nikki noticed my look of disgust. "Of course, no one does it anymore!"

"But you can understand why they did—the evil eye can be deadly. Just look what happened to your father," Antonis Makos chimed in. "Everyone noticed how quickly your grandparents' house is being built and they all talked about it, giving him the evil eye. So he crashed the car. It was fate that he was unharmed; it wasn't his time to die."

"I don't know," I objected. "It may have been fate, or the saint himself, who saved him, but it was my father's own fault that the accident happened."

Antonis slammed down his glass of red wine, sloshing some onto the tablecloth. "Look, I know you're educated," he blurted out. "But you may not know that we lose consciousness for three seconds every twenty-four hours—it's a fact, I saw it on TV. *A total lack of consciousness.* Now, that's fine if you're just sitting in a chair, but if you have the misfortune of it happening to you while you're driving . . ."

Fanis, Nikki, and I nodded. None of us could argue with an as-seen-on-TV fact. Antonis had called both science and media as witnesses for fate and convinced us. Liotes may have stopped burning babies in ritual scarification, but they still managed to clear a place for the evil eye in their modern lives.

The next morning, still feeling vulnerable to fate after my bout with the evil eye, I read my journal entry from October 8 to see what Thitsa Kanta had told me in my birthday coffee-ground reading—divination that she said would be especially accurate given the auspicious date. "You gonna get a good piece of paper in the mail, maybe money or something from you work," she said.

No dice there.

"This week you gonna get a phone call with some good news, a big surprise."

Nope, that one hadn't happened, either.

"And here, a big cross right where you drank—that's the man who gonna come make you life complete."

I laughed. I had moved to Lia and started the rebuilding to make my life complete, to fill a perceived void. In doing so, I removed myself from virtually any men my age, the very people whose presence Thitsa Kanta felt would make me whole.

"Don't laugh, honey," Thitsa Kanta chided me. "It's true. You gonna have a happy life. There's a five next to the cross—see—so you gonna meet the man in five days, five weeks, or five months."

By now, five days and five weeks had already passed. And I was beginning to have doubts about five months. In October I had laughed at Thitsa Kanta's suggestion that I needed a man; now I was thinking, *Don't let it be five years!* Maybe divination was really a sophisticated brainwashing technique to make you desire what the reader thinks you should want.

The American side of me scoffed at predictions, but once I moved to Lia, the Greek side insisted on taking advantage of every chance at prognostication that came my way. I had some standards, guidelines I followed to keep me from sliding down into crackpotdom. I never paid for my fortune, thus justifying my habit as (a) being social and (b) studying folklore, just as I did back in college. On my first foray into "research," Kaity's friend, an Albanian Cher look-alike, flipped her long hair behind her chiffon-clad shoulder, picked up my coffee cup, and predicted that this was the year I would get engaged. "But I'm not even dating anyone," I told her, hoping for a more realistic do-over.

"The cup doesn't lie," she insisted. "Within the year you will make a serious commitment to someone you already know but are not dating yet."

I thanked her. But when she was gone, I complained to Kaity about her trite prediction. Cher was simply saying what she thought I wanted to hear. This was a marriage-minded society. It wasn't just Thitsa Kanta; at every holiday, all the old ladies in my village automatically wished me, "Next year, may you be here with a groom!"

"If I'm getting engaged this year, how come I'm not even dating my future husband?" I complained to Kaity. "Because he doesn't exist!"

Still, Kaity's fortune-telling friends kept dangling bachelors in front of me as if my life were a psychic game of Old Maid. "Write this down," said her neighbor Noula, slapping down dirty playing cards, the reading of which was her specialty. "Your husband will be Greek but educated abroad. You will lead a happy double life, between America and Greece."

And where will I meet this international jet-setter? I thought. *Out picking oregano?* But all I said was, "How can you tell?"

"Just look," Noula said. "This card represents weddings, and this one your name, which is Eleni. That sounds like *Ellinas*, a Greek, so your husband will be Greek."

"From your mouth to God's ears," Kaity said, in between puffs of her cigarette.

Noula didn't know that none of my serious boyfriends had been Greek, a fact that was almost a point of pride. "I don't want to be the best *Greek* person some racial profiler can find," I'd tell people who wanted to set me up with other Greek Americans. But now that I was so attached to Lia, I saw how unlikely it was that any of my American exes would have agreed to spend at least a month each year surrounded by old people on a mountaintop instead of, say, summering in the Hamptons like everyone else.

In the last few months before I left, I had dated someone of Greek origin, although I tried to keep that information from the overly excitable *thitsas*. But he was even less interested in my plans to live in Lia than the others would have been. "I get so sick of my father's friends asking why I don't speak Greek that I developed this really clever answer," he told me shortly before I left. "I say, 'I do something even better, something that you can't do. I speak English properly.' "

I immediately understood that our points of view were so different, it wasn't even worth explaining that no one gets points for speaking his native tongue; I'd be gone soon anyway. Remembering this and all the other moments when I thought to myself, *Yeah, this isn't going to work*, I wondered if Noula might be right, and the answer was to marry someone from Greece who wouldn't mind visiting Lia occasionally, as long as his cell phone got reception.

When I told Dina about Noula's prediction, she insisted that I do my best to spur my husband's arrival. On August 27, Agios Fanourios's Day, she and Athina taught me to bake a *fanouropita*. "Agios Fanourios is the saint who finds things," Dina explained.

"Like luggage after the airline loses it?" I asked.

"Sure, like luggage, but also more important things, like health," Athina clarified. "Or, for example, you could ask him to find you your destiny."

"My destiny?"

"Your husband!" Dina explained. "All you have to do is pray for the soul of Agios Fanourios's mother while the cake is baking. She was a wicked woman, so she needs all the prayers she can get."

"Wicked?" I asked, intrigued. "Really. What did she do?"

"It doesn't say it in the book about the saint's life, but everyone knows she was a prostitute. Still, that doesn't matter," Dina said, keeping her eye on the prize. "What matters is, you bake and pray for his mother, then distribute the cake to twelve people. The saint returns the favor by finding what's missing in your life. For you, that's a husband."

Is that what was missing? And if I had a husband, would he be as thrilled as I was to sit in Lia, learning how to bake magic cakes? I wasn't totally convinced a spouse was what I needed. But I baked a delicious get-me-a-man cake anyway. And still my lover with a fancy foreign degree never appeared. Undoubtedly, while I was slaving over a hot stove, he was jumping off his yacht, hand in hand with his Eurotrash girlfriend.

It wasn't that I hadn't met anyone at all in Lia. A neighbors' sweet nephew passed through town, and I enjoyed talking to him. A month later his mother visited to explain that he made enough money in six months in Athens to support us living in New York the rest of the year. But I wondered, since he didn't speak English, what could he do in New York while I worked all day? Of course, I wouldn't consider marrying a man I hardly knew, although I might entertain dating him. But I worried that once he stopped teaching me obscure Greek vocabulary, I'd find our conversations a lot less interesting.

Then there was the man from Ioannina who had recently moved back to Greece after a decade in Australia. It wasn't our age difference or the fact that he had a son half my age that was my real objection to him, but rather that he'd said to me, "You'd be perfect to act in a screenplay I wrote about a guy who marries an Australian girl and has a horrible divorce. You'd play the simple village girl he should have married."

If I wasn't willing to be someone's token Greek girlfriend in America, I certainly wasn't about to sign on for that role in Greece.

"You're too picky," Thitsa Kanta chastised me when I'd complain about the men I met. "You can't keep saying this man smells and that one stinks!"

I disagreed. "My life is good," I insisted. "I'm interested only in someone who makes it more exciting, not less." But as I looked around me and saw long-married couples who relied on each other—Spiro and Atheena, Dina and Andreas, Grigoris and Athina—I knew I wanted that kind of companionship, too. And that by moving to Lia, and making it a part of my life, I had decreased my chances of ever finding the right person, someone who would be willing to live in a metropolis or a mountain village with me, and be happy in either place.

By September I was annoyed with clairvoyance. "Good predictions never come true, or at least not fast enough," I complained to a family friend at an art opening in Ioannina. "And bad ones are depressing, even if they don't happen! It's a no-win situation."

"Oh, you mustn't listen to any kind of fortune-telling," she warned. "Not only is it a sin in the eyes of the church, but it's also very dangerous. My mother-in-law read coffee grounds, and one day she told my brother-in-law that she saw an accident: he shouldn't go out on his motorcycle. He zoomed off, got hit by a truck, and almost died. Later he told me that when he saw the truck coming, he didn't try to avoid it, because he remembered his mother's advice. He made it a self-fulfilling prophecy."

I saw her point—I didn't want to be a slave to divination. But on the other hand, maybe the moral of the story is that a boy should listen to his mother.

After that warning, I asked Kaity where she had learned to read coffee cups. "From my mom," she answered. "She was from Asia Minor; they're the best fortune-tellers."

"And she learned from her mother?" I asked.

"I guess so," Kaity responded. "It's an inherited gift. But you can't read your own cup or see yourself in someone else's. When I was fifteen and taking exams, my mother told my fortune every morning, to see how I'd do. One day she said, 'I see a death in this cup!' By the time I returned home, she had died of an aneurysm."

I almost choked on my own coffee. "Aren't you afraid you'll see something horrible one day?" I asked.

"What is there to be afraid of?" Kaity shrugged. "It's all in God's plan." She stood up and disappeared into the kitchen. In a minute she was back, giggling, holding a yogurt container. "You have to promise not to tell anyone," she said, handing it to me.

I flipped off the top, extricated a bundle swaddled in tissue and bubble wrap, and began undoing it. Underneath all the neat layers was a coffee cup, covered in lacy-looking grounds that were now hard and crumbly.

"My daughter sent it," she laughed. "From grad school. I got a notice that I had a package at the post office, and it turned out to be this. She wants advice on her breakup."

"But she's an engineer . . . a mathematician," I sputtered. "She's too logical for this."

"Please," Kaity scoffed. "Even engineers break up with their boyfriends."

As for me, I decided that Mr. Right, Ph.D., could stay on his yacht. It was time to start concentrating on aspects of my future that I *could* control, such as rebuilding the house. Back in Lia, I stood watching Vlad and Xalime lay flagstones on the veranda of the Gatzoyiannis house, in between the stone banquettes that Yanni had finished the week before. There were still no doors or windows, but the front of the house was really starting to look polished, I thought, glancing over the flat, irregularly shaped stones. Suddenly I realized that something was missing: the *plistario*, the little kitchen, had no stairs leading from the ground to its outside door, or vice versa. You would have to jump from the veranda to the ledge in front of that door, risking possible death and certain ankle-twisting. The dog in the dream had tried to warn me that there was a problem with steps! This was exactly what Zervas was worried about, what he had wanted to work on when Vlad refused. If I didn't think of a solution before he arrived the next week, my architect was liable to pass out when he noticed the oversight.

"Eleni!" a voice called from below the property. A sickeningly familiar voice. I moved to the edge of the wall. There was Zervas, standing below, waving up at me.

"You're a week early!" I trilled.

"Yes, to make up for all the times I was two weeks late," he answered, walking toward me. "No, I was checking on another job in a village nearby and I thought I might as well come now and save myself a trip. I'm glad I did. How beautiful this all is—the benches, the columns. I was worried that they were going to be too thick, but they look even better! The flaw turned out to be an improvement!"

At least he was in a good mood. "Yeah, the place looks amazing," I said. "It's getting close to done now. Just a few details, the doors, windows, and, um, the stai—"

"And you look wonderful!" Zervas continued. "I must look different, too. Because when you take unshapen rock and turn it into a piece of art, something changes, both in the rock and in you. We are both forever changed because of this house."

I stared at him, then at the house, a gray stone cottage that looked as if it should always have a puff of smoke rising from the chimney. I had been so concerned with the steps, I had forgotten about the complete transformation of the place, from ruins to a thing of beauty.

"When Solzhenitsyn was sent to Siberia, the convicts were forced to work nonstop, building rock walls," Zervas continued. "Everyone was exhausted and miserable, but occasionally he would step back and say, 'Look what a beautiful wall we're making!' He knew it was art, and he was glad to be creating something."

Zervas seemed so happy. I couldn't deceive him any longer. "But look at the door to the *plistario!*" I wailed. "There are no steps to get to it."

"Oh, that's nothing," Zervas said, beaming at the rock. "Vlad, if you cut into that wall, three steps curving up from the courtyard, that would look perfect. Very organic."

"Sure," said Vlad. "Good idea."

They were agreeing with each other for the first time since the hedgehog incident. I couldn't believe my luck—maybe Scrappy had more white fur than black after all.

"Eleni, let's go," Zervas said. "The man whose house I came to check on, he's driving up to meet us at the Xenona in an hour and I promised him fish."

We drove on, through golden fall sunlight that intensified the rust-colored trees and azure sky, to the trout farm just before Kefalovriso, a tree-lined spring that resembled an enchanted grove so much that I expected naiads and dryads to pop out from behind the branches. "Barba Lambro!" Zervas called. A white-haired hunchback scuttled across wooden grids sticking up through his trout pond. Using a net, he pulled up twelve long, shimmering gray trout, dropped them into two plastic blue bags, and tied the handles together tightly. I heard the fish flapping in the double bag and felt a twinge of guilt.

"These trout are lucky," I told Zervas as we drove toward the Xenona with the bagged fish thrashing in the back. "Now they won't have to survive the cold winter."

Zervas looked at me. "You're an optimist," he said. "Just like Solzhenitsyn."

At the Xenona, Nikki cooked the trout as we drank wine with Zervas's friend, who turned out to be a master carpenter—this was a business lunch, hence all the effort to secure the fish. "I just came from your house," the carpenter said, pumping my hand. "It's so beautiful, I want to contribute something to it. I'd like to build the wooden door for the outer gate. Zervas told me about your grandmother; I want to leave my mark on her monument."

Zervas had called this man the best carpenter in Greece but said he was way out of my price range. And now he was offering a gift, a tribute to the house and the people who had loved it. Maybe *this* was the news Scrappy had tried to tell me as he ran through the empty outer gate frame and up the steps toward me in my dream. I couldn't be sure. That's the great thing about divination—you hear some shadowy hint of your fate, but when the predicted event actually happens, it still manages to surprise you.

After lunch our guest drove off to measure the pagoda-like frame of the *exoporta*. As he walked out, he passed a young monk in a black robe and a long red ponytail. "Father Gerasimos is the abbot of the monastery of Giromeri, outside of Filiates," Nikki said, introducing us. "He's here to pick up the slate tiles we took off when we fixed the roof, because the monks are doing some renovations."

"It is so important to refurbish the monasteries of Epiros in their traditional style," Zervas said, shaking the monk's hand. "They deserve to be showplaces. After all, we have so many significant local saints."

"We do?" I'd been to church in Epiros hundreds of times, and this was news to me.

"Of course," Father Gerasimos replied. "Agios Donatos is the most beloved. He worked miracles, killed a dragon. But the scholar, Agios Deodochos, is more important in the history of monasticism."

"Isn't that always the way?" I asked. "The flashy dragon-killing saint gets all the kids named after him, and the ascetic gets no love."

"Oh, but Agios Deodochos is very inspiring," Zervas said. "It was after reading his work on poverty and celibacy that my wife left me to join a convent."

I almost choked on my ice cream. I knew Zervas didn't have a wife even though he wore a wedding ring. But I assumed she had died or run off with another man—and I didn't mean Jesus.

"The thing is, Father," Zervas was saying to the monk, "when you get so wrapped up in something, there comes a point when you have to decide if you're going to move forward or stay where you are. If you move forward, you know you can't go back again, but if you stay where you are, you feel as if you're drowning."

I couldn't believe it! Zervas sympathized with his wife's internal struggle. This struck me as being even more generous of spirit than Solzhenytsin. I didn't know how to respond. I looked at the redheaded abbot expectantly. Wasn't counseling people about this sort of thing his job?

"Well, in true Christianity, nothing is irreversible," Father Gerasimos said, finally. "Because nothing is unforgiven." Then he went into the kitchen to strike a deal for the roof slates, leaving us to our coffee.

"What was your wife like?" I asked Zervas, who seemed still tangled in the complicated knot of his feelings about her.

"She was beautiful," he said, smiling. "She looked just like Jackie Kennedy, so elegant. That's why she left—it was the evil eye. Everyone coveted her and drove her away."

"Do you really think that's why?" I asked gently, not wanting to suggest that the cause might be less paranormal: she simply wanted out of her old life.

"Why else?" He sighed. "She regrets leaving. I know she's ready to come back."

"Oh." I was shocked for the second time in this conversation. "So you talk?"

"No, never," Zervas answered. "But she told people she was ready to return, and they told me. I could go get her today, when I leave Lia."

"So, will you?" I asked. Maybe fate would morph this tragedy into a love story.

"Probably not." Zervas sighed. "Not today, maybe never. It may be better this way—she's peaceful where she is; I'm calm as I am." He put down his drained cup. I longed to be able to turn over Zervas's cup and see his future, and his wife's, in it.

"I could try to read your cup," I said, to lift his mood. "Or do you think it's a sin?"

Zervas thought for a moment. "Most religions teach us we shouldn't try to learn the future, that we should leave that to God and be satisfied," he said. "But if we stop yearning to know how our lives will unfold, it's a little like not yearning to live. It's such an ancient desire. Look at Dodona." He glanced at me skeptically.

"The oracle, right?"

"The oldest oracle in Greece, right here in Epiros," he clarified. "It's just outside of Ioannina. Surely you've been there."

A few days later, Zervas left after approving Vlad's undulating stone steps that curved toward the *plistario*. Vlad began laying flagstone on the floor of the tiny bathroom. And I drove to Dodona on a spiritual field trip. This didn't count as divination, I reasoned. It was sightseeing. Ruins. A perfectly wholesome, purely academic exercise.

I sped through Ioannina and turned onto the exit for Dodona, a seventeen-kilometer drive that took me right in front of University Hospital, where I was expected for a sonogram the next day. I had successfully ignored my ovarian cysts for four months, and thought it in poor taste of the oracle to drag me past the scene of my impending medical tests. But all was forgiven when I arrived at Dodona, a field surrounded by solid green hills, silent witnesses to eons of earnest pleas. To my left an amphitheater from the third century B.C. stood in a smug semicircle, embracing the stage with its perfect acoustics and illustrious history. I wished I had taken the time to see a performance there over the summer, to have had the breeze rush past me at a particularly dramatic point in the play, functioning like the scary music in a made-for-TV movie about a woman in jeopardy. How had I let time rush by as quickly as the Kalamas River? It was mid-November; I had a little over a month left, and I hadn't even made it to a performance at Dodona, although in nine months in New York I could manage to fit in several made-for-TV movies about women in much less jeopardy than, say, Medea. Was I making the most of my life, or just marking time? I whirled away from the theater, angry that I had turned into a cliché. Here I was, at a sacred oracle, having a little existential crisis. That was old hat even in antiquity. On his way home from Troy, Odysseus had come to ask this oracle if he should return to Ithaka in secret, or out loud and proud. The oracle was a tall oak tree in which Zeus and the local incarnation of his wife, Dione, were said to live. Back then, supplicants such as Odysseus asked a question and the Selli, the oracle's priests, interpreted the answer from the rustling of the sacred oak.

That oak tree had been uprooted in the fourth century by either proselytizing Christians or anti-environmentalist souvenir seekers. But a stately oak had been replanted in its place long ago, so I hurried over. There were no Selli to interpret, but that was just as well. I wasn't sure what to ask. I was anxious about my sonogram tomorrow, but "Will the tests go well?" seemed like a wasted opportunity; I'd know soon enough. What I really wanted to know was whether I was healthy, whether I would have children who would one day visit their great-grandparents' house, which I had spent so much time rebuilding. But that was too important a question to ask; I didn't want to risk a negative answer. Besides, I knew that any answer I'd interpret would be too vague to satisfy my New York skepticism. I wanted an oracle that not only knew the future but also spoke its mind in pithy sound bites, one that might answer the question "Will I meet the man of my dreams?" with "Not in that outfit, honey."

The wind blew and a white card fluttered on one of the massive stone blocks surrounding the oracular oak. There, in English, was written the query "Will the Hearts win the cup?"

Sports? Someone trekked to the oldest oracle in Greece and wasted his question on sports? I stared at the oak, which looked strangely familiar, like the white image of the tree that Kaity had discerned among the brown residue in my coffee cup. Maybe the tree I was planting to bloom for future generations was an oak. I didn't need Selli; I had interpreted an answer on my own. Of course, it was the answer I wanted to hear and I could have been reading my own hopes into the leaves' rustling. But making people feel better is what has kept Dodona in business for almost four thousand years.

I still felt confident the next day as I entered the ultrasound room at Ioannina University Hospital. But afterward, the radiologist said, "The cysts haven't gotten bigger, but they're still there. Since you're staying another month, you should consult a gynecologist here. If I were you, I wouldn't wait until you return to the United States."

Kaity pulled some strings and got me an appointment with Ioannina's best gynecologist for the following week. I was grateful for the referral. At least, I knew I should be. But really I was annoyed that I had to submit to more humiliating tests, and worried that the doctor thought they were necessary. I had been ignoring my cysts, hoping that they'd disappear on their own. Now I was scared that these tests could lead to more sonograms, CAT scans, even another operation. Even the best doctors have to give bad diagnoses sometimes. That evening, back in Lia, I was planning a quiet night at home when the phone rang.

"Lenitsa, where you been?" a familiar voice shrieked forth from the receiver.

"Hi, Thitsa Kanta," I said. "I was at the hospital, checking up on my cysts."

"But I thought you done with that after the operation in March?"

"I thought so, too," I said. "But since it turned out that the tumor they took out was a low-malignant potential, you know, this really weak form of cancer—"

"I don't want to hear that word!" she shrieked. "You're healthy! I read your cup and I didn't see nothing, so don't worry about it—and don't tell anyone in Greece, or they'll think you can't have babies!"

I knew Thitsa Kanta meant well, but this was not exactly the kind of moral support I had in mind. So I called my mother, Joanie, and vented. "I know it's annoying that you have to keep doing all of this," she consoled me. "But at least the test results were good—the tumors haven't gotten any bigger!"

Joanie's upbeat chirping comforted me as little as Thitsa Kanta's wild shrieking. I explained that the results *weren't* good; the tumors were still there. Okay, they weren't growing wildly and I wasn't going to die, but at twenty-eight, "not dying" isn't a great diagnosis. I hung up and went over to Dina's, where I listed my troubles: I hated doctors, I had nagging cysts, and no one I talked to understood that this was a big deal, at least to me. Right now it was just another test. But bad results from this test might mean that not just my health but also my fertility was compromised. If that was the case, all the magic cake baking in the world couldn't guarantee me the family I hoped to have one day.

"Your mother just said the test results were good because she wants that to be true so badly," Dina said. "You can't do anything until after you see the gynecologist, so you might as well stop thinking about it. Self-pity is like a loose tooth—you can keep worrying it to make sure it's still there, or just ignore it so you don't make things worse."

She had a point. I would try to move on, starting by setting her table for dinner. Then Vangeli Panagiotou showed up. I told him I had visited Dodona, and he said that when he was a traveling salesman after the war, villagers near Dodona kept digging up ancient coins. "So I show up in town, and kids run up, yelling 'Hey, peddler, what do you buy?'" he recalled. "I say, 'Old bronzes, silver, coins,' and they take me to this geezer who shows me five ancient coins. Ancient—I mean older than Jesus, older than Jesus' grandparents! I offer to buy all five, thinking I'm really putting one over on poor grandpa. But on the way out of town, three policemen are blocking the road, doing random checks for the Archaeological Services."

"They knew the town was full of old coins?" I asked.

"Please, a farmer couldn't plow a field without digging up ten, fifteen old coins that he'd throw out, or make a hole in for his daughters to wear on necklaces. Anyway, the cops say, 'We're looking for old coins, turn out your pockets.' I had to give up the coins, but I convinced them I had no idea they were antiques." Vangeli smiled. "I pretended to be a stupid hick. Of course, I *was* a stupid hick—I should have hidden the coins in my shoe. Then I could have taken them to Athens and made a nice profit."

I hadn't realized I'd been hanging out with would-be scam artists. Having dealt in antiques before dowry linens, Dina and Andreas shared their own stories about bending the law. "But one thing we never did was take icons," Dina said definitively.

"You mean from a church?" I gasped. "People do that?"

"Not from a church, but from an old lady, say," Andreas explained. "Plenty of peddlers would go and say, 'I want to make a copy of this beautiful icon—I'll leave you a deposit, then when I return the original you'll give me half back.' And then they'd take off, and no one in the village would ever see them again."

"That's terrible!" I said.

"And dangerous," Dina added. "You don't want to risk the wrath of the saint."

She was right, of course. Outside of Konitsa I had visited a monastery that contained a buckled Byzantine icon of the Panagia; it had been stolen by a man who removed its gold covering to melt down, then threw the icon into the Aoos River. One day a shepherd heard screaming, followed the sound to the river, and retrieved the sunken icon. The icon stealer, consumed by his own guilt and grief at having been found out, drowned himself in the same spot where he had thrown the icon.

Listening to them, I realized that there was a major power source I hadn't tapped in my attempt to control fate—divine intervention. As a tourist, I had visited icons, churches, and monasteries all over Greece. In every church, I lit a candle and prayed for my family or dead relatives. But now I had a more specific request. I decided to visit Father Gerasimos's monastery at Giromeri as a pilgrim, to light a candle for my health.

The next day I set out with Foti, who had promised Thitsa Kanta he'd accompany me wherever I wanted to go, as long as it wasn't on a hunting day. The monastery of Giromeri turned out to be an impressive brick castle on a hill. Father Gerasimos served us coffee in the flower-filled piazza, then led us to the old church, which was covered with wall frescoes and ornate wood carvings. In the center, in a two-sided glass case, stood a miracle-working icon of the Panagia, which was reversible, with Peter and Paul on the back. I lit a candle and prayed, "Panagia, Peter, *and* Paul, I ask that you safeguard my health and one day bless me with children, and I promise to bring them back here to visit you."

A week later I arrived at the hospital early. Then it turned out that my doctor wasn't in the gynecology wing, as I assumed he would be, but in the *maieutiko*, a word that I had never encountered but turned out to mean "obstetrics." By the time my manhunt/impromptu vocabulary lesson was over, I had run up and down four floors, avoiding old men with canes, patients in gurneys, and breast-feeding Gypsies, before arriving ten minutes late. The doctor performed an ultrasound, then sent me for blood tests to check the presence of cancer hormones in my bloodstream. "If the tests come back negative tomorrow, you can wait until you return to the United States to discuss the cysts with a doctor there," he explained.

Lighting candles and saying prayers had felt good when I did it—at least I was taking some sort of action. But now I felt paralyzed until the next morning. The following day, just after the hospital opened, I arrived at the blood center and waited my turn. "Your results aren't ready," the nurse said. "Come back in an hour, and go straight to the lab."

Hot tears of frustration filled my eyes, but I nodded and walked, blinking, toward the parking lot. "Excuse me, miss," a shrill voice called behind me. I turned around. "Are you going into Ioannina?" A wrinkled gray-haired old woman in a wrinkled gray cardigan was tugging on my arm.

"Yes," I said, not able to lie when a direct question is asked.

"Well, can you take me into town?" she demanded, the thin mustache on her upper lip twitching.

"Yes," I said again, not able to think of a reason why I couldn't. We drove toward the clock tower in the center of town as she explained that she had left her wallet at home and had used the last bus ticket in her cardigan pocket that morning. She was worried she might have to walk back into town, when she saw me, may God bless me and grant me good health and good luck in the future. I was grateful for her chatter and her blessing. I knew I wasn't doing anything heroic. But it felt good to be able to provide an answer to a question, even one as simple as "How am I going to get home?"

I dropped off my elderly hitchhiker, then returned to the hospital. This time I pushed past the geezers, gurneys, and Gypsies and went straight to the lab, drumming my nails on the counter until the technicians dug slowly through their files to extract my results. I stared at the computer printout: five test results, which consisted of a number on the left and a range of normal responses on the right. At the bottom, a summary was printed in block letters: WITHIN NORMAL RANGE.

I had been granted a reprieve. I might need surgery someday, but not yet—certainly not before I returned to the United States.

I called Kaity and told her the good news and that I would be heading straight back to Lia. I wanted to stop at Agios Demetrios, to light a candle in gratitude for the test results being good but also for the old lady. Because as much as I was glad about the results, I was also grateful to have had someone with me who cared enough to bless my future, even if it was an old woman with no wallet.

In Lia, after visiting Saint Demetrios, I walked up to the Gatzoyiannis house to check on the building site. It was mid-November, but the weather was turning the corner slowly, ambling from the bright light of autumn to the muted gray glow of winter. It would be cold and rainy soon enough. The interior of the house needed to be finished, the bathroom installed, and doors and windows put in place and locked up tight before I abandoned the house to the isolation and rains of late December. I had to be firm with Thomas, to insist that the interior get finished fast.

As I strode into the house, rehearsing my opening line ("Everything looks exactly the same!"), I heard a noise in the room to the right, which was once the *mageirio* and would become a bedroom in the house's new incarnation. There was Thomas, leaning against the wall. He turned toward me and suddenly, behind him, I saw it. A beautifully formed fireplace with a carved gray decorative stone just below the mantel, etched with a diamond and the date 1914. "It's perfect," I whispered.

"It is," Thomas said, grinning. "I was just trying it out." The charred remains of crumpled paper glowed in the fireplace as smoke rose up the chimney. "Come into the main room," he added, halfway there already. I ran in and found Vlad standing next to another, even larger fireplace, whose decorative stone was painted a patriotic Greek blue, with a white compass rose design in the middle and the date 1922 above that.

"It's so beautiful!" I said.

"Fireplace in other room from your great-aunt Nitsa's house," Vlad informed me. Apparently, they had slipped into the crumbling ruins of Yiayia Nitsa's house and removed her fireplace stone for use by her descendants. She was no longer around to approve the permanent loan, but then again, there was no way she would miss it.

"Where is this other fireplace stone from?" I asked, staring at the compass rose.

"I was hoping you wouldn't ask," Thomas answered. "I can't tell."

"Oh come on—it's my house!" I insisted. "I have to know!"

"Let's just say it's from the village," Thomas answered. "A gift ... from an anonymous donor who is happy to see this house rise again." I went on a mental stroll through town, futilely trying to locate a house where I might have seen a stone with a white compass rose on it.

"Can you tell me someday?" I started to negotiate. But when I tore my eyes away from the fireplace, Thomas was no longer standing there. I ran out to the veranda in time to see him pull away and zoom off in his pickup truck.

I had watched this house grow from the beginning, and still it held secrets I might never learn. And I had spent nine months in Lia, but there was still so much I didn't know about the village. Soon I'd return to New York, my old home, but a city that would have changed in my absence. Friends had moved, my editors at magazines had found other writers, and the city itself continued morphing at its nonstop pace. Part of me was tempted to stay in my cozy village forever, but I knew I couldn't live there indefinitely. That is a privilege reserved for the elderly, who have already successfully completed the difficult tasks of creating families and careers, then returned to Lia to claim their reward. By the time I reached the Haidis house I was desperate for more divination—I needed reassurance that my time there had been worthwhile and that when I returned to the United States, I would be as happy as I had been in Lia. I was ashamed to admit it, but I was jonesing for a coffee-ground reading. I went home to call Kaity, but as soon as I got back to the Haidis house, the phone rang.

"Where you been?" It was Thitsa Kanta, calling about the tests. I told her that the results were good, and she said, "Didn't your *thitsa* tell you?" She paused—an uncharacteristic silence emanated from the receiver. "I got bad news," she said, finally.

"What?" I asked. "Thitsa Olga and Thitsa Lilia didn't like the house?" I knew that a *thitsa* caucus had been scheduled to view Thio Angelo's documentary on Lia.

"They don't know," Thitsa Kanta cried. "Ange's tapes were all blank. Your *thitsas* couldn't see the house, the Babouriotes couldn't see Panagia church, and Jimmy Bazooka, he no see his village in Albania."

"But that can't be true!" I insisted. "I saw some of those scenes on playback!"

"It was the metal detector in the airport, erased all of it," Thitsa Kanta replied. "They stronger now for the goddamn terrorists."

Some people coerce fate into blessing their future. Despite my best efforts, I couldn't even control the images of my past. I hung up, depressed, and went to sleep, but my dreams held no messages for me.

The next morning I woke to the jubilant peals of church bells, although it was just a regular Thursday. I quickly dressed and ran to the church of Agia Triada. After the service, on my way out, Ekavi, a widow with high cheekbones and short white hair, tapped my arm. "Come over for coffee," she insisted. "You know why I like you?" she added as we walked to her house. "Because you go to church. I was just saying to my neighbor, Eleni Gatzoyiannis is a young person who loves the church."

"Well, I go more here than in New York," I admitted, worried I might not live up to this pious image. "I don't even know why there was church today—is it a holiday?"

"Saint Phillip's Day," she said, leading me inside to a chair at her oilcloth-covered table. "Forty days before Christmas, the last chance to eat meat before the fast."

Wait a minute—there's a *Christmas* fast? I was proud of myself for kind of keeping the Easter Lent. I chewed my lip, confused.

"You know Saint Phillip," Ekavi prompted, boiling our coffee in a shiny metal *briki.* "He was a farmer in a poor village and had only one ox to plow his field. One year no one had meat to feast on before the fast. So he killed his ox and distributed the meat to his neighbors." She set a steaming cup in front of me, then sat down. "The next day he went to yoke himself to the plow, and his ox was there! The Lord returned it to him."

Aha! Here was the religious expert I was looking for, having been too embarrassed to bring my latest question to Father Prokopi. "That's fascinating," I said, before glancing down at my cup. "So, do you think reading coffee grounds is a sin?"

"That's what they say," she said, nodding. "So I don't have my grounds read."

I shrugged as if to indicate "Oh yeah, me neither."

"Why sin when you can just read the egg?" Ekavi continued. "That's all right, because eggs come from God."

So do coffee beans, I thought, before realizing that I had no idea what she was talking about. "What do you mean 'read the egg'?" I asked.

"Oh, it's like coffee grounds, but you pour the white of an egg into a cup of water and go from there—then you can use the yolk for baking," she explained. Economical *and* ecclesiastically approved! "Do you want me to read yours?"

"You know how?" I asked. Maybe fate was starting to smile on me, however shyly, after all—one simple trip to church and I had a fortune-teller right in front of me.

"Sure," Ekavi replied. "When I was fifteen in my hometown, I worked for a dressmaker. A client, a rich, beautiful girl a few years older than I, said, 'Will you do me a favor? Bring this egg to Kyria Maria and tell me what she says.' She wanted to know who she would marry, because she loved a Gypsy but her parents opposed the match."

"Kyria Maria was an egg-reader?" I asked, trying to keep us on topic.

"Oh, yes," Ekavi went on. "She was a widow who lived in the

shell of a bombed-out house—this was just after the war. Her daughter died during the bombing, and her son, in his sorrow, threw himself off the bridge. Kyria Maria was left to make a living reading eggs by candlelight, because there was no electricity. So I went to see her, and she must have liked me, because she told me to come back and she'd teach me to read the egg."

"What about the heiress?" I asked.

"Oh, I had to tell her that Kyria Maria said she'd marry the boy her parents had in mind. And she did. But ten years later I bumped into her, and she told me that her husband had died, and she had remarried—her Gypsy boyfriend." Ekavi raised an eyebrow.

"Kyria Maria hadn't seen *that* coming," I said, taking a last sip of coffee.

"Oh, no," said Ekavi. "Only God knows *everything* that is going to happen. But I could tell you a few things if you'd like."

She shuffled out to the chicken coop and returned with a smile on her face and an egg in her pocket. "This is yours," she said, pulling it out. "Five letters in *Eleni*, right?"

She filled a glass with water, then tapped the egg on four different spots along its rim, making the sign of the cross. Reserving the yolk, she dumped the egg white onto a plate, splashed her fingers in it five times, then poured the unsettled egg white into the glass. A ginger-ale-colored layer settled at the bottom, then slowly white stalagmites rose through the water, some hitting the top of the liquid and turning to drip down into it again. Air bubbles were trapped in the middle of the glass, shining like silver balls. "That's you," she said, pointing to one. "See, it's a full face." I looked but saw only an orb—this was trickier than a coffee cup. "You recently passed through a serious worry," Ekavi whispered. I nodded. "You worry a lot," she continued. "But you shouldn't. Everything in life will open up before you. See those shoes on the floor?" she asked, pointing across the room. "Let's say they seem out of place. Don't worry, just say, 'Shoes, I am going to put you right where you belong!'"

She made more predictions about my family from the floating

white swirls. But it was the shoe advice that stayed with me. Regardless of what fate had in store, it was up to me to put my angst in its proper place, under the bureau. I thanked her and strolled home, eager to tell Kaity about this new method of divination.

I dialed her number but couldn't tell at first if it was Kaity who answered, because she was sobbing. "You heard?" she said when I identified myself. I hadn't, so she told me. Her favorite brother had died of an aneurysm, unexpectedly, and in a few hours she would be driving across the country to attend his funeral.

"And the worst part is that it's such a shock," she whispered. "I had no warning."

"You didn't have a dream, like with your parents?" I asked.

"No, nothing at all," she said. "It's the strangest thing."

"There was nothing you could have done," I said. "Even if you'd been warned."

"No," she answered. "It might have helped me, but it wouldn't have helped him; this was his fate. The end of our lives is written at the beginning of them."

"Do you really think so?" I asked.

"Oh, I know it's all predestined, because when I was fourteen, my mother read my coffee cup and told me that I'd have three children and take many trips abroad," Kaity said. "How could she have known that then, if it wasn't already programmed for me?"

"I guess you're right," I replied. It seemed to comfort her to know her brother's death was meant to be, even if it was a tragic event.

"No one really knows their fate," she said. "None of us knows when we'll die. All we can do is make sure we spend time with people we love while we're alive."

I offered my condolences and hung up. Dina called to me and I stepped onto the veranda. She wanted to make sure I'd come for dinner; Vangeli would be there, too. She went inside, but I stayed, watching the swathes of pink that still stained the sky long after the sun had disappeared behind the mountain. I was in a place I loved, and it kept handing me gifts and inheritances, from friends to fireplaces. People die and even videotapes get erased, but memory persists and the places where we met and lived and loved remain. No matter where I went, or whom or if I married, Lia would always be there, a place to which I could return, as it had been all along, even before I realized it. It must have been predestined.

TEN

THE STONE POMEGRANA

<<Σπίτι μου, σπιτάκι μου, φτωχοκαλυβάκι μου.>>

"MY HOUSE, MY LITTLE HOME, MY POOR LITTLE SHACK.

November 20

I'm staring at the loveliest toilet bowl in the world. It's smaller than the average bowl in circumference—a little squat, but in a cute "I'm a little teapot, short and stout" kind of way. It's not a working toilet yet; it's currently lying on its side on the flagstone floor of the plistario. *But the plumber has just arrived to install it, along with the other chic little fixtures, in the tiny bathroom we added onto the back of the Gatzoyiannis house. Since a bathroom didn't exist in the original house, we're keeping the new one small—only five feet, four inches square. It will be basic but beautiful, with a corner shower set apart by two clear doors, a white porcelain sink, and, of course, this lovely toilet.*

"It's the wrong toilet," a voice behind me announces. I turn to see the plumber, who removes a cigarette from his mouth, the better to shake his head grimly.

"What do you mean?" I demand. "The guy at the store said that Ideal Standard is the best. He just drove all of this stuff up the mountain."

"The toilet itself is fine," the plumber responds, taking another puff. "It just doesn't work with the pipes I laid. This toilet has a receptacle for a wall pipe. In that little room, we've got a floor pipe. You should have consulted with me on the fixtures."

What I should have done is realized that, like all the other steps of construction, the bathroom was going to be a huge migraine. I look around. Yanni is gone, finished with the stonework, and Thomas is off hunting. We are down to a skeleton crew of Vlad and Xalime. I have to handle this myself, and I refuse to panic in front of the plumber.

"I don't know the first thing about construction," I sigh. "What do you suggest?"

The plumber smiles. "Well, I have to go to Ioannina next Monday to pick up supplies. I could get the right version of this toilet, and install the bathroom after that."

"Perfect!" I actually clap my hands in an effort to massage the artist's ego. "I'm so lucky to have an expert like you on the job! Thank you so much!"

I think the plumber is blushing, but with his beard, I can't tell. "May you be well," he says as he walks to his pickup truck, stubbing his cigarette out on the road.

High on Thitsa Kanta's extensive list of reasons why Greece is inferior to America was her complaint that "no one in Greece says, 'Have a nice day!'" It's true that shopgirls often acted as if I was dragging them away from their real job of nonstop gossiping in order to force them to sell me something, but other Greeks I met more than made up for the missing "Have a nice day" with continual blessings. Instead of "You're welcome," people respond to "Thank you" with "May you be well." On the first of every month, people wish, "Have a good month!" And when I set off for a trip, everyone would say, "God be with you." If I actually did anyone a favor—say, gave them photos I had taken or bought them a coffee—a shower of blessings would rain on me, something like "May you live happily for a thousand years, as strong as the tall mountains, and with a good husband." Aware that fate is tempted by the request for so much luck, I'd respond, "Good health and joy for *all* of us," so that the blesser would rein in her expectations and say, "Yes, health is everything. Let us be healthy." Now I worried about returning to New York. With no one to bless me there, was I less likely to have health, luck, love, and a thousand years of a happy life? Because I would much rather have all that than a nice day.

In the meantime, I had my more immediate future to worry

about. My parents were arriving in two days to spend Thanksgiving with me and to celebrate the expected completion of the house on my father's nameday, Saint Nicholas's Day, December 6. I had invited everyone in town months before, eager to return their hospitality and sure that by December the project would be completed. But now, just a few weeks before D-day, there was no bathroom and the electricity had not been activated. The carpenter was supposed to have come that day to start installing the floors, doors, and windows, but Vlad had been working alone, buffing the grout between the flagstones on the kitchen floor. I was upset about the setbacks. But I was also grateful for the distraction. If I had too much time to sit around, thinking about leaving Lia, I would get morbidly depressed. Soon I would have to return to my old life in America, and after a year in the cozy confines of Lia, that prospect so intimidated me that I wasn't sure I wanted to face it before I left. I didn't need reminders of America watering down my last few weeks in Lia—even if those reminders were my parents. The next day I would harass the carpenter, hassle the electrician, and start packing up a year's worth of clothes and books. But right now, I decided, I would take a walk through my village. The last walk I could take alone, without tourists like my parents hanging around.

It was the kind of clear, sharp day that makes early winter beautiful, when the hint of frost and rain to follow are presented as a cool, silver glow, illuminating everything. I decided to dress up for the occasion, changing out of my jeans into a black shirtdress and paisley shawl. Shutting the gate to the Haidis house, I looked up at the walnut tree, ready to cover my head if irate squirrels started lobbing nuts my way, their second-favorite pastime after walnut-bowling tournaments in my ceiling. But they were busy in the upper branches, so I stood under the tree, where my grandmother had been working in her father's garden when my grandfather walked by and saw her for the first time, her hair shining in the sun. Later my grandfather told me that walnut trees can steal your brain and turn it into a walnut; he had a brother who slept under one and went crazy. But that afternoon, when he first saw Eleni Haidis, he didn't even notice the tree, and in that glance was the beginning of my family. I gazed at the tree, straining to see if my own future might be coming toward me on the road above. Suddenly, a car zoomed down the asphalt path. But when the car door opened, the driver wasn't Prince Charming, just Vangeli Panagiotou, the only man who ever dared drive off the road and down the steep incline.

"Eleni, how come you're dressed like a *vavvo?*" he asked. I looked at my chic ensemble—black dress, large shawl—and saw that I was the height of Lia widow fashion.

"Oh, you know, it's cold," I mumbled. "And I'm going for a walk."

"Well, I came by to give you a present," he announced. He opened the trunk and pulled out a faded blue wooden cradle with pink roses painted on its round headboard.

"It's a *sarmanitsa!*" he beamed. "See these holes on the side? Women used to pull swaddling cloth through those and tie the *sarmanitsa* to their backs. Then when they got home, they could put it on the ground and rock the baby. We were all rocked in these things—me, your father. You can't get them anymore."

"Thank you!" I said. "It's amazing! Where did you find it?"

"Oh, I stole it," Vangeli said, smiling, as he carried the *sarmanitsa* to the veranda. I thought he was joking, but I couldn't tell.

"Well, at least you didn't steal the baby along with it," I remarked.

"Don't worry about how I got it," he insisted. "It's a going-away present."

"I'm not leaving for three weeks!" I protested, not wanting my departure rushed.

"I know, but I'm leaving tomorrow," Vangeli replied. "It's the Christmas season, and I have to help my son with the store in Athens."

"Do you have to go so soon?" I cried. Vangeli's dramatic stories had us laughing so hard every night that we could barely manage to eat Dina's delicious dinners.

"It's not soon," Vangeli responded. "All the summer people are gone already, and most other folks will leave before Christmas, to spend the holidays with their kids. Soon only Dina, Andreas, and a few others will be left."

I thought I was doing a good job disguising how much this thought depressed me. But I'd forgotten about Vangeli's degrees in psychology from the University of the Street. "Don't be so sad," he consoled me. "We'll all be back in a few months. Give me a hug good-bye."

I trudged up the path. I was sad to lose my eloquent dinner companion, but I also worried about Vangeli, who once confided that since his wife died, he couldn't fall asleep if he hadn't had enough to drink. How would he fare in Athens without our company? And if one good-bye depressed me this much, how could I handle three weeks of farewells? At least Vangelis would return in a few months. I didn't know when I'd be back, and I worried that the people I now loved would forget I had ever lived in Lia.

I forced myself to try to remember things I hated about living in Greece. Having to run through the rain in my pajamas at eight A.M. to move my car for a honking bus to pass. Visiting the IKA office in Filiates every month and having to wait in line for hours to pay Social Security for the workers. And that certain breed of young man I'd bump into in Ioannina, known as a *mangas* (a blowhard), who wears his anti-Americanism as proudly as his Armani manbag.

I tried to drum up righteous indignation that would make me glad to leave, but I softened when I passed a cluster of lacy spiderwebs, wet with mist, framing the bushes like embroidered collars. And I had to laugh at the House Divided Against Itself, whose ceiling was split in half—one side was orange tile, the other gray slate—because the brothers who inherited it couldn't agree on anything, not even repairs to the ancestral home they seldom visited.

By the time I made it to the *kafenion*, I needed a drink. I ordered retsina and looked at the grim faces of the men, and the happier expression of Laokratia. Costa was busy doing his second-grade homework, filling a regulation blue notebook with neat facsimiles of the letter Π that his teacher had drawn at the top.

"Why's everyone so down?" I asked Costa, after checking his penmanship.

"This morning the pretty doctor said it was her last week," Costa reported. "We get a new man doctor now."

Even the doctor was abandoning Lia. An era was coming to an end. My neighbors seemed to like me, as they did the lady doctor, to appreciate our young, blond nonlocal presence. But as I prepared to leave, I began to wonder if I had really become a lasting part of the village, or if the house I had rebuilt here would remain as an unwelcome reminder of the painful history of the civil war and the stubborn naïveté of the American who insisted on reviving it.

The next day I drove to Ioannina to pick up two more outsiders, NickGage and Joanie. They were tired, so I suggested we stay overnight. But I had a hidden agenda.

"Tomorrow, on the way home, we can stop at the supermarket and stock up for Thanksgiving," I said over dessert in a tiny old *kafenion* inside Ioannina's *kastro*.

"We don't need that much stuff," Joanie responded. "There's only three of us."

"Actually," I said, attempting a winning smile, "I invited a few friends to join us."

"How many?" my father asked.

I did a mental count. "Oh, eleven."

"Eleven!" Joanie screeched, causing the owner behind the bar and two weathered blondes at the next table to snap their heads toward us. "But your father smuggled in only one package of cranberries! And I can't cook for expert chefs like Dina!"

"No one is going to judge the food!" I insisted, at a slightly lower decibel. "These people fed me all year; I think we can prepare one little meal for them."

"What do you mean *we?*" Joanie said, sneering. "How many turkeys have you roasted?"

"Greeks don't like turkey anyway," my father added. "Or sweet sauces with meat—they have really specific ideas about food. Remember the ice-cream store?" That summer NickGage had been outraged when he tried to order plain ice cream—no sauces, whipped cream, or nuts—from a waiter who clearly felt that ice cream cries out for embellishment the way village ladies feel flat surfaces beg for a doily.

"There won't be any ice cream at Thanksgiving," I promised. "Everyone will love it. We could serve these people peanut-butter-and-jelly sandwiches and say, 'This is our tradition,' and they'd all tell us how delicious it was. You forget how friendly people are here. Whenever I traveled, strangers would stop me to say, 'Are you visiting? Come to our village next—just go to the main square and ask for Lambros; you can stay with us.' "

"You never took them up on that offer, did you?" my father demanded. Joanie was still stuck in her own personal circle of hell, muttering, "Fourteen people . . ."

The bartender, feeling my pain, slipped out from behind his wooden cage and walked over to us. "I'm sorry, I couldn't help but listen—it's a small café," he said in his excellent university English. "Your daughter is right; villagers tend to be very friendly. Perhaps you haven't been to Epiros before."

I laughed; this was the wrong thing to say to NickGage, son of Epiros, who liked to refer to himself as "the Fred Astaire of the Balkans." My father opened his mouth, but before he could educate the waiter as to his heritage, one of the middle-aged blondes at the next table leaned over. "I'm Danish, but I live in Parga and lead Danish tour groups around Epiros—it's such an interesting cultural area, this, especially for foreigners."

"I'm not a for—" NickGage began, but was cut off by the other lady.

"Most Danes just go to the islands," she said. "But for me, Epiros *is* Greece."

"I was just explaining that to my parents, but they're tired after their trip, so we have to go." I insisted, hoping to get out of there before NickGage began a lecture on the pre-Christian history of Epiros, which the Danish lady might find helpful for her tours.

She was right: so much of what makes Greece unique existed in our obscure province. On her last visit, I had taken Joanie to the Ambracian Gulf, the largest wetlands in Europe. At a state-of-the-art wildlife center we watched live video of silver pelicans and herons frolicking on one of the twenty-two coastal lagoons while tiny, tube-like cameras spied on them. Driving along the coast, Joanie chatted with a little boy watching his father spearing eel with a trident, while I ducked into a chapel covered in frescoes using the Byzantine cobalt that modern paints seem unable to equal. "That's what's so amazing," I told my parents. "You can be in a seaside chapel where monks still draw water from the well out front, and ten minutes later, spy on pelicans using the latest technology."

"So where are we going on this visit?" Joanie chirped.

"Well, nowhere," I answered, flustered. "I've got only two and a half weeks left in the village. And not only do we have Thanksgiving, then there's the nameday."

"The nameday!" NickGage yelled. "We're having two parties?"

"It's the least we can do!" I insisted. My father was born in Lia; I was born in Manhattan. But when they got all prissy, whiny, and worried like this, I couldn't help but think of my parents as "the Americans." It was best to table this discussion until their jet lag wore off. I kept my mouth shut and started unloading their luggage from the car.

"I can't believe you had me smuggle cranberries," NickGage muttered, lifting his bag.

The next morning, back in Lia, we unpacked the groceries as Scrappy trampled us to see what was in our bags. Then I suggested we drive to the Gatzoyiannis house to check on the carpenter.

"I can't leave—Thanksgiving is in two days!" Joanie cried. She boiled potatoes to mash as I drove my father up the mountain. I was eager to produce NickGage because, after watching construction stagnate, I had been forced to admit something: the workers thought of me as a nice girl who really cared about the house, but they never forgot that NickGage was actually paying for the production. NickGage was a man and he had been born there, so they were more inclined to listen to him anyway. Now that he was there, I expected the house to be finished at lightning speed. The crew was probably working away right now.

But when we arrived, the house looked deserted. I panicked silently. Then I heard the hollow *thwack* of a hammer hitting wood. "The carpenter's here!" I cheered. "Let's go." My father marveled at the roof, the stone-covered columns, the flagstone veranda, and, when we went inside, the 1922 fireplace. A lot had been done since his last visit, I just hadn't realized it, because I watched, like a parent, as the house grew inch by inch, and he, visiting it months apart, was shocked at how much it had matured. In the 1914 room, as I now called the *mageirio* with Yiayia Nitsa's dated fireplace stone, a bald man dressed entirely in camouflage stopped hammering and grinned, revealing a few missing teeth. He had set up frames of four-by-fours on the cement and was nailing narrow planks together on top of them, forming smooth wooden floors. "These look great," I said.

"But what about the doors and windows?" NickGage demanded, slipping comfortably into his bad-cop role. "I thought the carpenter said he'd install them today."

"He's coming tomorrow," the floor man assured us. "He was delayed on another job, but just for a day."

With things in order at the house, I drove my father to the *kafenion* so he could catch up with old friends and give Foti the jeans, Tylenol, and stack of Social Security checks Thitsa Kanta had sent him. I joined Costa by the potbellied stove and admired the stars his teacher had drawn on the page of perfect *Π*s. "What's new?" I asked.

"At the Xenona, Fanis and Nikki are treating everyone to sweets because they have a new grandson," he reported. "You can hear music coming from there every night—Christmas songs, even the Chipmunks."

"The Chipmunks?" I asked. "Singing in Greek?"

"Of course." Costa eyed me suspiciously. "That's what they speak."

Over dinner at the Xenona I explained to Nikki and Fanis that Thursday was Thanksgiving, an annual American holiday commemorating how the settlers gave thanks to God for surviving their first year in the new land and invited the Indians to join them in a feast. "I love traditional customs like that!" Nikki exclaimed, as if I'd just described something as bizarre and ancient as sacrificing a rooster to build its severed head into your new home. But I realized both rituals involve killing poultry for the greater good, so I just continued my pitch. "We'd like to have the ceremonial dinner here at the inn, with you as guests. Our house isn't big enough to hold everyone, so we want to use this dining room. If you provide wine and salad, we'll bring the food, including two turkeys."

"You have turkeys in America?" Nikki asked.

"Turkeys are a Thanksgiving symbol," I explained. "They're *native* to America."

"I thought they were French," Fanis said. "We call them *gallopoules*, French birds, because they go *glou, glou, glou*, which sounds like French people talking."

The man had a point. "In America, turkeys say *gobble, gobble*," I informed him. Fanis and Nikki laughed uproariously at this ridiculous idea.

I soon discovered I had misinformed everyone about the true meaning of Thanksgiving. I told them it was about Pilgrims, Indians, and turkey, but it seemed it's really all about Joanie, who was still convinced no one would like her food. At least she was trying to get into the Thanksgiving spirit. NickGage had turned into a conscientious objector, chiming in with phrases like "Greeks don't eat boiled green beans!" as we rushed around the kitchen. I knew he was more excited about the house than about the holiday, so I tried to be understanding. Then he went too far. We had forgotten to buy ready-made crust for the pumpkin pie, so Joanie needed a recipe to make it from scratch. "Don't worry," I called to the kitchen. "I'll e-mail Mrs. Kalber—she taught home ec."

My father looked up from his book. "No one's going to eat pumpkin pie; these people have never even heard of pumpkin pie. Why go to all this trouble to make it?"

"Because, NickGage, Thanksgiving without pumpkin pie is un-American!" I shouted, leaping up out of the *taverna* chair I had set in front of the first computer in the Mourgana mountains. "This is going to be a traditional Thanksgiving, and you can love it or leave it, mister!" He lay low for the rest of the afternoon.

Eventually I forgave my father for his culinary critique and drove him up to the Gatzoyiannis house. The carpenter had come and gone, installing a wooden front door with a wrought-iron handle as well as small wooden shutters in the basement. On the veranda lay the other shutters, unfinished wood with diamond-shaped peepholes covered by sliding wooden diamonds. Resting there, the shutters seemed to have magical powers; they were the ingredient that would transform the house into a cozy home.

Thanksgiving dawned bright and sunny. Up in Perivoli the Dick Clark–like carpenter, his two handsome sons, and his dentally challenged employee were installing windows, doors, and three built-in cabinets in the walls, just like those in the original house. Even the plumber had arrived—three days ahead of schedule—bearing the platonic Ideal Standard of a toilet. He had gone to Ioannina early and decided to drive up today, since it was such nice weather. I knew it was a Thanksgiving miracle, but I kept this to myself; I wasn't about to explain about the turkey all over again.

At the Xenona, Joanie and I helped Nikki push enough tables together to seat fourteen. Joanie created a centerpiece starring a pineapple surrounded by a chorus of plums, grapes, apples, and pears, and I set the table using paper napkins that showed a cornucopia pouring out Thanksgiving treats, including a cooked bird. "So it really is all about the turkey," Nikki muttered as she passed by.

At eight P.M. people started trickling in dressed in their best— after all, it was their first Thanksgiving, except for Foti, who had spent years in the United States. On his first November in America, when Thitsa Kanta told him she was going to roast a "turko" in- stead of a "French bird," he thought she planned on doing some- thing nasty to a Turk. "I wouldn't put it past her," he said, laughing.

As we started in on the wine, Thodoris Panagiotou, Vangeli's younger brother, started in on NickGage, needling him the way all these men who had been boys together joked about one another's false teeth, thin hair, and other perceived deficiencies. "Niko, you were born here," he began. "So why does Eleni speak Greek so much better than you? She speaks it like it was Farsi."

Passing by with a tray of rolls, I helpfully added, "That's an idiomatic expression that means really well—like a native."

"I know what it means!" NickGage snapped in English. Then, in Greek, he answered, "I left here in the fourth grade; Eleni studied Greek in college. Of course she speaks it better. But my English is better than hers."

I opened my mouth, then shut it, deciding to let that remark slide. It was Thanksgiving after all. And I knew that even if I gave an entire lecture series in *alafiatikia*, I still would never have spent as much time in Lia as NickGage, who had been born and raised there as a central figure in a tight-knit community. He must have known it, too, but I could tell he was annoyed, as he started mocking Thodoris's comb-over. And understandably so; I didn't mind it when people corrected my imperfect Greek, but if one of the villagers had ever implied that my mother or sister belonged in Lia more than I did, I know I would have thrown a roll at him, Thanksgiving or not.

Finally, Dina and Andreas arrived, bearing a second turkey, which she had prepared in the traditional Greek style, with pepper and lemon juice, cooked until its skin was blackened. "Mine looks more tender!" Dina trilled when she saw our pale bird. Joanie was right; these were competitive chefs! "Who made these?" Dina asked, fondling a warm brown 'n' serve Pillsbury roll.

"I did," I jumped in, not wanting to let on that half of the meal, from Uncle Ben's wild rice to the biscuits, came out of a box. An imported box, but a box nonetheless.

"Did you hear, Atheena?" Dina beamed. "Eleni made these with her little hands!"

Just as I was about to confess, my father tapped on his glass and we took our seats. "Thanksgiving is about giving thanks, being grateful that God has blessed you with such good friends," he began. "Which is why we're so glad you're here to celebrate with us. These are the same dishes the settlers in America shared with the Indians. The Indians taught them how to cook the local turkeys, to turn cranberries into a sweet sauce for the meat, and to harvest wild rice, which grows along riverbanks. Even today only Indians harvest it, in canoes along the river."

Was NickGage for real? I thought Uncle Ben, in his infinite wisdom, had invented wild rice. But our guests were eating this stuff up—literally. "The black rice is delicious!" Atheena said, passing it to her husband, Spiro.

"But I don't like the cranberry sauce with the turkey," Dina announced as an evil grin of triumph spread across my father's face. "It's so tasty, I'm eating it on its own!"

"Everything on this table has such meaning behind it," Antonis Makos whispered.

I wanted to tell them that every meal they had served me had just as much meaning, was the product of as many years of history, and had been cooked with as much care as I had carved orange rinds into sauce baskets and as Joanie had cut butter into flour to make a home-ec-approved piecrust. But I didn't, because it was most people's first Thanksgiving, and I felt it was better if they found out for themselves that sharing customs, foods, and lives is what Thanksgiving is about. Because nobody's really in it for the succotash.

Sure, there were a few glitches: Dina kept telling people on our side of the table that there was "spicy turkey" down at the other end, because "they don't cook theirs like we do." And I felt a little guilty about stealing the Pillsbury Doughboy's intellectual property. But overall, it was a resounding success, judging by the reactions of our guests, who pocketed their place cards and napkins as souvenirs. I knew the napkins with overflowing cornucopias would appeal to them. Atheena had told me that when she was starving in Hungary, a friend of hers found an unattended orchard and stole as many cherries as she could stuff into her bag. "She dumped them into a tin basin until it overflowed. It was so beautiful," Atheena recalled. "Since then, I've always liked large displays of fruit." But more than appreciating the abundance of Thanksgiving food, our guests seemed to enjoy the wealth of lore—the noble Indians canoeing up rivers, searching for black rice; the noble Joanie, standing at Dina's food processor to make potato soufflé. The event was exotic to them, and familiar to us, a photo negative of my experience all year.

The next morning I awoke to a high-pitched moaning coming from the courtyard of the Haidis house. *It's the ghost of the woman the Germans burned here,* I thought. As the sound continued and the possibility of sleep diminished, I gave myself a little mental lecture. "You know this house is ghost-free; you can't possibly still be scared after all this time," I insisted. "It's just the Americans snoring."

But when I sat up and looked over at the empty bed next to mine, I realized I was the laziest American in the place. My father had gotten up early to go check on the Gatzoyiannis house, and my mother was down in the kitchen, making coffee.

"Joanie!" I yelled—she couldn't hear much above the running water. "Meet me in the courtyard." Fully awake now, I knew there was no such thing as ghosts. But I might need protection from whatever was howling in that otherworldly way. Outside, the only suspicious-looking character lying in wait for us was Scrappy, who had been moping around for days and was now whimpering in front of our gate. I worried that the turkey leftovers had done him in, but on closer inspection, I saw that he was missing half a toe; a ring of red flesh circled the lower half of his claw. "That looks infected," I said to Joanie. "We can't leave him here to die on the doorstep."

We stared at each other for a moment before agreeing to follow the course of action we always chose in times of crisis, like power outages or locking ourselves out: call on Dina and Andreas. Armed with rubber gloves, sterile wipes, and Bacitracin from our first-aid kit, Dina swabbed Scrappy's toe as Andreas held and petted him. Joanie and I looked on helplessly. "Don't worry, we're not going to hurt you," Andreas cooed. "That's a good dog." Much improved after the procedure, Scrappy limped off to more leftovers.

"It's good that they bonded," Joanie mused as Dina and Andreas returned home. "Now they can look after Scrappy and he can look after them once you're gone."

These people had been looking after me all year. Now they

would have each other and I would be back in New York, without Dina's advice, Andreas's tender heart, and Scrappy's leaping enthusiasm. When I thought about leaving, I felt a knot of barely controlled panic. So I concentrated on my to-do list: packing, checking on the house, and, of course, getting ready for the nameday/housewarming party.

The next day, en route to Ioannina, Joanie and I stopped in Leptokaria to see the electrician. "You're all set," he said, handing me a receipt and some forms. "You just need to get this signed by the contractor, that signed by the plumber and workers, have them all stamped in Filiates by the IKA office and then in Ioannina by the prefect who gave you the building permit."

"Is that all?" I joked, lamely.

"Well, once that's all done, then you drop it off at the electric company in Igoumenitsa, and when they've approved it all, they come and power up the house."

I looked at the electrician. "There's no way I'll be able to get all that done in the next two days, before my father's nameday, is there?"

He laughed so hard that I could see the pointy tips of his incisors. "Not a chance."

"But then I leave for America," I sighed.

"I could take care of this for you, for a small fee," he said. "If you leave it with me, the electricity will be working by spring. You will be coming back then, won't you?"

"Of course I will," I said, deciding that the housewarming/ nameday would be even lovelier in the glow of candlelight. I left the papers in his hands and continued on to Ioannina, where Joanie and I picked up foil-wrapped chocolates, boxes of pastries, and the main ingredient for the nameday party—the celebrant, who had spent the past few days at meetings in Athens. After getting NickGage at the airport, we had one more stop, a frame shop with a small sign that read ICON FACTORY. "I need to see the iconographer," I told a tall redhead about my age.

"That's me," she answered, pointing to an icon in progress.

"We'd like to order an icon of the Prophet Elias ascending to heaven—for a chapel," I explained to the foxy iconographer. "The saint saved his life." I pointed to NickGage.

"Then you definitely need to offer an icon in gratitude," she agreed. After we paid our deposit, NickGage turned to me. "How did you know we should offer an icon?"

"It's common knowledge. You have to be thankful for your blessings," I replied as we drove away from Ioannina toward Lia for the last time that year. I kept imbuing every event with significance: my *last* church service at Agios Demetrios, *final* chance to watch the news at the *kafenion*, *ultimate* sighting of a wild boar carcass tied to the back of a truck. But on this last drive Joanie drowned out my sighs with her more powerful whining. "What if we got the wrong liqueurs?" she moaned. "What if cognac is just for memorial services? I'm not a Greek; I can't be expected to know these things!"

"Take comfort in being a honky, Joanie!" I encouraged her. "If someone says we're doing it wrong, just shrug and say, 'What do we know—we're Americans!' "

All year I'd enjoyed the leeway afforded guests who are forgiven for serving, wearing, or doing the wrong thing. But this party was my debut as a homeowner in Lia, a fellow villager, and I was suddenly, albeit quietly, worried. The stakes were now higher for me, and I didn't want to blow it.

The next day was devoted to the one aspect of restoration I felt I could handle on my own: decorating. The house wasn't actually ready; there was still no electricity and no furniture, and the cement ceilings had yet to be covered in wood. Although the toilet flushed, Thomas hadn't dug the septic tank, so the water emptied out into the backyard. I knew the house wasn't perfect, but I still wanted it to be as pretty as possible. I scattered candles on the windowsills and in the glass-fronted cabinets and wall niches, arranged bottles of booze and platters of foil-wrapped sweets, then rested an elaborate icon of the Virgin Mary above the 1922 fireplace and set a table in front of it. Just before I locked the doors with my shiny new gold keys, I placed my grandparents' wedding

photo on the mantel so that they could enjoy the next day's ceremony, the blessing of their new old home.

Saint Nicholas is the patron saint of unmarried girls, so he blessed
me with clear weather for my housewarming and his feast day.
While Joanie arranged orange and burgundy mums from Dina's
garden and pale green hydrangeas from Atheena's, NickGage and I
heeded the church bells for the Saint Nicholas Day service. We were
nearing the end when Stella ran in and whispered in Athina Ganas's
ear. Athina and Grigoris were up from Athens for the weekend; his
health was improving and the weather was good, so they came to
celebrate. But now Athina's face fell, and her smile crumpled into
tears. I watched whispers pass in a chain throughout the church.
Dina, standing next to me, called Stella over to learn the news.

"Aspasia Daflakis died of a heart attack in Athens last night,"
Stella reported. "Her daughter called. They're on their way here
with the body; the funeral is tomorrow." An image of the white-
haired woman appeared in my mind; Aspasia used to walk past the
Haidis house every evening in summer, taking the air with some of
her girlfriends. I didn't know her well, although she had kissed and
blessed me on several occasions.

"If her daughter calls again, tell her we're going to ring the
death bell this afternoon, after the celebration at the house," Antonis Makos, who was passing the offering basket, decreed. The next
day, another Liote would be buried behind the Panagia church. But
this day was for the resurrection of a house. Antonis had made an
executive decision; sorrow could wait a few hours.

By the end of the service, the whispering had stopped, as had
Atheena's tears. Having lived long, eventful lives, the villagers
were used to this continual cycle of endings and beginnings.
"Happy Saint Nicholas Day and many years to all of you," Father
Prokopi announced. "We're all invited to the home of our co-
villager Nikos Gatzoyiannis up in Perivoli, at eleven, with lunch at
the Xenona to follow."

As we streamed into the churchyard, people descended on me, wishing that I be overjoyed in my father on his nameday and that I return next year with a husband—the villagers were clearly eager for more beginnings to celebrate. But I couldn't listen to people who had just remembered a nephew in Athens I must meet, or a godson in Thessaloniki. I had forgotten a key ingredient to the party's success: the oranges.

I left my father basking in blessings and drove home to collect three oranges and the three blue-bordered handkerchiefs I had bought in Ioannina. Up at the house, Thomas and Foti had already dropped off a four-foot-tall wooden cross. I knotted a twenty-euro bill into each handkerchief, tied them onto the arms and top of the cross, and, after much struggling, secured the oranges to the cross with wire. Thomas climbed onto the roof and rested the cross against the chimney. Months earlier we buried a rooster head into the house; now we were setting up the ritual that indicates a house is finished—when the cross is placed on the roof and the workers climb up to collect their handkerchiefs, oranges, and accolades. The oranges glowed against the Greek blue of the sky, and the handkerchiefs blew in the wind. This ritual was definitely prettier than the decapitated rooster.

But despite the beautiful day, I still felt nervous, and not about having the wrong liqueurs. What if the villagers were offended by the house's reconstruction? I knew well that the home had the power to bring sorrow as well as joy. I was re-creating a building that was new to me but fearfully remembered by my neighbors for the tortures and killings that went on there. What if their pain and anger returned when they entered the gate? In trying to do something good for me and my family, to change our feelings about the past, perhaps I was doing wrong to the villagers, digging up memories that they'd rather let lie. The Liotes were not shy about expressing unflattering opinions, telling visitors, "Oh, you gained weight since last summer!" or "You're too thin, you should eat more!" but I thought it unlikely that anyone would criticize the house's reconstruction directly to my face; I was their hostess, after all. Instead, I feared having them smile tensely at me, then comment on my foolishness after I left, the way people in the *kafenion* waved at a patron stumbling out into the darkness, then, as the door shut, sighed and clucked, "He drinks too much. One day he'll fall off the mountain and the wolves will find him, but what can we do? We told him he's being ridiculous and he won't listen."

My thoughts were interrupted by a black-clad white-haired old widow who floated in, told me that she had many memories there, and touched my cheek, smiling through tears. Then she wandered off, crossing herself as she entered each room. Soon more villagers started filing in, many bearing gifts for the house—a decorative plate, a set of glasses, a bottle of Vassili Deppis's homemade *tsipouro*. "It looks just like the old house," Grigoris Ganas marveled. "I remember it from when I was a boy."

Through the open front door I spotted Father Prokopi's long black frame striding toward us. He pushed through the crowd, arranged a bowl and censer on the table in front of the blue and white fireplace, and stood there, facing east toward Jerusalem. "Ready, Spiro?" he asked the cantor. "The service should take an hour."

"Are you trying to starve us?" Foti was indignant, his admirable gut growling.

But the priest would not be dissuaded. "This is an important event—a nameday *and* a blessing for the house," he insisted. "I looked up chants in two different books!" The table was set with three offering breads, an icon of the Panagia leaning against them, and a bunch of basil resting in a bowl of holy water, which Father Prokopi would soon sprinkle on the faithful. Fifty people were crowded into every corner of the room as Father Prokopi chanted, intoning the names of everyone who would live in the house. A sweet trail of incense rose in front of my grandparents' wedding photo. I had never met my grandmother or known my grandfather when he was young, but their faces seemed as familiar as those of the people I had come to love, who were now in the room, watching raptly as Father Prokopi turned a construction site into hallowed ground.

These people had seen me once a year for decades, watching as I grew up. Now that we had lived together for a year, I knew almost as much about them as they did about me. There was Grigoris, who had just finished chemotherapy but said the scariest experience of his life was when, as a boy, he walked past a priest who had been buried up to his neck by the invading guerillas and left to die. And Athina, whom he courted in Hungary, where they lived next to each other in refugee housing projects, both mourning the same lost home. They made it back home together and were now standing next to Andreas and Dina, who had lost two sons in traffic accidents and spent their lives nurturing other people, from a hungry American neighbor to a stray dog with a sore foot. Next to them was Foti, who showed me both wild boars and unexpected waterfalls and who had been so in love with Thio Angelo's sister when he was a young shepherd that, Thitsa Kanta told me, "he almost killed his mule trying to get down from the flocks faster so he could see her." Now his beloved was dead, their sons lived in America, and he had returned home to the village where he had once been a lovesick shepherd.

An elbow in my back knocked me out of my reverie. "Go over to that corner, too," Atheena whispered in my ear. "So you can take a picture of us." I scuttled across the room, cutting through a wafting cloud of incense, to photograph Atheena and the other ladies and record their participation in this significant event. I stopped remembering stories of the villagers' past and noticed how absorbed they were in the present, how attentively everyone watched and prayed. It wasn't enough to simply attend the event; they wanted to be a part of the house's transformation, to see it in a new way.

Soon Father Prokopi dipped a silver cross into the holy water and offered it to me, Joanie, and NickGage to kiss. "May you live many years to enjoy the house," he said. "Have a safe trip, and may we meet again in health and happiness soon." The cluster of celebrants broke into smaller groups, some heading into the 1914 room to try Vassili's *tsipouro*, others veering toward the sweets table, where Stella pocketed several gold-wrapped chocolates for Costa before kissing me and running back to the *kafenion*.

Looking at the photograph of my grandparents on the fireplace, I realized that the ceremony couldn't be over yet. I went up to Father Prokopi, who was sipping a glass of Vassili's homemade wine. "Would you mind blessing the basement?" I asked.

"Not at all," he said, smiling.

Father Prokopi, Joanie, NickGage, and I walked through the crowd of well-wishers on the veranda and down to the small, dark basement, where thirty-one prisoners had once huddled in fear. He began chanting, then dipped the basil into the holy water and flicked it around the dark room. A drop splashed my forehead, and relief washed over me. For the first time, the constriction I felt in my chest when thinking of the basement failed to appear as I stood there. I still shuddered at the thought of my grandmother's pain, but I no longer felt it trapped within the walls.

Father Prokopi finished and stepped outside, now inspired to bless the bathroom, kitchen, even the mulberry tree, in a fit of overconscientious beatitude. Dina walked up behind me, her footsteps echoing on the flagstones. "This is nice," she said, indicating the basement. "You could use it as a room, too."

I nodded but knew I would never do that. I wasn't afraid anymore, but because it was the last room my grandmother and so many others lived in, it could never be a regular basement, a place to store suitcases and ironing boards. The house might be a home now, with fireplaces to lie in front of and cabinets that already had glasses in them, but the basement would remain a monument to those who had lived and died there. It was where I planned to display the treasures Vlad had unearthed, the physical artifacts of my grandmother's life—the rusted spoons and broken plates, the tools, mangled headboard, and used hand grenade.

"Eleni—I'm about to climb up on the roof myself!" Foti yelled from the veranda. So I scrambled up and called everyone outside. Thomas, Vlad, and Xalime climbed a ladder onto the roof of the *plistario*, then the men strode over to the cross resting against the chimney, and Xalime, in a smart navy pantsuit and heels, followed shakily. Thomas untied each kerchief and held it up as the crowd clapped and yelled, "Bravo!" and "Long life to your hands, which created such a beautiful home."

Once they descended back to the veranda, Spiridoula grabbed Thomas's arm and asked, "Eleni, will you take a picture of us?" I agreed. "And now one of the three of us," she added, pulling Net into the photo. "I'm going to baptize Net, you know, so now he's part of the family." As I snapped photos of Thomas, Spiridoula, and Net, a childless couple and their already beloved surrogate son, I asked the boy how school was.

"Good," he answered.

"Great," Thomas clarified. "Next year Net is going into the vocational class, specializing in plumbing."

"One day he can take over your business, Thomas," I joked.

"That's the idea," Thomas smiled. I felt proud to have employed Net and Thomas on their first joint job; the house had already brought one family closer together.

The Net shoot led to other photo requests: Athina and Grigoris wanted one, then Vlad and Xalime. All of Lia was ready for their close-up, and had been all year, ever since I passed out the photos I snapped at the *panegyri*. From toothless old crones to three-year-old toddlers, everyone wanted his Kodak moment. A stranger at a *panegyri* once asked me, "See that *yiayia?*" pointing to a three-foot-tall kerchiefed lady. "She raised me. Would you take her picture and send it to me?"

I had been surprised to find everyone so camera-ready. In New York my unwrinkled young friends seldom let me photograph them. "I hate being in pictures," they'd whine, offended that I wanted to remember them as they were rather than as they looked in their minds, artfully made-up and illuminated with flattering lighting. In Lia everyone just wanted to be remembered.

Foti tugged on my arm. "Here," he said, handing me a small bundle. "I had a guy in Babouri join these together." I unwrapped the paper and saw two curved wild boars' tusks, joined into a crescent by a filigreed silver band. "It's to hang from the rearview mirror of your car for good luck," Foti said, blushing.

"In the car—no way! I'm going to wear this," I said, stringing it onto my necklace. I felt instantly empowered by my barbaric-looking pendant.

Foti walked away, laughing, as Ekavi, the old woman who had read my future in egg whites, pulled me aside conspiratorially.

"I don't know if you noticed," she whispered, looking around to see if anyone could overhear us. "But on Holy Thursday, while the priest read the Gospels, I was kneeling on the floor, praying and knitting. Then during the year, I cut up that piece of knitting and sew it into little bundles for good luck and divine protection." She pressed something about the size of a piece of bubble gum into my hand. "This is to bring you good luck—and a husband! Wear it in your bra."

For now my pocket would have to do, because Vlad was tapping on my back. "I bring you things from our yard in Albania that we find last month when we go to visit, see Dorina, and fix house," he said, handing me a blue plastic bag stuffed with dented tin cups, caved-in canteens, and the metal bases of lanterns, antiques that he had unearthed and lugged across the border into Greece for me. "I know you like the old things." I thanked Vlad, promised I would take the artifacts to a tinker in Ioannina to have them shined so I could display them in the house, and hugged him, causing the bag of tin to rattle. He blushed and scurried toward Xalime as Atheena walked over to me.

"I have something ancient," she said. "I don't know if you're interested in having it, but I wanted to give it to you." She pulled out the long vest I remembered seeing in her old family photograph. "This was my mother's," she said. It was a black wool sleeveless garment called a *sengouni*, heavily embroidered in scarlet and gold curlicues.

"I love it—but are you sure?" I asked, holding it up. Given its age and its history, this was something precious and irreplaceable. But then, so were all the other gifts.

"Of course," she replied. "Who else but you would care about it?" I hugged her and didn't speak. I loved the gift, but more than that, I loved her reason for giving it to me—she knew that I would appreciate it and that this piece of her past would be treasured in the future.

"I'll hang it in the house as decoration, when I'm not wearing it," I finally said.

Spiridoula interrupted. "I'm making something for the house, too," she said. "A crocheted wall hanging like the ones I have in our home. It's a pair of swans; they stand for fidelity. I'd love to have something of mine up in your grandmother's house."

Dina looked pained. "Don't leave our neighborhood to move here," she pleaded.

I told her not to worry; I couldn't stay in the Gatzoyiannis house until it was furnished anyway. Even then, I'd go back and forth between my grandparents' house and my great-grandparents', hiking from generation to generation. The important thing was that the house had risen from a pile of rocks and would always call me back to Lia—and it would be filled with the specially chosen gifts of the villagers who didn't hold its tragic past against the house but welcomed it as they had me, and wanted to embellish the interior with pieces of their own past. I knew I would visit the house often. But even if I never made it back, the fact that it existed would comfort me, making me as happy as all my memories of those villagers who came to celebrate its completion.

Zervas, of course, had made the trip to see his architectural drawing realized in stone and wood. At the Xenona, he approached me with tears in his eyes. "It's even better than what I saw in my imagination," he said, holding my hand. "Your father must be so happy." NickGage was almost too happy to speak—except to say that it was the first time he had celebrated his nameday in the village in fifty-four years. But when we arrived at the Xenona, I suspect that the villagers were happier than any of us.

First there was the amazing spread of food: Nikki and Fanis had set up a lavish buffet, complete with a whole roast piglet, whose eyes they covered with orange slices to prevent him from seeing the lusty looks he inspired. There were the usual salads, *pitas*, and rice, along with two platters of lamb. Within fifteen minutes the buffet was cleaned out by fifty Liotes who took plates two at a time, in case the delicacies were gone when they came back for seconds. Apparently, it is unwise to put a table groaning with food in front of people who survived a decade of starvation.

Most of all, the villagers seemed to enjoy celebrating a new beginning in a place where memorial services and funerals were all too common. This event was surprisingly free of the discussion that had taken place at every *panegyri* all summer: the Death of Lia dirge. An old person looks around and says, "In the old days, the *panegyri* would draw a thousand people. Tonight there are only four hundred." Sigh. "Take a good look around, because when this generation dies, that will be the end of Lia."

In 1945, Lia had twelve hundred inhabitants, Barba Prokopi had said. Now it's three hundred in summer, fifty in winter, with six hundred Liotes in Athens and three thousand the world over. But I had watched Thitsa Kanta and other Liotes engage in enough suffer-offs, where each maligns his or her own fate, trying to win the coveted position of most downtrodden, to suspect that the oldsters exaggerated the death of Lia in order to feel irreplaceable themselves. After all, sixty years ago Lia had plenty of people but no electricity, roads, or toilets. Now Lia has an inn, streetlights, and indoor plumbing; I'd say things are looking up. Over the next half century, Lia will change, but maybe it will improve. Perhaps those three thousand people across the world will also return to restore their family homes.

The next morning we went to Panagia church to say the one good-bye we knew would be final. Aspasia's husband, children, grandchildren, and siblings stood behind her coffin, where she lay surrounded by so many bouquets that I could barely see the white top of her head. Father Prokopi led us in chanting to her everlasting memory, then held an icon of the resurrected Christ for us to kiss as we circled the coffin, kissing the dead woman good-bye.

When the service ended, Aspasia's husband stepped forward. "I just want to thank all of you, my fellow villagers, for being so nice to Aspasia," he said, then collapsed, weeping, into the arms of his children, who led him out of the church.

As we sat in the *kafenion* afterward, I thought about what Aspasia's husband had said. It had been his wife's last chance to let everyone in Lia know how much she had enjoyed sharing her life with them.

Father Prokopi leaned over, interrupting my thoughts. "Eleni," he said, "you'll come back for Easter, won't you? It's April twenty-seventh next year." I nodded. "I hope you'll stay until May twentieth, the other day we celebrate Saint Nicholas, when we hike to the chapel near where your grandmother was killed. I'd like you to take a photo of me there, so that I can have one to remember the place by."

That night, at our final dinner at Dina's, Joanie told Dina how wonderful her meals always were. "But it's company we want," Dina answered, smiling sadly. "You can't enjoy your food unless you have someone to share it with."

"Now you're leaving," Andreas sighed. "And we got used to having you here."

"Don't worry," I promised. "I'll be back at Easter to turn the spit for the lamb."

The next morning Joanie, NickGage, and I frantically loaded the car. We still had so much to do, to pay IKA in Filiates, then drive to Ioannina to bid farewell to George and Kaity, drop off the car, and catch the plane to Athens, then to the United States. I was grateful that my emotions were swallowed up by the chaos as we locked the house, left the key with Dina and Andreas, and kissed them; that the sorrow of the good-bye was mitigated by millions of last-minute concerns. As we packed up the car, a light snow began to fall, the dusty, powdered-sugar-like flakes that make you think you're inside a snow globe.

"Where are you going?" Joanie demanded as I set off, turning up the mountain.

"I want to see the house in the snow," I answered.

I had a set of keys, so I unlocked the door. The house was still glowing, filled with the *kefi*—party spirit—of the people who had celebrated there a few days earlier. I walked over to the fireplace, where the photo of my grandparents stared back at me. I had overseen the rebuilding of their house, and in return the house had stopped time for me, allowing me to live in a village full of grandparents, a place where people treated me like a beloved daughter. As I looked at the photo of my grandparents, who died oceans apart, I realized that every happy family is a tragedy, because it exists for a limited time only. Children grow up to form their own families, parents die, and the original family is lost forever. Every family is a civilization, and all of them decline too quickly. Immersing myself in the village had allowed me to extend my family a little longer and to expand its sphere to include many people who had been there at its beginning. I might be leaving, but the affection I had for my new extended family would travel with me.

In Lia, people who didn't recognize me never asked, "Who are you?" but "*Whose* are you?" because they suspected they would know my family, and therefore understand why I was there. After almost a year there, I began to feel I belonged to Lia itself. I watched snow fall on my grandmother's mulberry tree and smiled, because although I was leaving, I knew I'd return. I had lambs to roast and photos to take. My card reader had been right, at least partly. I didn't need a bicultural husband to have the lucky fate she predicted. I could live my own transatlantic life, between two happy homes.

After ten months in Lia, I suspect that Persephone knew exactly what she was doing when she ate the seven seeds of the juicy red pomegranate. She hadn't asked to be sucked into the underworld, but once fate brought her to a kingdom she feared, maybe she began to embrace her strange but familiar new home, to feel she belonged there. By consuming the seeds, Persephone ended up blessed with two homes and the ability to travel between two very different worlds. The pomegranate was the pawn, the excuse she created so that she would always have to return.

I discovered Persephone's secret because fate gave me a second home, too, a place that I once saw as a sinister, dark side of my personal history but that I came to love and found myself unwilling to leave for long. I knew that I would always be torn between two different worlds, but having lived in Lia, I realized that this fact enriched my life instead of just complicating it. This house that I had rebuilt was a stone pomegranate, my reason to keep returning.

A TASTE OF LIA

Spiridoula's Wine-y Rooster

As a contractor, Thomas may do the heavy lifting in the family, but I have to hand it to Spiridoula for turning a skinny old fowl into a nutritious, delicious, celebratory meal. This dish is worth eating even if you haven't watched the rooster being beheaded yourself.

One rooster, plucked, cleaned, and cut into pieces
One large onion, finely chopped
Oil
Butter
Salt to taste
Pepper to taste
One glass red wine
½ can diced tomatoes, or 2 large tomatoes, finely chopped

Stirring continuously, sauté rooster and onion in oil, butter, salt, and pepper until onion is melted and rooster is browned. Throw in the red wine and turn down the heat to simmer. Add tomatoes (either canned, diced tomatoes or fresh, chopped ones, whichever you have handy—Spiridoula does not judge). Add enough water so that the rooster is covered, and let simmer over a low flame until most of the water is absorbed by the rooster, with just a little juice remaining.

Serve over macaroni, and you'll find that the occasional rooster sacrifice is good for the body *and* the soul.

274 A TASTE OF LIA

Marcia's Kosher-for-Passover Spanakopita

Romaniote Jews traditionally prepare this dish for the Pesach holiday, but it's delicious any time of the year. Spinach and matzo—two great tastes that taste great together. Who knew? Marcia Ikonomopoulos, the president of the Association for Friends of Greek Jewry, knew. Along with Isaac, she led the tour group I spent time with in Ioannina. Marcia gave me this recipe and very kindly allowed me to reproduce it.

3 lbs. fresh spinach
½ lb. fresh dill
½ cup olive oil
4 onions, finely chopped
6 cups matzo meal
Salt and pepper
15 eggs
Juice of 2 lemons
Additional matzo broken into small pieces

Preheat oven to 350°. Clean spinach and dill well and chop very fine. Combine. Heat oil in heavy frying pan and sauté onions until soft. Then add spinach mixture and stir until wilted and well mixed with the onions. Stir in matzo meal. Add salt and pepper to taste. Remove from heat and put in large bowl. Beat eggs with lemon juice and add to spinach. Stir in well.

Oil bottom of large baking dish (10 × 14 inches). Line bottom with broken matzo pieces and sprinkle with oil. Pour in spinach mixture. Bake at 350° for 45 minutes, until brown on top.

Serves 6–8.

Mmm-mmm, matzolicious!

Dina's Kollyva in Memory of Andreas's Son

I hope you never have to make *kollyva*, because it is served by people who are hosting a funeral or memorial service. But if the time comes, here's what you need to know: The wheat berries symbolize the resurrection of the soul. With all the advice about reaping what you've sown, wheat is a common image in the Bible. But it has symbolized resurrection since pre-Christian times, as Demeter would let the wheat grow only in the spring, once Persephone had reemerged from the underworld. Similarly, the pomegranate seeds represent Persephone's time spent in the underworld and, therefore, life after death.

All the other trimmings are there to make the *kollyva* sweet and encourage people to eat it, as accepting the treat indicates that you've forgiven the dead for any trespasses he may have committed against you in life. I wish I could give you a recipe for garnering forgiveness while you're still alive, but I'm still looking for that one.

At the service, several sympathetic ladies should spoon the *kollyva* into a cup and pass it out along with plastic spoons. When Dina made *kollyva* for the one-year memorial service of Andreas's son, this recipe easily served forty Liotes.

If you're on the receiving end of *kollyva*, and it's handed out by a family member of the deceased, say, "Long life to you," or "May you live to remember him."

2 lbs. boiled wheat berries
1 cup sliced almonds
1 cup chopped walnuts
1 cup raisins
1 cup golden raisins
1 cup sugar
1 cup finely chopped parsley
1 cup pomegranate seeds
2 cups toasted breadcrumbs
2 lbs. powdered sugar

White or silver Jordan almonds, and assorted spun sugar decorations for trim.

Bring a large pot of water to boil, then add the wheat berries, reduce heat, and simmer for about 2 hours.

Drain the wheat berries and mix in a large bowl all of the other ingredients *except* the breadcrumbs, the Jordan almonds, and the powdered sugar. Once mixture has cooled, arrange it on a silver tray so that it rises into a slight mound, like an ancient grave tumulus, in the center.

Shortly before the service, cover this mound with a thin layer of toasted breadcrumbs, then a thick, smooth layer of the powdered sugar (the crumbs prevent moisture from seeping through the powdered sugar in ugly wet splotches).

You can decorate the mound with the Jordan almonds (usually placed around the border and in the shape of a cross in the center) or with a cross or leaves made of spun sugar, which are sold at pastry shops for this purpose.

Long life to you.

Patsavouropita— *"Dina's Dishrag Pie"*

This recipe is easy and fun—it is to *pita* as Rice Krispie Squares are to dessert. It's called "dishrag pie" because it involves scrunching store-bought phyllo up into balls that resemble wadded-up dishrags. You want to be careful when tossing around the term *dishrag*, however; it can also be used to refer to a lady who is not so skilled at the domestic arts but has other, more salacious talents. Another word of caution: this pita can't be made with homemade phyllo (it's too thick), so don't get all ambitious and start rolling out dough. And it's rather oily—don't eat it if you don't want to leave telltale fingerprints anywhere.

500 grams (just over a pound) feta cheese (in the United States I have been known to use half regular feta, half low-fat—not that Dina would approve)

500 grams (one box) of store-bought phyllo dough

Oil

200 grams (almost a cup) melted butter

5 eggs

1 can club soda

Grate a scattered, thin layer of feta over one sheet of phyllo. (If you run out of feta, you can use other salted cheeses instead—go crazy!) Fold the sheet in half, then scrunch it up so it resembles a discarded dishrag or deformed Cinnabon. Repeat with the other sheets of phyllo.

Place the packets in an oiled casserole dish and pour the melted butter over them, making sure it gets stuck in all the crannies. In a bowl, beat five eggs. Beat in one can of club soda. (This will make the final product fluffy, more like a soufflé than a *pita*. It is Dina's secret ingredient—when people ask her for this recipe, she gives it to them but leaves out the club soda. But I couldn't do that to you, dear reader. My apologies to Dina.)

Pour this mixture over phyllo, again so that it oozes into all the folds of the dishrag blobs. Bake at 400° for 1 hour. When it starts to brown slightly, lay a sheet of tinfoil on top of the dish so that it won't burn—you can remove it for the last five minutes or so, to watch it turn into golden brown goodness. When the mass is brown and fluffy, remove from heat and serve.

Fanouropita
(Get-Me-a-Man Cake)

Dina taught me how to make this cake in the hopes that Agios Fanourios would find me a mate. It hasn't worked for me—yet—but my friend Anna has made the cake several times, then brought it to church to be blessed, and left a piece of paper with the names of all her unmarried friends on it for the priest to read during the ceremony. And all the people on Anna's list have since gotten married. (Don't worry, the priest just reads the names and doesn't say what the supplicants are seeking—for all the churchgoers know, you're hunting for lost jewelry or asking for good health. Of course, churchgoing old Greek ladies are not stupid, so if you're young and single and they hear your name, they might suspect.)

You have to drop off the cake at a Greek church for this to work—if you bring it to the Unitarians, they'll be very polite but have no idea what to do with it other than serve it during the coffee hour. If you want to sidestep church altogether, you can simply distribute the cake to friends and family, but make sure that twelve different people eat it (twelve being a very important number, I'm guessing because of the apostles).

Not to go too Kabbala on you, but speaking of numbers, this cake must have nine ingredients to work (nine being, like twelve, a multiple of three, the most important number of them all, thanks to the Father, Son, and Holy Ghost). So if you remove one, add a substitute (like, say, almonds instead of golden raisins, which I've never liked anyway).

1 cup sugar
1 cup oil
1 tsp. baking soda
2 cups orange juice
1 tsp. vanilla extract
1 shot of cognac (like Metaxa)
4 cups sifted cake flour (not regular flour, or it won't rise)

¾ cup chopped walnuts

¾ cup golden raisins

Beat sugar and oil together until creamy in texture and yellow in color. Dissolve the baking soda into the orange juice and pour it into the sugar mixture. (This is what makes the cake rise—it's science. Science, magic, and religion in one tasty cake!) Mix in vanilla, cognac, and flour. Stir in walnuts and raisins. Bake for 1 hour at 350°, and while it's cooking, say a prayer for Agios Fanourios's mom, something like "Dear Lord, please forgive the mother of Agios Fanourios for her wicked deeds and grant her peace." Let the cake cool, then distribute it or bring it to church, but don't reveal what you're hoping to find (as if I didn't know!).

Because it has no dairy, *fanouropita* is also good for fasting during Lent (except on days when you can't have oil) and for the lactose intolerant. Something to keep in mind if the man the saint nabs for you suffers from dairy issues. Happy hunting!

Greek Coffee Recipe

Any fool can make Greek coffee (no, we don't call it Turkish coffee in this house). All you need are the right ingredients:

Greek Coffee This is finely ground so that it is powdery, as opposed to granular. It is to American coffee as confectioners' sugar is to regular sugar. The *thitsas* favor either Loumidis's Papagalos brand or Bravo, both of which you can get at ethnic groceries such as Bahnan's in Worcester, or online at sites such as www.greekgrocers.com.

One Metal *Briki* This looks something like a beaker with a long handle, which lends a mad-scientist air to making coffee. Again, try an ethnic market or website.

Sugar If desired. NO MILK EVER.

Flitjanis Cups for serving. The thick plain white ones they use in *kafenions* look less sissy than the traditional French demitasse, if you're worried about that sort of thing.

To make one cup of Greek coffee, fill one *flitjani* with water and dump it into the *briki*. For two cups, dump two *flitjanis* in—you see where I am going with this. You've probably thought of this already, but if you start with hot water, the coffee will be ready faster.

Add heaping teaspoons of coffee, one for each cup you're making. Add sugar as desired. No sugar leaves your coffee *sketo*, plain. A scant teaspoon makes it *metrio*, medium. And a heaping teaspoon makes it *glyko*, sweet. If people get fancy on you and ask for it *me oligi*, they just want a little bit of sugar, like a pinch. Yes, this endeavor is full of subtleties. Do not try this at Starbucks.

Mix everything together with spoon.

Place *briki* on a hot burner. Let boil until the coffee rises and is about to overflow (but doesn't, because that would be a huge mess). Now remove the *briki* from the burner and pour the coffee into the waiting *flitjania*. Serve with a tall, cold glass of water.

For the advanced coffee maker: Once the coffee boils up, take the *briki* off the burner for a few seconds until it subsides, then put it back on until it starts to boil up again, but snatch it back off just in time. Repeat a couple of times. This will make for more *kamaki*, foam, on top of your cup, which is a good thing. And bubbles in the foam represent eyes that are admiring you, which is even better.

Drink down to the mud at the bottom of the cup, but don't drink the mud, even in an attempt to look tough—no one does.

If you have the connections, secure a *flitjanou* to read your fortune in the grounds. She'll turn your cup over, make the sign of the cross on top of it (although this act is in no way sanctioned by the church, so don't be thinking it is), and let it dry as you all chat. Then she'll flip it back up, and all your secrets will be revealed in the lacy patterns inside the cup. Good luck!

BIBLIOGRAPHY

Antoniades, Anne Gault. *The Anastenaria Thracian Firewalking Festival.* Athens: Thracian Archives, Society of Thracian Studies, no. 36, 1954.

Baker, D. S., comp., *Αρχαίες Ελληνικές Παροιμίες, Greek Proverbs, Ελληνίκες Παροιμίες.* Belfast: Appletree Press, 1998.

Dakaris, Sotirios. *The Nekyomanteion of the Acheron.* Athens: Ministry of Culture Archaeological Receipts Fund Direction of Publications, 2000.

Dalvin, Rae. *The Jews of Ioannina.* Philadelphia: Cadmus Press, 1990.

Danforth, Loring. *Firewalking and Religious Healing: The Anastenaria of Greece and the American Firewalking Movement.* Princeton, N.J.: Princeton University Press, 1989.

Δημητρίου, Σωτηρης. *Τους τα Λέει ο Θεος* Athens: Εκδοσεις ΜΕΤΑΙΧΜΙΟ, 2002.

Economou, Steven G. *Greek Proverbs,* vol. 1 and 2. Copyright: Steven G. Economou, 1976, 1978.

Gage, Nicholas. *A Place for Us.* Boston: Houghton Mifflin, 1989.

Gage, Nicholas. *Eleni.* New York: Ballantine, 1983.

Graves, Robert. *The Greek Myths,* vol. 1. London: Penguin, 1955, 1960.

Leigh-Fermor, Patrick. *Roumeli: Travels in Northern Greece.* London: Penguin, 1983.

Megas, George. *Greek Calendar Customs.* Athens: B. and M. Rhodis, 1963.

Παυλή-Κορρέ, Μαρία και Σπανούλη, Ρίτα. *Τσιγγάνες Μύθοι, Έθιμα, Παραδόσεις.* Athens: Εκδόσεις ΟΛΚΟΣ, 1991.

Plutarch, *The Age of Alexander: Nine Greek Lives.* Ian Scott-Kilver, trans. London: Penguin, 1973.

Sakellariou, M. B., ed. *Greek Lands in History: Epirus, 4,000 Years of Greek History and Civilization.* Athens: Ekdotike Athenon S.A., Demetrius and Egle Botzaris Foundation, 1997.

Stoneman, Richard, ed. *A Literary Companion to Travel in Greece.* Malibu, Calif.: J. Paul Getty Museum, 1994.

Made in United States
North Haven, CT
30 November 2021

11741625R00188